T0121150

*f*P

Blocking the Courthouse Door

How the Republican Party and Its Corporate Allies
Are Taking Away Your Right to Sue

STEPHANIE MENCIMER

Free Press
New York   London   Toronto   Sydney

*f*P
FREE PRESS
A Division of Simon & Schuster, Inc.
1230 Avenue of the Americas
New York, NY 10020

For information about special discounts for bulk purchases, please contact Simon & Schuster
Special Sales: 1-800-456-6798 or business@simonandschuster.com.

Designed by Davina Mock

Manufactured in the United States of America

1   3   5   7   9   10   8   6   4   2

Library of Congress Cataloging-in-Publication Data

Mencimer, Stephanie.
Blocking the courthouse door: how the Republican Party and its corporate allies
are taking away your right to sue / Stephanie Mencimer.
p. cm.
Includes index.
1. Justice, Administration of—United States. 2. Frivolous suits (Civil procedure)—United States.
3. Damages—United States. I. Title.
KF8700.M46 2006
347.73'53—dc22 2006050967

ISBN-13: 978-0-7432-7701-3
ISBN-10:   0-7432-7701-5

For Erik

CONTENTS

Representative government and trial by jury are the heart and lungs of liberty. Without them we have no other fortification against being ridden like horses, fleeced like sheep, worked like cattle, and fed and clothed like swine and hounds.

—John Adams, 1774

Blocking the
Courthouse Door

Introduction

The story of Frank Cornelius would be funny if it weren't so awful. In the mid-1970s, Frank Cornelius worked as a lobbyist for the Insurance Institute of Indiana, an industry group that was trying to change the state's medical malpractice laws. Back then, doctors across the country were protesting rising medical malpractice insurance rates, which they blamed on escalating jury verdicts in lawsuits filed by patients injured by bad medical care. The doctors staged white-coat protests at state capitals and buttonholed legislators with their claims that lawsuits and rising insurance costs were forcing them to stop delivering babies and to give up their practices.

Cornelius hand carried these gripes to the back halls of the Indiana statehouse. His goal was to win legislation limiting the amount of money injured people could receive in malpractice lawsuits, awards that were generally paid not by the doctors but by the companies that employed him. As he made his rounds, Cornelius told stories about frivolous lawsuits and ambulance-chasing lawyers. He argued that a cap on lawsuit damages would help the state rein in health care costs.

Indianapolis's governing class was persuaded. In 1975 the legislature passed one of the strictest medical malpractice laws in the country. The new law capped all awards at $500,000, including actual losses like wages and bills related to botched medical care, regardless of how much those bills actually amounted to. And legislators abolished pain-and-suffering awards entirely. In the places you'd expect, the champagne flowed.

The new law made Indiana, and Cornelius, early pioneers in tort "reform," an emerging movement led by insurance companies, doctors, big corporations, and conservative ideologues who sought to restrict personal injury and other lawsuits.

Cornelius's work on the medical malpractice bill was just one item in a long and quirky professional resume. He went on to lobby for several years on behalf of a state police group to ban cop-killer bullets, then later moved into journalism and, eventually, to running a car dealership.

But in late 1988, the forty-three-year-old Cornelius fell and injured his left knee. A few months later, he went to the hospital for routine arthroscopic surgery to fix the problem. When he went home, however, he suffered a great deal of pain. He called the surgeon several times that day without reaching him. The surgeon finally called back the next day, told Cornelius's wife, Cathy, to get him a bedpan, and then left on a skiing trip, saying he'd see Cornelius when he got back.

Cornelius continued to suffer, so he consulted another surgeon, who immediately diagnosed him with reflex sympathetic dystrophy, a degenerative nerve disorder brought on by an accident or medical prodecure. The condition is so painful that many sufferers desire to amputate the affected limb rather than endure the torture that comes with it, according to Stephen B. Caplin, Cornelius's lawyer.

To deal with his condition, which at that point was still treatable, Cornelius sought care from a physical therapist, who a few months later, Cornelius claimed, accidentally jolted his leg with a current of electricity from an improperly used medical device. The zap rendered his condition incurable and cost him the use of his leg. A year later, Cornelius had surgery to install a filter in his leg to catch blood clots, but the main vein from his leg to his heart was punctured. Cornelius would have quietly bled to death were it not for a visit that evening from his wife, who sounded the alarm. Another doctor intervened to save his life, although Cornelius suffered a punctured lung in the process.

The series of medical mishaps left Cornelius unemployed, a wheelchair user, and dependent on bottled oxygen and a continuous morphine drip to dampen the pain. His medical expenses and lost wages were estimated at more than $5 million should he live to retirement age.

Following the three-word American tradition known as "sue the bastards," Cornelius consulted a lawyer and filed a medical malpractice lawsuit against the physical therapist, the hospital, and some of the doctors. That's when he discovered exactly what he'd accomplished back in 1975. The medical malpractice bill he'd helped pass through the Indiana legislature as a lobbyist ensured that he could recover only a fraction of the $5 million in losses the health care system's failures had cost him. In 1990 Cornelius settled his lawsuits against the hospital and physical therapist for $500,000, the most he could get.* The experience transformed Cornelius into something of a consumer advocate, and he used his lobbying skills to help Ralph Nader and others across the country campaign against further restrictions on lawsuits. He went on *The Phil Donahue Show.*

In 1994 he wrote a mea culpa in the *New York Times* in which he wrote, "I have received last rites from my church. . . . At the age of 49, I am told that I have less than two years to live. . . . All of my suffering might have been worthwhile, on some cosmic scale, if the law had accomplished its stated purpose. But it hasn't." He went on to note that the argument he'd used to persuade legislators to cap malpractice awards—that it would reduce health-care costs—had proved to be a sham. Health care costs in Indiana had soared 139 percent between 1980 and 1990, he wrote, noting that it was just about the national average.

Cornelius's public act of contrition couldn't erase the severity of his condition. The daily dose of narcotics prevented him from driving, and the pain left him unable to work steadily, according to Cathy Cornelius, who became the breadwinner for a family of seven. Depression plagued him. His marriage fell apart, and as Cornelius wrote in the *Times,* "The emotional fallout on our five children has been difficult to witness, to say the least."

On March 1, 1995, Cornelius died, after intentionally overdosing on morphine. Along with his suicide note, he left behind one last piece of written testimony for the Indiana state legislature, which was considering a new bill to restrict lawsuits even further.

For years, the tort reform movement was something of a fringe element in Washington and elsewhere, a special-interest group that popped up every ten years or so when insurance premiums got out of whack. Democrats have historically opposed it, and Americans have never put lawsuits at the

---

*Many of the lawsuits discussed in this book ended in settlement. It should be noted that parties settle lawsuits for a variety of reasons, and settlements typically do not contain any admissions of liability.

top of their list of national concerns. They're far more concerned about education, crime, and Social Security. Even the term itself, *tort reform,* is largely meaningless outside of Washington and certain legal and business circles. (*Tort* is the legal term for "injury.") As the famous Mississippi trial lawyer Richard "Dickie" Scruggs reportedly once said, "Most Americans don't know what tort reform is, and if they did, they'd be against it." But when President George W. Bush and Senator John Kerry sparred over the issue in front of fifty million TV viewers in the second 2004 presidential debate, tort reform went mainstream, joining the Iraq war and illegal immigration as top issues facing the nation.

During that debate in St. Louis, audience member Norma-Jean Laurent posed a tough question for the Democratic challenger. Laurent noted how Kerry had bemoaned the rising cost of health care for Americans. Yet she wanted to know how the candidate could reconcile this concern with his choice of a running mate who had made millions of dollars successfully suing medical professionals.

The question reflected the ongoing debate over high rates for doctors' medical malpractice insurance. Bush had turned this into a major campaign issue by blaming the problem on greedy trial lawyers and frivolous lawsuits and calling for restrictions on jury awards. It also presented Kerry with a tremendous opportunity. As a lawyer himself, Kerry had a powerful opportunity to deliver a spirited defense of the civil justice system. He could have argued for the good sense of American jurors, who know a frivolous lawsuit when they see one, without needing the heavy hand of Washington to tell them what to do. He might have suggested that people need the legal system to hold doctors accountable for the injuries they cause, which number in the hundreds of thousands every year. Most important, he might have pointed out that malpractice awards had little to do with rising health care costs.

Instead, Kerry simply said, "John Edwards and I support tort reform." Kerry then referred Laurent to his website, where he said she could find a tort reform plan outlining his proposals for limiting lawsuits.

Kerry's dodge reflected just how much success the business lobby has had in framing the nation's conversation about the civil justice system. In putting himself and trial lawyer John Edwards on record as tort reform supporters, Kerry was explicitly endorsing the conventional wisdom put forth by Bush and his business backers that Americans are too litigious, that an epidemic of frivolous lawsuits is driving doctors out of business, and that lawsuits are hindering America's economic progress.

Kerry's office never responded to several requests to interview him for this book to clarify his position, but in truth, Kerry and Edwards did not support tort reform, at least not as it's commonly articulated by its major proponents. In the Senate, neither man had ever voted for a major tort reform bill, and Kerry would go on to vote against a bill to restrict class actions in 2005. Apparently, though, not even the $33 million donated to his and Edwards's campaigns by plaintiff lawyers, whose primary issue is fighting off limits on lawsuits, or the fact that his kid brother is a trial lawyer, could persuade Kerry to rise to the defense of the beleaguered American civil justice system on prime-time TV. And why would he?

Thanks to three decades and millions of dollars' worth of careful marketing by corporations and their paid legions of lobbyists, pundits, and think-tank hacks, it's hard to find an American who hasn't heard the story of Stella Liebeck, the woman who spilled McDonald's coffee in her lap and won a $3-million jury verdict against the company. Poll after poll shows that Americans overwhelmingly support limits on "lawsuit abuse" and believe that out-of-control litigation is just another symptom of the decline of personal responsibility in America.

Persuading Americans that the "litigation crisis" is a myth was a losing battle, and one that would take a lot longer than the brief time Kerry had to respond in the televised debate. Besides, as it's currently packaged, tort reform sounds so reasonable. Who could be against reform?

But the self-described "reformers" Kerry was rhetorically linking arms with are anything but. They are a retrograde alliance of insurance companies, corporate interests, and political operatives—mostly Republican—who seek to do away with many of the consumer, worker, and environmental protections established in the 1960s and 1970s. They have manufactured a litigation crisis that does not exist, to support their efforts to limit or even abolish average citizens' right to sue for damages when they have been wrongfully injured. And the legal rights they seek to curtail are things that most people take for granted, at least until they really need them.

It's hard to think of another public policy issue where the reality is so far removed from the myths that dominate the public discussion. Popular culture regularly leaves the impression that justice in the courtroom is alive and well. Movies like *Erin Brockovich* or *A Civil Action* suggest that David regularly bests Goliath in the courthouse and that great legal heroes are still fighting the good fight on behalf of the little guy. That impression, though, couldn't be more wrong.

New state laws pushed by anti-lawsuit crusaders and slanted media coverage are partly responsible for pushing jury trials to the verge of extinction, and the trial lawyers who lead them are an endangered species. Sober government data repeatedly show that plaintiffs' success rates at trial are at an all-time low, and they're winning ever smaller amounts of money. The right to a civil jury trial—guaranteed by the Bill of Rights—is in serious jeopardy. Personal injury lawsuits, the kind most despised by Bush and his business supporters, are on the decline. Punitive damages awards, which are given only in cases involving really egregious conduct, are equally rare events. The notion that Americans who take on deep-pocketed defendants or health care providers are making out like bandits is belied by numbers showing that plaintiffs in civil cases are taking it on the chin, losing far more often than they win.

Yet the perception of the legal system as out of whack has proven highly resistant to correction by the truth. This is by design. The movement against greedy trial lawyers and irresponsible plaintiffs is the result of a concerted and successful campaign by large corporations (especially the tobacco and insurance industries, but many others besides), to get this issue on the table and limit their vulnerability in the civil justice system. They have spent decades, and many millions of dollars, on focus groups and Madison Avenue public-relations research. They have funded institutes, sponsored academic research, bankrolled politicians, set up phony "Astroturf" grassroots organizations (with chamber of commerce return addresses), and fed copy to journalists. And in 2004, they succeeded in making the issue the stuff of a presidential debate, after having funneled millions of dollars into every one of Bush's political campaigns since 1994.

For corporations, the self-interest involved is fairly plain. Tobacco companies, no longer able to dodge the bullet of liability for knowingly selling poisons, are making an end run around the civil justice system. If they can't win a class-action suit, they'll make suing itself illegal. Insurance companies, drowning in red ink from mismanagement and bad investments, hike insurance rates by huge sums and blame malpractice suits. The doctors, in turn, blame greedy lawyers—and their own injured patients.

In larger terms, the tort reform movement is just the logical sequel to the war against government regulation. Unable to fully dismantle popular consumer-protection and environmental laws in Congress, corporations have changed tactics and instead gone after trial lawyers and the suits that give teeth to those laws. This has proved to be an effective strategy, achieving the same results without mobilizing political resistance. After all, who can really come to the defense of lawyers?

Tort reform also draws on the ideological backlash against the 1960s-era policies that expanded civil rights and protections for various minority groups and added new legal remedies for people injured by defective products and environmental degradation. The language of antilawsuit propaganda is rich in calls for "personal responsibility." The welfare queen of the 1980s has been replaced by the fat guy suing McDonald's. The movement is populated by people who want to return to the golden years when elderly women who spilled coffee on their laps got sympathy, not punitive damages.

Even so, tort reform for many years had been a hard sell. Most of the companies looking for protection from lawsuits had such dismal safety and environmental records that they were case studies in the need *for* lawsuits. Tort reform might have remained on the fringes were it not for the beauty of polling data. In the early 1990s, based on polling and focus-group research largely underwritten by the tobacco industry, Republicans discovered that tort reform offered an ideal wedge issue in competitive campaigns. When framed as "lawsuit abuse" and focused on greedy trial lawyers rather than polluting and negligent corporations, it played wonderfully as a populist notion with voters.

As Bush also discovered, it made for a fabulous fund-raising vehicle as the "chronic defendants" in the business world happily anted up to support lawsuit restrictions. Even more importantly, though, GOP strategists realized that by attacking lawsuits and trial lawyers, they had a tremendous opportunity to undermine a principal source of Democratic support. Limit the earnings of plaintiffs' lawyers through caps on damages and other restrictions on lawsuits, and you limit a major source of income for the Democratic Party.

This book is in part about that marriage of corporate desire for immunity from lawsuits and the new breed of GOP politics. It's also the story of how big businesses succeeded in taking bad public-policy proposals, packaging and stage managing them, and selling them to the public through well-paid "experts," gullible journalists, and intensely misleading propaganda—all to the detriment of the average citizen, who still thinks that if he ever needs the legal system, it will be there for him. Unfortunately, as this book will show, in many parts of the country today, that is no longer the case.

Since 1986, forty-eight states have passed some type of restriction on lawsuits, ranging from limits on lawyers' fees, to restrictions on plaintiffs' access to expert testimony, to caps on noneconomic and punitive-damage awards. Since 1995 Congress also has passed legislation to rein in shareholders' lawsuits and class actions, and it has attempted to grant legal immunity to favored industries, from defense contractors to pharmaceutical companies to gun manufacturers to fast-food chains.

None of these restrictions on civil lawsuits and the power of juries that have come over the past twenty years would have been possible without the complicity of the media. The vast majority of the reporting on the civil justice system has been lazy and gullible. Reporters have bought into the propaganda, the spoon-fed story tips and bogus research generated by the tort reform movement. Respectable outlets like *60 Minutes* and *U.S. News & World Report* have reported outright falsehoods about lawsuits and the legal system, without apology. There are reporters who have questioned the conventional wisdom, but they are few and far between.

In one sense, it's easy to see how it happens. Few newspaper or TV reporters ever cover the civil side of the legal system as a beat, so they rarely understand its complexities. They only report the occasional big verdict, which skews the coverage by suggesting that such events are commonplace, when they aren't. Unlike most Americans, journalists are also frequently threatened with lawsuits, and occasionally sued. The same goes for their employers, which are increasingly the same types of huge corporations that have long backed the tort reform movement.

The truth is that the corporate war on the courts is also a war on journalists. It's an effort to keep the lid on potentially damaging information. Journalists are deluding themselves if they think they can produce important and groundbreaking investigative reporting without the documents and other information that is produced in discovery through private lawsuits. The Catholic Church wasn't about to turn over its files on pedophile priests just because the *Boston Globe* asked nicely. Most of the documentation on the scandal, including the names of the victims and the errant priests, came into the public eye because those victims sought out lawyers, who then forced the church to come clean under the threat of court sanctions.

Indeed, much of the country's greatest investigative journalism over the decades has relied heavily on information produced in the very private lawsuits that tort reform seeks to restrict. Who can forget the story of the Ford Pinto, where lawyers turned up the written cost-benefit analysis the automaker used to decide whether it was worth $5 per car to prevent passengers of the Pinto from going up in flames? The 1977 story in *Mother Jones* magazine that turned the Pinto into a national scandal would never have been written without the information produced in those lawsuits.

Only through private lawsuits did the public learn the extent to which asbestos companies hid the dangers of their products—products that have caused the deaths of more than 250,000 people since the 1960s, with numbers increasing daily. Ditto for tobacco litigation, which forced the release of millions of internal documents from big tobacco companies showing just how much they were lying to the public. All of this litigation produced award-winning journalism, which in turn created the impetus for change for the public good.

The same big businesses that want to put caps on medical malpractice lawsuits also want to limit plaintiffs' ability to request documents in discovery, and they want to keep those documents that are released sealed away from the public view. While they claim to fear the financial implications of litigation, they are just as afraid of the outrage that might occur if the public really knew the truth about how they run their businesses or treat workers and consumers.

In a country with a weak regulatory system, moreover, it's rarely the Food and Drug Administration or the Department of Justice that sheds light on these critical public concerns and generates calls to withdraw dangerous drugs, ban toxic substances, or address rollover risks on SUVs. It's private citizens through lawsuits. In fact, not only do journalists rely on these lawsuits for information, so do government regulatory agencies that lack the resources or the power or the political will to investigate themselves. Oftentimes, the most important function of civil lawsuits, even beyond compensation or justice for injured victims, is their role in unearthing critical health, safety, and financial information about the workings of private institutions.

Perhaps more than anything, tort reform is a frontal assault on the civil jury. It's designed to limit the power of average citizens to set community standards, mete out justice, and to hold wrongdoers accountable in the courts. That's why tort reform, at its heart, is an elitist notion based on distrust of the intelligence and good sense of American citizens to sit in the jury box and make a decision. That same logic can be used to make a case against voting, as voters and jurors are one and the same. With its current emphasis on caps on damage awards, tort reform creates arbitrary limits on a jury's power and vests judges—some who have lifetime political appointments—with vastly more authority over the outcome of a trial.

No system of justice is perfect, but the American civil jury system is close to perfect democracy. As a lawyer once explained to me, jury verdicts are like having 100 percent voter participation in elections; except in the case of the jury, the "voters" are much better informed. On a jury, everyone has to listen to the evidence presented by both sides, hopefully by articulate advocates, and then they have to vote. The jury is a tremendously powerful institution, powerful enough to prompt businesses to spend millions of dollars trying to disarm it. The Founding Fathers saw the jury trial as a protection against imperial judges, and the Constitution was nearly scuttled because it didn't include a provision for civil jury trials. (One was later added in the Seventh Amendment.) The French author and statesman Alexis de Tocqueville thought the civil jury was evidence of Americans' great faith in their ability to govern themselves.

In supporting the tort reformers' agenda, Americans don't seem to realize that they are hastening their own exclusion from the democratic process and creating yet another impediment to meaningful participation in public affairs. It's not just the ability to recover financially from a wrongful injury that's disappearing as a result of restrictions on lawsuits. Fundamental constitutional rights are dying a quiet death, as the thousands of serious lawsuits that never got filed are eclipsed by one or two big ones that did. The irony of the tort reform movement is that even as it's convinced Americans that the nation is in the midst of a litigation crisis, it's reinforced their misguided belief that the system will work for them if they need it. Like Frank Cornelius, a great many people have discovered the hard way that this just isn't the case. This book, I hope, will tell some of their stories and serve as a wake-up call about what's been lost—and what else we are about to lose—as the nation embraces the corporate war on lawsuits.

CHAPTER ONE

Too Good to Check: Media Myths about the Civil Justice System

U.S. News & World Report editor-in-chief Mort Zuckerman, in a June 2003 column titled "Welcome to Sue City, U.S.A.," made a startling claim: "Litigation," he wrote, "has become our national pastime." As proof, he offered several examples of asinine lawsuits. Zuckerman wrote, "A woman throws a soft drink at her boyfriend at a restaurant, then slips on the floor she wet and breaks her tailbone. She sues. Bingo—a jury says the restaurant owes her $100,000! A woman tries to sneak through a restroom window at a nightclub to avoid paying the $3.50 cover charge. She falls, knocks out two front teeth, and sues. A jury awards her $12,000 for dental expenses."

The anecdotes were catchy but—at least in several instances—unsubstantiated. The stories had been circulating for two years and had made it into several mainstream news outlets, including another Zuckerman property, the New York *Daily News,* which had published an item containing one of the lawsuits in the sports section a year earlier. When the *Washington Post*'s Howard Kurtz called him on the *U.S. News* error, Zuckerman's spokesman noted that the stories had been reported in a variety of other reputable publications and that "few Americans would disagree with the proposition that there are far too many frivolous lawsuits filed." The magazine later published only a brief clarification about the fictional suits, noting that the original article mentioned several lawsuits "originally cited by reputable publications as examples of absurd jury awards. However, after further research, two of the lawsuits could not be independently substantiated." When I contacted his office, a spokesperson for

Zuckerman refused to discuss the lawsuit anecdotes or to offer an explanation as to why Zuckerman would publish this stuff without checking it out first.

Zuckerman was hardly the only journalist to get duped by the bogus stories. Small-town papers seem even more vulnerable to such fabrications than the national media. For instance, in February 2003, the *Weirton Daily Times* in Weirton, West Virginia, published an editorial supporting tort reform legislation that was pending in the state and blaming juries for outrageous decisions in frivolous lawsuits. Among the examples was the story of an Oklahoma man who put his Winnebago on cruise control at 70 miles per hour and "calmly left the driver's seat to go into the back and make himself a cup of coffee." Naturally, after the crash, the man sued Winnebago for not advising him of the dangers of cruise control. A jury awarded the man $1.75 million and a new motor home, the paper said.

Every one of the lawsuits mentioned in the *Daily Times* editorial stemmed from an anonymous email and could not be corroborated as true. A local attorney, Michael Nogay, called *Daily Times* managing editor Richard Crofton and alerted him to the error. But rather than print a humble retraction, Crofton argued in print that the *essence* of the editorial was true and published several examples of "real" frivolous lawsuits.

"What really killed me was that they didn't even say, 'We're sorry,'" says Nogay, who notes that the column came a week or so after the state chamber of commerce had run a full-page ad in the paper calling for tort reform while the legislature was in session. When I asked Crofton what made him write about the suits without checking their veracity, he replied, "We're a small paper, and I don't have the resources to track down things all over the country."

No one ever claimed responsibility for the email, but it's safe to say that the media had been well primed to buy into it. For nearly thirty years, insurance companies, the tobacco industry, and corporate-funded think tanks and advocacy groups have been plying reporters and the public with fictitious or badly misleading stories that purport to show that the nation suffers from a crisis of frivolous litigation.

The campaign has worked according to plan. Nearly everything Americans think they know about the civil justice system is but a caricature of the reality that takes place inside the nation's courthouses—or, more likely, just flat-out wrong. The ability of tort reformers to boil down a complex policy issue into a catchy sound bite, and to actively mask the true identity of those pushing this particular view of the system, is devilishly shrewd. The media have fallen into line, for the most part, creating a steady drumbeat for nearly every state in the union to restrict citizens' rights to sue.

★ ★ ★

The current PR campaign had its origins in the 1950s. Its first target was informed news consumers, who just happened to double as jurors in abeyance. Ads sponsored by the insurance industry appeared in *Life* magazine and the *Saturday Evening Post* as early as 1953, declaring, "ruled by emotion rather than facts, [jurors] arrive at unfounded or excessive awards—verdicts occasionally even higher than requested!" The ads implored would-be jurors to remember that "you pay for liability and damage suit verdicts whether you are insured or not."

The insurance sector had strong bottom-line imperatives for getting its message out. In the '50s, plaintiff lawyers started breaking down some of the legal barriers that had long protected industry from responsibility for injuries to workers and consumers, and opened up jury pools to make them more representative of the general public. The bloodbath on the nation's highways during the postwar auto boom also created a whole new arena of litigation over who should pay for the injuries and deaths caused in car accidents. Auto insurance companies were frequently in the middle of these disputes (as they are today; insurance companies are the defendants in 90 percent of all auto accident lawsuits). Indeed, the insurance industry is the self-acknowledged "banker of the tort system," responsible for paying the legal bills and any settlements and verdicts in nearly every type of litigation imaginable today.

Plaintiff lawyers viewed the insurance companies' advertising offensive not as a legitimate act of free speech but as jury tampering. In several states, lawyers unsuccessfully brought suits against the insurance sector on this basis. In one of those cases, the plaintiffs offered up an article in *Shop Talk*, an American-Associated Insurance Companies publication. The piece described just what the industry hoped to achieve with the ads, outlining how the campaign was designed to "combat the important problem of unjust jury awards," and bragged that "more than one out of every three potential jurors will see at least one of these advertisements."

These early years of clashes over tort reform foreshadowed what would become a pattern in subsequent decades: namely, the resourcefulness of the insurance lobby and the weak counterpunches of the plaintiffs' bar. For instance, the insurance industry successfully planted articles in national magazines and TV shows that were designed to look like investigative reporting. In 1962 CBS broadcast *Smash-Up,* a fictionalized docudrama that portrayed sleazy lawyers faking auto accident cases. The Insurance Information Institute, the industry's public-relations arm, helped write the script.

In 1977 the venerable insurance company Crum & Forester sponsored one of the first print ads that included what would become a staple of anti-lawsuit rhetoric: the fictional lawsuit horror story. The ad told the story of a guy who collected a $500,000 jury verdict after he was injured using a lawnmower as a hedge clipper. The agency later conceded that it had no reliable source for the alleged incident.

The industry occasionally abandoned its shotgun approach to PR and went straight after jurors. Once, in the 1950s, an insurance company mailed reprints of an article called, "Why Your Auto Insurance Costs So Much"—which claimed that excessive jury awards were driving up insurance rates—directly to jurors on a car crash case. The company's executive vice president was found in contempt of court and fined $1,000.

The industry knew what it was doing. In 1979 Elizabeth Loftus, the famous memory researcher and University of California psychologist, tested the effects of this kind of advertising on potential jurors and their decision making in the jury box. At the time, the industry was spending $10 million on a series of ads in a host of national magazines. In an article in the *American Bar Association Journal,* Loftus reported that potential jurors who were exposed to even one insurance ad awarded much less for pain and suffering than those who weren't.

The tort reformers' appeals gained in sophistication as time wore on. In 1986 *Newsweek* ran a series of ads sponsored by the insurance industry under the heading "We All Pay the Price." The ads warned that lawsuits were driving ob-gyns out of business, shuttering local school sports programs, and scaring the clergy out of counseling their flocks—though few of these assertions turned out to be true.

Around the same time, fake or misleading lawsuit stories began to pop up in respectable news outlets. In 1986, *60 Minutes* profiled the owner of a ladder manufacturing company who claimed that his company had been hit with a $300,000 jury verdict in a suit by a man who fell off a ladder because he set it in a pile of manure. According to the business owner, the lawsuit alleged the company should have warned buyers of the dangers of setting ladders in dung. In fact, the real lawsuit had nothing to do with manure; the ladder had broken with fewer than 450 pounds on it, even though it had a safety rating that said it could support up to 1,000. According to a spokesman for the network 60 *Minutes* never ran a correction.

The campaign to spread litigation myths got a huge boost in May 1987, when President Ronald Reagan, appearing before the newly launched American Tort Reform Association (ATRA), told an old litigation horror story that would become a staple of tort reform rhetoric for years to come. According to Reagan, a California man was making a call in a public phone booth when a drunk driver crashed into the booth. "Now, it's no surprise that the injured man sued. But you might be startled to hear whom he sued: the telephone company and associated firms."

As with many of Reagan's favorite anecdotes, this one wasn't quite complete. There was, in fact, a California lawsuit involving a man injured in a phone booth. But the case transpired a little differently. In 1974 custodian Charles Bigbee was indeed making a call in a public phone booth outside a liquor store, but he had seen the speeding car coming and tried to flee. The door to the phone booth jammed, and he ended up severely injured, losing a leg in the accident. Bigbee later learned that the same phone booth had been totally destroyed a year and a half earlier by another car, and that the phone company had simply replaced it without any additional safety features. His injuries left him broke, depressed, and unable to walk. It took eleven years of litigation before the phone company and the booth manufacturer finally settled Bigbee's claim for an undisclosed amount.

Bigbee actually tried to set the record straight with Reagan and came to DC to testify at a congressional hearing on tort reform. But Reagan never responded, and members of his administration continued to recycle the misleading version of the story as part of their broader campaign to restrict lawsuits.

Reagan was a chronic offender in spreading litigation myths. He also liked to tell the famous story of the psychic who won a million dollars after she claimed that a CT scan caused her to lose her psychic powers, another perennial in the annals of tort mythology. The psychic story had been kicking around for some time before Reagan got to it, but he gave it new life. As with the phone booth tale, the psychic story was based on a

real case, but in the condensed version, the facts were badly miscon-
strued.

The psychic in question was a woman named Judith Haimes, who at
thirty-three was suffering from tumors in her ears. She went to Temple University Hospital in Philadelphia for a CT scan. Haimes told the radiologist
that she had previously suffered a bad allergic reaction to the dye sometimes
used in CT scans. The radiologist dismissed her claim and proposed giving
her a small dose of the dye to see what happened. Almost immediately,
Haimes started vomiting, lost control of her bladder, and had difficulty
breathing. She broke out in hives and for the next two days was extremely
sick. The hives hung on for several weeks afterward. After the reaction, she
suffered from debilitating headaches when she performed tasks involving
intense concentration.

Haimes sued the doctor and the hospital for the injury. As part of her
claim, she sought compensation for the loss of her psychic abilities, because
she had been unable to work after suffering from the allergic reaction.
When the case went to trial in 1986, eleven years after the incident, the
state court judge instructed the jury to ignore that part of her claim because
she'd failed to offer an expert witness who could testify that the dye had
caused her headaches. The only thing the jury considered was whether she
should receive an award for pain and suffering during and shortly after the
dye injection. The jury awarded Haimes $600,000 in damages, but the judge
threw out the award as excessive. Haimes went through a second trial, and
a different judge dismissed the case entirely, and she never got a dime.

The psychic and the CT scan story has been endlessly recycled, pre-
served for posterity in the introduction of Peter Huber's book *Galileo's Revenge* attacking science in the courtroom. "The most fantastic verdict
recorded so far was worthy of a tabloid," wrote Huber, a fellow at the Manhattan Institute for Policy Research. "[A] soothsayer who decided that she
had lost her psychic powers following a CAT scan persuaded a Philadelphia jury to award her $1 million in damages." Huber did note that a judge
had thrown the case out, but claimed that "scientific frauds of similar character if lesser audacity are attempted almost daily in our courts, and many
succeed."

Steve Brill, founder of the *American Lawyer* magazine, first wrote about
litigation myths back in 1986, when, as a journalist, he traced several examples of the allegedly frivolous lawsuits and found that many of them were
simply urban legends. Reporters' perpetuation of the litigation myths has
become one of Brill's pet peeves, even though, as a business owner himself,

he supports legal changes that would protect businesses. "Reporters are basically lazy," says Brill. "You can always find a ridiculous lawsuit to make the system look crazy."

Such tales have been so effective that today, feeding myths to the media about the legal system has become a cottage industry. There are dozens of think tanks and advocacy groups, mostly created by some of the nation's leading PR firms, dedicated to the cause. These groups are constantly culling the wires for examples of frivolous lawsuits or outrageous plaintiffs and their lawyers, which they frequently repackage in simpler terms to heighten the outrage factor. The internet has only extended the reach of such stories.

One group active in such pursuits is the American Tort Reform Association, the nation's leading tort reform advocacy group. Founded in 1986 by the American Medical Association, ATRA—as with all tort reform groups—sells itself as an organization devoted to protecting average Americans from lawsuits. In one of its early fund-raising letters, it claimed that ATRA was "not a wealthy special-interest group backed by vast cash resources. . . . ATRA is the home owner tired of paying exorbitant insurance premiums for minimal coverage. ATRA is the average citizen looking for an end to the threat of being sued."

Of course, ATRA's funding actually comes from most of the nation's largest corporations, particularly pharmaceutical, insurance, and tobacco companies, which ante up $50,000 or $75,000 apiece for their membership, according to a report in *Legal Times*. ATRA's website features a "Loony Lawsuit" section that includes such recent entries as "A viewer has sued NBC for $2.5 million over a *Fear Factor* rat-eating episode, alleging the episode made him dizzy, lightheaded, and caused him to vomit and run into a doorway." ATRA doesn't mention that in the *Fear Factor* lawsuit, plaintiff Austin Aitken had filed a four-page handwritten lawsuit in a federal court in Cleveland in January 2005, without the aid of a lawyer. By March, a judge had thrown it out, a sign that the system was working as it should be.

Gretchen Schaefer, ATRA's communications director, says she compiles the entries from submissions from various sources: defense lawyers, tips from state leadership groups, random readers. She says that there are dozens of state-level civil justice reform groups that have their own newsletters, for which they also compile examples of crazy lawsuits; many of those work their way up to the national level. But she concedes that she doesn't confirm the veracity of the reports, check out the actual legal complaints, or call any of the lawyers involved to check on the suit's fate.

"There's not a research component to it other than checking if it's a valid source," she says.

The same groups that circulate outrageous lawsuit stories to the media have actively marketed many of the litigation myths directly to the public and elected officials as part of their organized efforts to pass legislation limiting lawsuits. There's no better example than the case of Stella Liebeck, the New Mexico woman who sued McDonald's after spilling hot coffee in her lap and won a $2.9-million jury verdict in August 1994.

The Liebeck case is the beginning and the end of what many Americans know about the civil justice system, even though the original verdict was rendered more than a decade ago. That jury verdict set off a flurry of media coverage and snide editorializing about America's "victim" culture. Jay Leno and David Letterman worked the story into monologues and other gags. Jerry Seinfeld later did a famous show in which Cosmo Kramer spills coffee on himself and hires a Johnnie Cochran—style lawyer to sue. (He settles for a year's worth of free coffee, much to his lawyer's chagrin.) The *New York Times* editorialized in 1995, "Life used to be blissfully simple: the coffee hot, the drinker sitting and sipping. But now everyone's hither and yon, perching takeout coffee in mid-dash. And spilling it. And suing someone."

The more the Liebeck story was retold on talk radio and in op-eds by antilawsuit crusaders, the more distorted it became. Of course, the cartoon version of Stella Liebeck and the hot coffee was significantly different than the actual case. The facts presented to the jury clearly showed that the famous frivolous hot-coffee case was anything but frivolous.

Stella Liebeck was an unusual poster child for the tort reform movement. At the time of her accident, in 1992, Liebeck was recently retired as a department store salesclerk. She hailed from a family of longtime conservative Republicans and had never filed a lawsuit in her life before her run-in with McDonald's. The whole mess started when the seventy-nine-year-old woman was riding in a car with her grandson. They stopped at the drive-through of an Albuquerque McDonald's, and Liebeck bought a cup of coffee. Her grandson, who was driving, pulled up to the curb so she could doctor up the coffee with cream and sugar. The Ford Probe didn't have a cup holder, so Liebeck put the cup between her legs and took off the lid. As she did, the coffee spilled onto her lap, and she started screaming. Her grandson figured she was going to be fine, as people spill coffee all the time. But a few minutes later, he realized that his grandmother was quite ill, nauseous, and possibly in shock. He took her to the hospital, where she was treated for third-degree burns on her thighs and private parts. The accident left her hospitalized for over a week, where she underwent painful skin grafts, and was permanently disfigured.

Experts would later testify that it was McDonald's policy to serve its coffee between 195 to 205 degrees Fahrenheit—liquid temperatures high enough to peel skin off bone in about seven seconds or less. As the bills mounted, Liebeck left the hospital earlier than her doctors recommended, so her daughter took time off from work to transport her back and forth for continuing treatment. The elderly woman suffered immensely, wasting away to a mere eighty-six pounds. She was partially disabled for about two years after the spill.

Liebeck didn't consult a lawyer initially. She attempted to contact McDonald's herself, to alert it to the dangers of the hot coffee in the hopes that the company would turn down the temperature to protect unsuspecting customers. She also asked the fast-food giant to pay for her medical costs. Liebeck's total demands added up to about $20,000. After six months, McDonald's informed Liebeck that it wasn't going to change its coffee policy, but it would send her $800 for her troubles. The callous dismissal prompted Liebeck to consult a lawyer. She eventually hired Houston attorney Reed Morgan, who filed a lawsuit on her behalf. Morgan had offered to settle the case for $300,000; a mediator suggested $225,000, but McDonald's refused to settle, so the case went to trial.

From the beginning, the jurors in the McDonald's case were skeptical of Liebeck's claim. But once they heard evidence that the company had received more than seven hundred complaints of serious burns from its coffee—including reports from the Shriners Burn Institute in Cincinnati, which had treated numerous coffee injuries, and another serious case that also led to a lawsuit—they realized that Liebeck had a legitimate beef with Mickey D's. McDonald's executives admitted that even though they had known for many years that the coffee could literally burn to the bone, they had done nothing to change their policies.

Jurors were outraged. They awarded Liebeck $200,000 for her actual economic losses and medical bills, but they docked the award by 20 percent to account for the fact that Liebeck was partially responsible for the injury. She had, of course, spilled the coffee on herself. On top of the $160,000 in actual damages, the jury awarded $2.7 million in punitive damages—about two days' profits from McDonald's coffee sales at that time—as a way of punishing the company for its casual disregard for its customers' safety.

The Republican judge who'd overseen the trial thought the punitive award was excessive and reduced it to $480,000, or three times the actual damages. Even so, Judge Robert Scott still believed that McDonald's deserved to be punished with the punitive award. He wrote, "I conclude that the award of punitive damages is and was appropriate to punish and deter the Defendant for their wanton conduct and to send a clear message to this Defendant that corrective measures are appropriate." The jury verdict apparently hit home; reporters noted that the day after the verdict, McDonald's coffee passed through Albuquerque drive-throughs had cooled to a considerably safer 158 degrees Fahrenheit. The Liebeck case eventually settled for an undisclosed amount, but far less than the $3 million advertised in the headline news versions of the story.

Some responsible news outlets reported all of this from the beginning, but the condensed version of the hot-coffee lawsuit was far more entertaining and enduring, particularly on the opinion pages. Typical of the media treatment was this 1994 editorial in the *San Diego Union-Tribune,* which said, "When Stella Liebeck fumbled her coffee cup as she rode in the car with her grandson, she might as well have bought a winning lottery ticket. The spilled coffee netted her $2.9 million in the form of a jury award. . . . This absurd judgment is a stunning illustration of what is wrong with America's civil justice system. . . . Our guess is that other greedy copycats in restaurants throughout America soon will be happily dumping coffee into their laps in a bid to make a similar killing in the courtroom."

Even so, the case might eventually have faded from the public eye as just another item in "News of the Weird" were it not for the well-oiled tort reform PR machine. By the end of 1994, most of the news coverage about the Liebeck case had died off. But in 1995, a new Republican Congress made lawsuit abuse an item on its Contract with America agenda, and tort reform suddenly became a looming battle on Capitol Hill. Republicans were focusing on restricting products-liability lawsuits. Products-liability law is complex, and the reforms sought on the Hill were equally mind-numbing. Legal terms like *joint and several liability* were resistant to sound biting; the hot-coffee lawsuit against the nation's most beloved fast-food chain, though, was something everyone could understand.

The Liebeck case was a gold mine for tort reformers looking to support the legislation, and they used it repeatedly in advertising and testimony. For instance, in 1995, a year in which the tobacco industry gave ATRA $5.5 million (nearly half its annual budget), the group spent hundreds of thousands of dollars buying TV and radio ads promoting tort reform. The radio ads intoned, "A jury awarded a woman $2.9 million in a lawsuit against McDonald's. She spilled coffee on her lap while sitting in her car and claimed it was too hot." ATRA wasn't alone. The nation's largest business lobbying group, The U.S. Chamber of Commerce also bought radio ads that said, "Is it fair to get a couple of million dollars from a restaurant just because you spilled your hot coffee on yourself? Of course not. It's ridiculous. But it happened."

Citizens for a Sound Economy (CSE), now known as FreedomWorks, is another right-wing think tank that invoked Liebeck in its lobbying efforts. Chaired by former George H. W. Bush White House counsel C. Boyden Gray, CSE counts among its members big chemical, oil, drug, telecommunications, and tobacco companies. It runs "grassroots" campaigns in favor of lawsuit restrictions and other favored libertarian industry policies. The group was founded by Charles and David Koch, the leaders of Koch Industries, one of the nation's largest privately held oil and natural gas companies. Koch has annual sales of more than $40 billion and has faced several lawsuits alleging environmental violations. At the time of the products-liability battle on the Hill, the Koch charitable foundation had given CSE more than $8 million. Philip Morris USA was also chipping in to CSE with $250,000 a year.

With that kind of funding, CSE had no problem spending $5 million in early 1995 on TV and radio ads supporting products-liability legislation in about sixty different congressional districts. It also organized a telemarketing campaign to contact thousands of voters in those districts, urging them to contact their congressional representatives to support lawsuit restrictions. The script for calls turned up in documents produced in the litigation against Philip Morris. Entitled "Lawsuit Abuse Patch Thru Script," the document describes how callers would contact a member of Citizens for a Sound Economy to ask for support for the Common Sense Legal Reform Act, a key element of the Contract with America. After a brief introduction, the script launches right into the Liebeck case, with, "Did you know that a woman in a civil court case got a jury to award her $2.9 million dollars from a restaurant chain because she spilled coffee on herself that was too hot? Cases just like this are being filed every day in courtrooms across the country."

The script goes on to insist that the legislation in question would bring "fairness" into the civil court system, decrease the number of frivolous lawsuits, and ensure that the punishment "more accurately reflects the actual damage caused." Then call recipients could be transferred to their own congressman to pitch the case themselves.

At least one other big corporation overtly took advantage of the Liebeck verdict to lobby for the products-liability bill. Mobil Oil ran a big ad in the *New York Times,* noting that "nearly $3 million was awarded to a customer who spilled hot coffee on herself."

The myth that Stella Liebeck actually received $3 million for her coffee spill has proved highly resistant to correction. During the debates over the products-liability law in 1995, the nonprofit consumer group Public Citizen brought Liebeck to Washington and held a press conference to try to set the record straight. Tort reformers organized a protest, so that when Liebeck appeared, she was greeted with protesters carrying signs that said, She Spilled It on Herself. An internet-based publishing outfit now compiles a list of the year's most outrageous lawsuits and dubs it the Stella Awards, ensuring that the poor woman's name will be forever associated with legal-system excess.

University of Washington political science professor Michael McCann has dubbed litigation myths "pop torts." McCann and coauthor William Haltom at the University of Puget Sound spent five years analyzing media coverage of the tort system. They thoroughly dissected the coverage of the McDonald's coffee case for their recent book, *Distorting the Law.* McCann believes that one reason the McDonald's coffee case gained such notoriety and enduring status as an urban legend is that the tort-reform groups had been working for at least fifteen years to create the public perception that lawsuits were out of control. "The public and the media were so primed for this to happen, it was like the perfect storm," he says.

President Bill Clinton ultimately vetoed the products-liability bill that was at the heart of all the media frenzy back in the 1990s. But the effects of all the marketing and media were still considered a success by at least one tort reform lobbyist. Victor Schwartz, the éminence grise of the movement and general counsel to ATRA, told *Legal Times* in 1996, "In 1967, when I first walked into a classroom, the only word associated with tort reform was 'arcane.' Now cabdrivers know about the McDonald's case."

★ ★ ★

In December 2003, *Newsweek* featured a cover story by Stuart Taylor and Evan Thomas that blared: "Lawsuit Hell: Doctors. Teachers. Coaches. Ministers. They all share a common fear: being sued on the job." Paired with a weeklong tie-in on NBC News and online chats on MSNBC.com, the article claimed that because "Americans will sue each other at the slightest provocation," the country is suffering from an "onslaught of litigation" that costs Americans $200 billion a year. The story was full of tales claiming to illustrate Americans' overarching sense of legal entitlement and desire to "win a jackpot from a system that allows sympathetic juries to award plaintiffs not just real damages . . . but millions more for the impossible-to-measure 'pain and suffering' and highly arbitrary 'punitive damages.'"

Among others, the story featured a softball tournament organizer, a minister, and a doctor who all claimed to have modified their behavior because they were terrified of lawsuits. Ryan Warner, an insurance salesman in Page, Arizona, told *Newsweek* that he had recently canceled an annual charity softball tournament because an injured player had sued the city of Page for $100,000. Warner said that he worried he might be added as a defendant.

The article presented Warner's story in one paragraph, leaving little room for certain details. *Newsweek* didn't mention, for instance, that the 1997 federal Volunteer Protection Act ensures that volunteers are immunized from damages in most of these types of lawsuits, so Warner's fear of being sued was not well-founded. The article also did not mention that the injured man, Richard Sawyer, was a locomotive engineer who suffered a dislocated ankle and a spiral fracture to the fibula, and missed months of work as a result—after he slid into a base that was supposed to break away on impact but didn't. According to Sawyer's lawyer, Kevin Garrison, the city hadn't followed the manufacturer's instructions for maintaining these fixtures properly.

The event organizers had insurance—required by the city—to protect against exactly this kind of situation, but Warner canceled the tournament anyway because he says the lawsuit was "a hassle." Canceling the tournament proved a smart PR move, as it brought out an immense amount of pressure on Sawyer from his friends and teammates to drop his suit, says Garrison. However, Garrison didn't drop the case. It was settled in January 2004 for an undisclosed amount, Warner was never named, and the tournament was revived shortly thereafter.

The *Newsweek* piece used the anecdotes to support its claim that Americans will sue each other at the slightest provocation. (The piece does note

that litigation has been a force of good, making companies and public officials be more responsible, for example—a position forcefully articulated by
Senator John Edwards in the same *Newsweek* issue.) And yet *Newsweek*'s
"onslaught" of lawsuits simply hasn't happened. Personal injury and other
tort filings fell 5 percent between 1994 and 2003 in twenty-nine states studied by the National Center for State Courts (NCSC), a nonpartisan research group funded by the state courts themselves. According to the
Congressional Budget Office (CBO), the NCSC numbers, when controlled
for population growth, show that personal-injury filings and other tort filings declined nationally by 8 percent between 1975 and 2000, and they've
been falling steadily in real numbers since 1996. The numbers are even more
dramatic in places with rapid population growth, like Texas, where the rate
of tort filings per 100,000 residents fell 26 percent between 1994 and 2003.

Jury trials are likewise on the decline. The most recent data from the
U.S. Department of Justice's Bureau of Justice Statistics (BJS) show that between 1985 and 2003, the number of tort trials in federal courts plummeted
by 80 percent. A similar phenomenon is at work in the state courts. In the
nation's seventy-five largest counties studied over the past decade by the
BJS, the number of jury trials fell by 23 percent between 1992 and 2001.

Taylor and Thomas also made short shrift of the many changes in state
laws that have taken place since 2001 that will accelerate this trend, including a constitutional amendment in Texas that allowed the state to radically
cap pain-and-suffering awards in medical malpractice cases, a change that
took place with a great deal of publicity three months before *Newsweek*'s
story was published. Just between September 2003 and September 2004,
the *Dallas Morning News* reports, medical malpractice filings in Texas fell 80
percent.

And those overly sympathetic juries *Newsweek* derides as so eager to
dole out big bucks to injured victims? In 2001 they voted against plaintiffs
in 75 percent of all medical malpractice trials, according to the BJS, and the
amount of money they're awarding is rapidly shrinking. Median jury verdicts in tort cases plummeted 56 percent between 1992 and 2001, from
$64,000 to $28,000.

In an interview, Taylor dismissed the declining jury verdict numbers as
insignificant compared with the tort system's $200 billion drag on the econ-
omy. "The costs of the tort system to society have gone up astronomically,"
he says. That figure, though, comes from the insurance-industry consulting
firm Tillinghast-Towers Perrin (TTP), whose occasional reports on U.S. tort
costs include in their definition of the tort system insurance-company ad-

ministrative costs and overhead, and all or a portion of the salaries of certain highly paid insurance company CEOs. One thing TTP *doesn't* include is court budgets, which makes its study seem a lot more like an assessment of the insurance industry than of the legal system.

The TTP study is so deeply flawed and largely meaningless that the consulting firm finally acknowledged as much in the 2004 edition of "U.S. Tort Costs," writing that "the costs tabulated in this study are not a reflection of litigated claims or of the legal system." The problems with this study have been repeatedly outlined in academic journals for years. But the primary reason for this admission by TTP is that its definition of *tort costs* includes such things as insurance claims where no lawsuits were filed—such as for auto accidents, including those in no-fault states, where lawsuits are in fact banned for certain auto accidents and for which people pay insurance premiums.

Their "tort costs" also don't take into account the profits that the insurance companies earn from premiums or the dividends paid to policyholders (like doctors), or the earnings from their investments—a net plus to the economy that should be used to offset any alleged "drain" on the economy caused by the tort system.

Taylor and Thomas also based lots of their article on information provided by Philip K. Howard, the founder of Common Good, a group funded by corporations and physicians seeking to limit their legal liability for wrongdoing. Common Good's agenda includes advocating for legislation that would end the civil jury's role in many lawsuits. To advance the cause, Common Good helps reporters generate antilawsuit articles by distributing colorful litigation horror stories from around the country—the story from the *Arizona Daily Sun* about Warner's softball tournament, for instance, was linked on Common Good's website a few months before the *Newsweek* story appeared. (Taylor insists that he did not take any information from Howard or Common Good without carefully checking its accuracy and completeness.)

In the end, the most discouraging aspect of the *Newsweek* piece is that its criticism of the civil justice system is the rule, not the exception. Every few months, one or another newspaper, magazine, or television show— often well-regarded publications like *Newsweek* or TV's *60 Minutes*—does a story just like it. They all hew to a familiar format, starting with the juicy but potentially misleading lawsuit story typically describing an irresponsible plaintiff, followed by "studies" on the economic damage of the tort system, and including profiles of those calling for reforms to rein in mushy-headed juries and greedy trial lawyers.

The *Newsweek* piece is a classic example of the tort reform movement's two-pronged assault on the media. Along with encouraging urban legends about the civil justice system, tort reformers have sought to create the public impression that hard data and objective researchers show the existence of a lawsuit crisis that the tort reformers' pet proposals would, of course, cure.

While advocacy groups like CSE and ATRA have spent millions ensuring that Americans are on a first-name basis with the McDonald's coffee plaintiff, other think tanks have supported the cause by producing what appears to be academic research that provides a more intellectual basis for their agenda. One of the most influential of those research groups is the Manhattan Institute of Policy Research, founded by the late CIA director William Casey and British millionaire Anthony Fisher. In 1986 the institute created its Project on Civil Justice Reform with funding from all the same insurance companies who'd been responsible for circulating bogus lawsuit stories. The project was targeted specifically at journalists.

In a 1992 memo, institute president William Hammett explained the strategy for molding reporters into a "pro–tort reform" position: "Journalists need copy, and it's an established fact that over time they'll 'bend' in the direction in which it flows. For that reason, it is imperative that a steady stream of understandable research, analysis, and commentary supporting the need for liability reform be produced. If sometime during the present decade, a consensus emerges in favor of serious judicial reform, it will be because millions of minds have been changed, and only one institution is powerful enough to bring that about: the combined force of the nation's print and broadcast media, the most potent instrument for public education—or miseducation—in existence."

Since the founding of its Civil Justice Project, the institute has produced a blizzard of reports, conferences, op-eds, books, and mailings all decrying the "litigation explosion" and greedy trial lawyers. It has targeted sympathetic and influential journalists such as *20/20*'s John Stossel, former *Los Angeles Times* editorial page editor Michael Kinsley, and *Weekly Standard* executive editor Fred Barnes. Stuart Taylor frequently cites Manhattan Institute work in his columns for *Newsweek,* the *National Journal,* and the *Atlantic Monthly.*

The "research" conducted by the institute usually purports to show how lawsuits impact the average consumer's daily life by raising the cost of groceries or auto insurance or driving their favorite physicians out of business. But some of the institute's "scholars" have played a little fast and loose with the facts.

Take the idea of a "tort tax," the financial hit allegedly taken by every citizen because of the legal system. It dates back to 1988, when Manhattan Institute fellow Peter Huber coined the term in his book *Liability,* and claimed that the tort system cost Americans $300 billion a year. After Vice President Dan Quayle mentioned the figure in a 1992 speech, several researchers examined the methods Huber had used to arrive at that figure. University of Wisconsin law professor Marc Galanter concluded that Huber's number had no legitimate basis. As *The Economist* observed in 1992, "the $300-billion figure has no discernible connection to reality." (In response to criticism over his methodology, Huber stated in a letter in the *Texas Lawyer* in 1993 that he had derived his numbers from 1986 *Wall Street Journal* and *Forbes* magazine articles, as well as a study by two New York University economists on the adminitrative costs of the tort system.)

Other experts peddled to the media by the Manhattan Institute hardly qualify as the dispassionate observers they're portrayed as when quoted in the media. The institute itself is funded by insurance companies and big corporations on the receiving end of many lawsuits, and attorneys for these corporations often provide research and write articles for the institute. Several of its affiliated scholars serve as expert witnesses or consultants to companies that have a huge financial stake in active litigation at the heart of much of its research.

Though the Manhattan Institute's corporate ties are plainly spelled out in its marketing materials, the media doesn't appear to have taken note. In 2002, for instance, the *Chicago Tribune* ran a 1,200-word front-page story on the institute's study of Madison County, Illinois, dubbing the county a "plaintiff's paradise." The story only briefly noted that John Beisner, the author, was "a lawyer who defends companies against class actions." The story failed to mention that Beisner worked for a law firm that was currently defending the Ford Motor Company in a lawsuit that had resulted in a $43.7-million verdict against Ford in the county. Nor were the reporters apparently clued in to the fact that the research director on the report was Samuel Witt III, the former longtime general counsel to RJR Nabisco, who handled industry tort reform projects for the tobacco giant and later as a consultant for Philip Morris and other tobacco-related interests. At the time Witt was overseeing work on the report, Philip Morris was facing a class-action trial in Madison County that resulted in a $10-billion verdict against the tobacco giant. Newspapers around the region gave the report similar play, creating a steady drumbeat for class-action reforms.

One reason for such favorable news treatment is that the Manhattan

Institute has more than succeeded in romancing a handful of pivotal media voices who put its work in front of millions of people. In fact, today, journalists' reliance on the Manhattan Institute and other corporate-funded tort reform groups for legal commentary and story tips is so common that several high-profile journalists who actively promote the cause don't even take pains to disguise their loyalties.

One of the most prominent offenders is ABC's John Stossel, who regularly attacks the civil justice system on his segments for the news show *20/20*. After starting his career as an enterprising consumer reporter who specialized in exposing rip-offs and scammers who victimized average citizens, Stossel has become a reliable mouthpiece for corporate-funded attacks on the legal system. His "Give Me a Break" features regularly focus on the latest outrageous legal claim and examples of greedy trial lawyers.

Stossel was one of the first mainstream broadcasters to jump on the McDonald's coffee case. Two months after the verdict, Stossel brought Stella Liebeck onto a *20/20* segment called "The Blame Game: Are We a Country of Victims?" where he proceeded to lump her in the same category as drug addicts scamming Social Security for disability checks. After feigning sympathy for her injuries, Stossel demanded to know whether Liebeck thought the burns she suffered from the coffee were partly her fault. "Shouldn't you know that that's going to be hot if you bought it?" he demanded.

He followed the interview with a quote from Roger Conner, director of the American Alliance for Rights and Responsibility, who said, "The word of these lawsuits spills out into this society, enters into the national conversation, and people start thinking that this is the appropriate way to live … It makes people think, 'I'd be a chump if I did otherwise. If I take responsibility for what I do and for what happens to me, I'm a fool.' Now, when that idea gets loose, America's in trouble."

Much of Stossel's work also bears the fingerprints of the Manhattan Institute. In early 1996, for instance, when Congress was still hotly debating several tort-reform bills dealing with products liability, Stossel aired a segment called "The Trouble with Lawyers," which bashed trial lawyers and blamed them for encouraging too much litigation. A few months after the broadcast, Manhattan Institute president Larry Mone sent out a letter to supporters bragging that senior fellows Walter Olson and Peter Huber were "heavily involved in helping John shape the broadcast."

A classic example of Stossel's bread and butter was his July 23, 2004, broadcast shortly before the Democratic National Convention. The seg-

ment was an attack on vice presidential nominee John Edwards for his career as a trial lawyer. In the lead-in, Stossel says that trial lawyers may be
the most powerful profession in America. "We always hear about how
they help the little guy. But we rarely hear about the unintended consequences of what they do. And they can be nasty."

He trotted out every old and discredited canard in the tort reform talking points, claiming that the fear of lawsuits is the reason drug companies
don't make vaccines anymore and that doctors order too many unnecessary
tests. Stossel claimed that lawsuits didn't help anyone but lawyers, who
only got richer, noting that before Edwards's election to the U.S. Senate, he
had made $26 million. "By being a consumer, you helped pay for [famous
trial lawyer] Dickie Scruggs's plane and John Edwards's three homes."

The segment was so one-sided that 20/20 cohost Barbara Walters said
at the end, "John, I just want to make it clear that, as with all of your
columns, this is your take on it, not necessarily the program's or mine."

The take on Edwards was, however, the same one being peddled by a
host of tort-reform groups that had been attacking Edwards from his entry
into the presidential primaries. ATRA had created an "EdwardsWatch.org"
website in October 2003 to discredit the "Learjet lawyers" associated with
his campaign. The Manhattan Institute, in late 2003, published a report en-
titled "Trial Lawyers, Inc.," full of similar attacks on lawyers, including Edwards and many of his financial supporters in the plaintiffs' bar. The
institute doesn't get credit on ABC, but in Stossel's 2004 book *Give Me a
Break,* he thanks Olson and Huber profusely as among those who "exposed
my small brain to the grand benefits of liberty."

Stossel's attacks on lawyers and so-called frivolous lawsuits go beyond journalism and verge into the arena of advocacy. While Stossel is on
the air bashing lawyers and the legal system, he frequently appears at fund-
raising events for groups actively lobbying for restrictions on Americans'
rights to sue.

In February 2004, for instance, as the Oklahoma state legislature was
considering a bill to put limits on lawsuits, Stossel was the keynote speaker
at a fund-raising lunch sponsored by an Oklahoma City business group
backing the legislation. The money from the fund-raiser was earmarked for
further tort-reform lobbying efforts. In April 2002 Stossel appeared at a
fund-raiser in South Texas for Citizens Against Lawsuit Abuse, a corpo-
rate-front group that was helping doctors seeking caps on malpractice lawsuit damages. He has also appeared at Manhattan Institute events on tort
reform. And, of course, millions of viewers watch his show every week.

Perhaps that's why, for one of its conferences in 1999, the Manhattan Institute promoted an appearance by Stossel by saying that he had "done more than anyone in the media to bring national attention to abuses in the court."

Most reporters don't understand the legal system any more than do their readers. Few newspapers or TV stations have beat reporters who focus on the civil side of the legal system. Most courthouse coverage is about crime and punishment instead. Rarely do reporters actually cover a civil trial; instead they focus on the filing of suits, without following up on the outcome, or simply report unusually large verdicts.

Authors Michael McCann and William Haltom found that, for instance, newspapers and magazines vastly overreport plaintiffs' victories, giving the impression that winning millions in court is both easy and commonplace. In looking at twenty years of coverage in five major newspapers, McCann and Haltom found three times as many stories about plaintiffs' wins than defense wins, despite the fact that plaintiffs lose more than half of all personal injury cases, and nearly 70 percent of medical malpractice lawsuits. The stories they studied focused almost exclusively on the gigantic awards and settlements. Settlements reported in the news tended to be about one thousand times larger than the national median.

With all the focus on pretrial maneuvering and big-dollar verdicts, reporters rarely focus on expert testimony or other evidence presented in the courtroom. Fewer than 20 percent of the stories about lawsuits in McCann and Haltom's research database included reporting on events that took place during a trial, as opposed to before and after. This lack of expertise and experience makes reporters vulnerable to spin by interested parties—on both sides—and an overreliance on think tank–based sources.

Indeed, McCann and Haltom coded the sources in thousands of news stories on the civil justice system to assess how balanced the stories were. After crunching the numbers, they found that the Manhattan Institute strategy of courting the press had clearly paid off. Reporters were nearly twice as likely to quote a pro–tort reform source as someone on the other side.

Lobbying groups and industry-financed think tanks have also taken advantage of an information vacuum. For years, most state courts never collected information on case outcomes and jury awards, so real numbers were hard to come by. Tort reformers have expertly filled this void with their own figures purporting to show a litigation explosion. "When there's no data, [people] can just make stuff up," Theodore Eisenberg, a law professor at Cornell Law School who specializes in empirical research on the legal system, said in an interview.

Even when there are relatively good data, they are easy to misread. The Rand Corporation's Institute for Civil Justice has reliable jury-verdict data for two counties in Illinois and California going back forty years. At one point, California's average jury verdicts showed a big jump. A tort-reform lobbyist might point to the same data as proof that emotional jurors are giving away a lot more money. In fact, what happened was that California raised the dollar limit for cases that could be filed in small claims court, taking the small cases out of the main court, thus pushing up its statistical average even when the actual awards stayed constant. "It's really, really hard to make any inferences about what's going on out there from jury verdicts," says Rand's Seth Seabury, an associate economist with the Institute for Civil Justice.

Indeed, the "onslaught of litigation" over the past thirty years decried by so many media accounts of the justice system is a relative term. In 1962, for instance, only about three hundred civil rights lawsuits were filed in federal courts. In 2000 there were more than forty thousand—an onslaught, to be sure, but that's because prior to 1964, racial discrimination was legal.

One thing that has exploded over the past twenty years is news coverage about tort lawsuits. In their study of media coverage of the tort system, McCann and Haltom found that the efforts by the tort reform movement to make lawsuits a national issue has been enormously successful. Between 1980 and 1999, the number of stories about lawsuits has increased sevenfold even though the actual number of those sorts of suits has been falling.

All of this badly slanted news coverage may be creating some unexpected consequences: some academic researchers suspect that all the hype about the litigation crisis might actually be making Americans *more* litigious by giving them the erroneous impression that compensation is available through the courts for most injuries. As McCann says, "Tort reformers may have produced more frivolous claims while making legitimate claims harder to bring."

At the same time, if Americans really are overcome with a fear of law-suits, it might be because they've been reading too many articles. At least, that's the rationale cited by the organizers of the annual Polar Bear Plunge in Page, Arizona, home of the softball tournament featured in *Newsweek* in 2003. In January 2004 organizer Paul Ostapuk told the local newspaper that he was canceling the annual event, in which participants take an icy winter swim, at Lake Powell because "given the rampant rise in frivolous lawsuits across the nation and the recent *Newsweek* article . . . I've had to play it safe and rethink the 2004 Polar Bear Plunge event." Ostapuk said he was plan-ning to reschedule for 2005—after buying some insurance.

CHAPTER TWO

When the Smoke Clears:
Big Tobacco's Secret Tort Project

Tobacco companies were latecomers to the tort reform game. But they had a lot to lose. So when their traditional legal defenses began to crumble in the 1980s, they joined insurance companies and doctors in the attack on the courts in earnest. Rose Cipollone was a key in the shift. In 1983, Cipollone, a fifty-seven-year-old New Jersey woman who was dying of lung cancer, filed a products-liability lawsuit against several of the nation's largest tobacco companies. Cipollone had smoked a pack and a half a day since she was sixteen years old. In the suit, she alleged that the cigarette makers had failed to warn her adequately about the dangers of smoking.

Cipollone was hardly the first smoker to make such a claim in court. Smokers had been suing tobacco companies since the mid-1950s, but at the time Cipollone filed her suit, no smoker had ever prevailed. The tobacco industry had never paid out a dime in damages, and it spent millions of dollars to ensure that its no-loss record remained pristine.

It wasn't uncommon for the industry to have thirty attorneys for every one on the plaintiff's side, and they left no stone unturned, no motion unchallenged. Investigators for the industry tracked down and deposed plaintiffs' former hairdressers, grade-school classmates, employers, and coworkers. They would comb plaintiffs' medical records for evidence of venereal diseases, ask deposition questions about infidelity and domestic violence. The industry tailed plaintiffs in surveillance vans. Ailing cancer victims would be subjected to days of grueling inquisitions about every piece of food that went into their mouths, if they used pesticides in the garden, or whether they had been stressed out by personal tragedy, as the lawyers tried to prove that something other than smoking might have caused their illnesses. Often the plaintiffs couldn't take it and would quit before the case ever went to trial, leaving their contingency-fee lawyers holding the bag for thousands of dollars in legal fees.

In documents turned up during one such lawsuit, R. J. Reynolds Tobacco Company outside counsel J. Michael Jordan once explained why, in forty years of tobacco litigation, the industry had never paid out a cent to a plaintiff: "To paraphrase General Patton, the way we won these cases was not by spending all of Reynolds's money but by making that other son of a bitch spend all his."

For years, tobacco companies had successfully argued in court that smokers understood the risk of smoking when they took it up. Therefore, if they got sick from smoking, it was, of course, their own fault, not the cigarette makers'.

Tobacco companies also fielded their own scientists to declare that there was no established link between smoking and cancer, and insisted for decades that smoking was not addictive. But by 1983, the scientific evidence that smoking was a deadly and addictive habit was mounting. The gap between the industry's legal defenses and science was growing. In addition, the law itself had begun to change, particularly in New Jersey, where Cipollone's case was pending.

New Jersey's laws were already among the most consumer friendly in the nation. But the year before Cipollone filed her suit, the New Jersey State Supreme Court ruled in an asbestos case that it didn't matter whether a company had 100 percent proof that its product was dangerous for a jury to find the company liable for injuries from one of its products. To win damages, the injured person need only prove that the company had evidence of a potential hazard and failed to provide adequate warning about the dangers to the public. That meant that even if science still couldn't prove conclusively that smoking caused cancer, the circumstantial evidence was enough for sick and dying smokers to bring potentially successful suits against cigarette makers.

Standing at the ready to exploit such rulings was a handful of aggressive plaintiff lawyers who had seen how asbestos litigation could prove extremely lucrative and rewarding. They suspected that tobacco litigation was the next frontier. Public health and antismoking activists also believed the time was ripe to take on the tobacco industry in the courts. They'd all but given up on the legislative process to address the dangers of smoking after watching the industry for years water down legislation and buy off public officials who might have imposed stronger warning labels on cigarettes and their advertisements. Juries, though, might be less susceptible to tobacco company influences.

The year after Cipollone filed her suit, Northeastern University law professor Richard Daynard founded the Tobacco Products Liability Project (TPLP) to help coordinate and encourage the efforts of the private contingency-fee lawyers. He believed, as the TPLP's mission stated, that lawsuits were "the best way to force into the media and the public consciousness a strong emotional awareness of tobacco's true degree of danger by focusing on the suffering of particular individuals, thereby helping to counteract the $2 billion spent annually . . . which promotes this catastrophic epidemic."

With considerable forces mounting against it and several serious lawsuits in New Jersey and Mississippi heading toward trial in the mid-1980s, the tobacco industry grew increasingly concerned about its future liabilities. Asbestos litigation had already pushed Johns-Manville, one of the nation's biggest companies, into bankruptcy in 1982, and there were a lot more sick smokers than asbestos workers.

So the tobacco industry pooled its resources and hatched a plan to attack the legal system itself. In 1986, three tobacco manufacturers—Philip Morris, Brown & Williamson Tobacco Company and the Lorillard Tobacco Company—hired the powerhouse DC law firm Arnold & Porter to help craft its defense against smokers' lawsuits. Arnold & Porter, in turn, hired the famous spin doctor John Scanlon, who started clipping newspaper stories about allegedly outrageous lawsuits and forwarding them to influential people in the media.

Scanlon was also charged with coordinating the media response to the lawsuits pending in New Jersey and Mississippi, putting the industry's spin on the events and badgering reporters who didn't hew to the industry line in their coverage.

Scanlon, who died in 2001, went on to work for Brown & Williamson, and later landed in front of a grand jury investigating his possible role in helping the tobacco giant discredit whistle-blower Dr. Jeffery Wigand, formerly the vice president for research and development at Brown & Williamson. After Wigand emerged as a major plaintiffs' witness in tobacco litigation in the mid-1990s, Scanlon delivered a five hundred-page dossier on Wigand to his many contacts in the media. The dossier, written by tobacco company lawyers, proved to be full of false or unsubstantiated charges against Wigand. (The 1999 movie *The Insider,* starring Al Pacino and Russell Crowe, painted an unflattering portrait of Scanlon in his role in the episode.)

Scanlon's early PR efforts, though, were designed to bolster lobbying in state legislatures to limit liability in smokers' suits. The cigarette makers were the masters of stealth, even as they poured millions of dollars into passing legislation, so that the public never really knew who was behind the bills. In a major victory for the industry, in 1987 tobacco lobbyists convinced the New Jersey legislature to pass a law outlawing products-liability lawsuits over products that everyone knew were dangerous, such as booze, guns, and, of course, tobacco. The new law didn't derail the Cipollone case, but it meant that there wouldn't be any more filed in New Jersey in the future.

A similar law passed in California that year after a group of trial lawyers, insurance executives, and other business lobbyists sat down at Frank Fat's Chinese restaurant in Sacramento and crafted a cease-fire between the lawyers and the business interests in the legislature. Known as the "napkin deal," the agreement was brokered by then-assembly speaker Willie Brown, who had taken more than $600,000 in campaign contributions from tobacco interests during his tenure in the legislature.

The agreement, drafted on the back of a linen napkin and passed by the legislature in nearly identical form, called for a five-year moratorium on attacks on trial lawyers in exchange for their support of sweeping changes in the state's civil justice system, including a law that essentially immunized the tobacco industry from lawsuits. Tobacco lawyers weren't at the table at Frank Fat's that day, but they were credited with drafting a portion of the final legislation, and after the bill passed, the Tobacco Institute, the trade association for tobacco companies, gave sixteen lawmakers who'd supported the bill more than a total of $23,000 in donations.

Despite those successes, litigation was still a major threat to the industry. In 1987 the *Wall Street Journal* reported that tobacco stocks were down by 20 percent because of concerns about smokers' lawsuits. The concerns proved well-founded. In 1988 a New Jersey jury awarded Rose Cipollone's family $400,000 in a mixed verdict against the Liggett Group in which the jury found the cigarette maker negligent for failing to warn smokers adequately of the health risks of smoking, and for misleading advertising. None of the money was awarded to Rose's estate, however, because the jury found that she was 80 percent responsible for her illness—she knew smoking was bad for her yet never even tried to quit—and New Jersey law required that the defendant be at least 50 percent responsible in order for a plaintiff to collect damages. The $400,000 was for Rose's devoted husband Tony, to compensate for the loss of his wife, who had died in October 1984.

Even with the convoluted verdict, which didn't come close to covering the nearly $3 million Cipollone's lawyers had invested, the case was a landmark because it was the first time that a jury had ever ordered a tobacco company to pay damages for a smoker's illness. Liggett would appeal the case all the way to the U.S. Supreme Court, which in 1992 granted the Cipollone family a new trial, but by then the lawyers were broke and the family exhausted. They threw in the towel rather than face the exorbitant costs of continuing the litigation—perhaps a smart move, as it turned out. Before it was over, the tobacco companies spent between $30 million and $50 million defending the case, making the money it would later invest in tort reform seem like a bargain by comparison.

It wasn't until well after the tobacco industry had settled more than forty lawsuits filed by state attorneys general recouping the Medicaid costs of treating sick smokers that its true role in creating and funding the modern tort reform movement really became apparent. The state tobacco litigation produced a treasure trove of internal documents from the country's major tobacco companies that provide a clear look at just how involved the industry was in the late eighties and most of the nineties in promoting tort reform. (The documents are now online at www.tobaccoarchives.com.)

The documents paint a portrait of a secret multimillion-dollar decades-long Madison Avenue quality advertising and marketing campaign devoted to convincing the public that the legal system was in dire need of reform.

Until the mid-1980s, tort reform had been the exclusive province of insurance companies, and occasionally doctors who were concerned about medical malpractice lawsuits. Despite lip service from some in the Republican Party, the issue really hadn't caught on. Overhauling the tort system was expensive. Tort law is largely the province of state, not federal courts. Few companies were willing to shell out the kind of money needed to lobby all fifty state legislatures to pass measures limiting lawsuits.

After the Cipollone verdict, though, limiting lawsuits became one of the tobacco industry's top priorities, and it had the deep pockets necessary to bring the crusade to a much higher level. It also had the marketing smarts that the insurance industry and its doctor allies had been lacking. Tobacco executives were savvy about stealth marketing, having hooked millions of teenagers on their products even though it was illegal for kids to actually buy them. They had made a smelly, dangerous habit cool, turning smoking into an emblem of rebellion and women's liberation. Tobacco companies simply applied the techniques they'd used to selling smokes to selling an idea.

The tobacco industry turned that marketing genius to reforming the legal system, one state at a time, with the goal of creating the impression that its agenda was the same as the average American voter's. The vision for the campaign was laid out early in a 1986 memo written by folks at the Tobacco Institute, the trade association for tobacco companies. "The primary purpose of [grassroots lobbying] is to substantiate and support Tobacco Institute positions presented [to] Congress, state legislatures or local councils by our lobbyists," it said. "In order to be totally effective, the grassroots effort must appear to be spontaneous rather than a coordinated effort."

In the mid-eighties, Philip Morris, the biggest tobacco firm in the country, spearheaded its own tort reform project out of Washington, DC. At the top of the management chart was Jack Quinn, an influential attorney at Arnold & Porter who specialized in "strategic counsel," and who would go on to become Bill Clinton's White House counsel. While Quinn directed the project, the specifics were carried out by an Arnold & Porter subsidiary, APCO Associates, which handled public relations for firm clients and was later sold in 1991 to Grey Advertising, a huge media-relations conglomerate. APCO PR wiz Neal Cohen, the firm's liaison to Philip Morris, was charged with coordinating its attack on the civil justice system and with "grassroots strategies" that would give the tobacco company's agenda the appearance of popular support.

One of the first targets of the new tobacco campaign was the state of Texas. The nation's second most populous state, Texas had a number of smokers' lawsuits in the pipeline and a reputation for a court system friendly to plaintiff lawyers, who also wielded formidable power in the state legislature and had successfully fended off past tort reform bills. (By 1992, Texas would have more tobacco lawsuits pending than any other state in the country, according to internal tobacco-company memos.)

Even so, Texas was well primed for a tort reform campaign. It housed the headquarters of a large number of big oil and gas corporations whose industrial operations were often the subject of lawsuits from workers injured in fires and explosions, or local residents poisoned by various environmental hazards. Those businesses were all potential allies in the tobacco industry's tort fight.

In 1986 some of those business leaders had created the Texas Civil Justice League (TCJL) to help push the tort reform agenda in the next year's legislative session. Today, TCJL president and CEO Ralph Wayne says that more than three hundred of the Fortune 500 companies are members of his group. But in the late 1980s, TCJL was strongly associated with Philip Morris. In journalist Richard Kluger's exhaustive study of the tobacco industry, *Ashes to Ashes,* the author describes the tobacco industry assault on the Texas legislature and other political officials during this time. He describes TCJL as an operation that allowed tobacco companies to funnel money to lobbyists, consultants, and elected officials without having to publicly disclose their spending. Kluger managed to find a former APCO executive who was involved in the campaign in Texas who told him that while TCJL claimed to be a broad-based coalition, it really "was Philip Morris's show."

TCJL went to work spreading the now-familiar themes that lawsuits were bankrupting businesses, killing off jobs, and costing the state $8 billion in corporate revenues because companies were leaving the state or refusing to come there because of the legal climate. As a result, in 1987 the state passed a limited products-liability bill that capped damages in some lawsuits. But the bill didn't go far enough for the tobacco industry, and neither, apparently, did TCJL. The league was an old-style lobbying group whose work was largely concentrated on the legislature and backdoor deal making, not radical change—especially radical change that would eliminate the need for its lobbyists' services. The group's business ties were obvious, making it hard to distinguish from any other chamber of commerce group.

TCJL president Ralph Wayne said in late 2003 that his group was perhaps more conservative than the tort reform activists who would come up after him. The League's goal was to achieve "incremental changes" to the tort law, rather than wholesale revisions, he said in an interview.

The tobacco industry, though, was impatient. It couldn't afford to wait for incremental change. It wanted a lobbying effort that was more cutting edge, something lower to the ground that would create a swell of support—

or at least the appearance of support—from regular people. In 1990 it found what it was looking for in Texas's Rio Grande Valley, where the seeds of a national tort reform movement were just taking root.

In 1987 two Mexican men who had illegally crossed the Rio Grande River were walking through a sugarcane field in South Texas. As they attempted to cross the field, employees of the Rio Grande Valley Sugar Growers mill allegedly saw the men and lit the field on fire. Both men were horribly burned. Two weeks later, one died. The ensuing lawsuit revealed a history of similar incidents, although none fatal. The sugar growers cooperative settled the suit for $8 million.

The lawsuit was just one of a string of suits against the mill, which had a reputation for being tight-fisted with injured workers and their families. In 1990 a jury awarded $2.5 million to two employees who were fired from the mill after filing workers'-compensation claims. The lawsuits against the mill prompted the owners to get organized. Within several months of the verdict, the mill owners had helped organize the nation's first Citizens Against Lawsuit Abuse (CALA) group, a "grassroots" organization that was run out of the Weslaco, Texas, chamber of commerce office and funded by valley businesses and doctors.

Sam Sparks is a board member of the Rio Grande Valley Sugar Growers co-op that owned the mill, and an original founder of CALA. Sitting in his tiny office at the foot of the Progresso International Bridge, where he keeps an eye on the Bloomberg ticker as he talks, Sparks recalls how the group got started. He says that in the sugar mill case, four employees had work-related injuries, but when the mill closed at the end of the harvest, the four didn't return to be rehired. Later, they came back and wanted to work, but they'd been replaced by then, he says. "They sued us because it is against the law to fire workers with compensation claims. The upshot was that we had to look at filing for bankruptcy. We were so fearful of that."

Sparks says the men agreed to settle, and the mill's liability insurance paid for it, but he says that the lawsuit was "a tragic thing." As a result, he says, "We started this Citizens Against Lawsuit Abuse, and it spread like wildfire." What made CALA so successful was its bumper-sticker language that turned legal jargon into everyday slogans. For most of its history, the tort reform movement had been handicapped by a huge linguistic problem. No one, not even the corporate world's biggest tort reform champions, could figure out a compelling way to explain exactly what the term meant in ten words or less. Complex legal principals were virtually impossible to explain in a sound bite.

Historically, too, attacks on the legal system were largely associated with the insurance industry, which was even less popular than the trial lawyers. The Weslaco business groups that created CALA changed all that forever, creating language the average Joe could relate to. They also revolutionized corporate lobbying by creating an advocacy group that, with its talk of protecting consumers from greedy trial lawyers, was hard to distinguish from a legitimate public interest group like those founded by consumer activist Ralph Nader.

CALA hired Jon Opelt, a political consultant who helped launch a barrage of advertising suggesting that lawsuits were going to bankrupt the mill and put people out of work. The slogans were simple and catchy. Billboards along the valley's busiest highways screamed, "Lawsuit Abuse: Guess Who Picks Up the Tab? You Do." TV ads replayed over and over showed clips of the mill, foreshadowing its imminent doom. More ads bashed trial lawyers; "Fairness, yes—greed, No." CALA created the impression that the valley was in the midst of a populist uprising against greedy trial lawyers and frivolous lawsuits, started by ordinary people who'd simply gotten fed up.

Of course, there were few ordinary citizens in the Weslaco CALA. Its original chairman was an executive with the local power company. Other members were wealthy doctors. Trial lawyers later would go to court to find out who the members were, prompting CALA to reorganize as a subsidiary of the chamber of commerce rather than a nonprofit group, so it didn't have to disclose its donors, according to Bill Summers, president of the Rio Grande Valley CALA. The mill never did go broke and continues to operate today. But the message honed by the Weslaco CALA proved to be influential, as was its organizational model.

The CALA concept got another big boost in 1992, from Vice President Dan Quayle. As head of the White House Council on Competitiveness, Quayle had been involved in recruiting then-solicitor general Ken Starr to come up with a plan to revamp the nation's civil justice system. Starr, who would later become the special counsel investigating the White-water affair during the Clinton administration, also handled appellate work for tobacco clients at his law firm, Kirkland & Ellis.

When the Starr report was released in August 1991, a coalition of insurance, tobacco, and other big corporations banded together to give it a boost of publicity by sending it on the road with the vice president, who had seized on tort reform as an issue he could call his own. Coordinating the effort were ATRA and Covington & Burling, the DC law firm that had long represented the tobacco industry. The group arranged for another lobbying firm to set up speaking engagements for Quayle to promote the report, and it included Weslaco on the itinerary.

With the national media attention brought by the vice president's visit and hundreds of thousands of dollars from the tobacco industry funneled through the national tort reform association, carbon-copy CALAs spread across Texas. (Eventually the state would claim ten different chapters.) They all sounded an identical message of a lawsuit crisis, even though, at the time, there was little evidence that Texas was suffering from too many lawsuits or big verdicts. In 1993 the state legislature passed a bill that limited lawsuits against tobacco companies, and the lawsuit-abuse groups took much of the credit for turning public opinion in favor of the legislation.

The Texas project was so successful that the tobacco companies decided to pump millions of dollars into expanding the groups in other states. The expansion plans were managed by the American Tort Reform Association. For instance, the Houston CALA received more than $360,000 from ATRA between its startup in 1992 and 1997. Along with the money, the faux grassroots groups would get all the prepackaged marketing materials: bumper stickers, billboard slogans, brochures, and other materials branded with the Stop Lawsuit Abuse motto. If there weren't any willing partners in a critical state, the tobacco industry would simply create a CALA on its own.

Such groups created enormous publicity and media coverage for an issue that was of real interest to only a handful of corporate executives in historically dirty industries.

They spent the bulk of their budgets on TV, radio, and billboard ads, and often targeted jurors directly: one Texas CALA put up a billboard about lawsuit abuse on the road to the county courthouse so that jurors driving in couldn't miss it. None of the ads, of course, ever mentioned the tobacco funding.

The CALAs provided an especially useful vehicle for distributing television ads produced by APCO, the tobacco industry's PR firm. Memos in the tobacco archives show that APCO and the tobacco industry clearly understood the power of TV advertising on changing public opinion, and as far back as 1991, they were hatching plans to unleash a barrage of TV ads about tort reform on the American public. The language in the ads was carefully crafted, with input from attorney Victor Schwartz, Philip Morris's legal tort consultant.

In early 1993 CALA groups in Texas, Louisiana, and Mississippi ran an ad featuring a man attempting to change a lightbulb while standing on a stepladder covered with safety devices and warning labels, while a narrator said, "Some people misuse products and then look for someone to blame." The ad claimed (without proof) that lawsuits boosted the cost of the ladder by 20 percent and ended with a toll-free 800 number for viewers to call to join the crusade.

The focus-grouped advertising proved a successful formula for the CALAs. Neal Cohen, who headed the CALA project, reported to the trade paper *Liability Week* in 1994 that APCO's system of creating grassroots advocacy groups had prompted major changes in state liability laws in Texas, North Dakota, Arizona, and Michigan in 1993. The magazine noted that "polls uniformly show high levels of public hostility to personal-injury lawyers, and the grassroots organizations capitalize on those findings to build public support for changes" to the law.

While the CALAs were the tobacco industry's baby, they didn't stay that way, in part because Philip Morris and the other cigarette makers didn't want to foot the bill entirely for pushing tort reform that might benefit other groups. In 1992 Cohen sent a status report to several Philip Morris executives about the tort reform "communications program," a project that entailed making a barrage of television commercials designed to promote tort reform. Philip Morris wanted to get other "investors" on board to help pick up the enormous tab for the national TV ads. It was apparently a hard sell at the time.

Cohen acknowledged some of the hurdles the company faced in marketing the "liability-reform communications program"—many of which, he noted, were the same problems they had in lobbying for tort reform proposals. "Only a very few companies are willing to spend even a relatively small amount of money on the issue. To date, none of the companies we have approached have committed to spend the money that they have designated for tort issues on an unproven communications program."

But once the CALA strategy started to show promise, the tobacco company's attempts to lobby other CEOs in different industries apparently paid off, particularly in Texas. Among the targets of Philip Morris's recruitment efforts were drug companies, Texas oil and gas companies, railroads, insurance companies, and doctors' groups. In a 1992 internal Philip Morris memo describing the "tort project," the company notes that its effort to recruit other players in Texas had been so successful that ATRA's budget was going to increase by 50 percent in 1993, while Phillip Morris's contribution was set to decline by a quarter.

By 1995 the tobacco industry's tort reform project was in full swing, and a memo from Covington & Burling from January that year shows that the program's budget for 1995 was projected to exceed $21 million. Of that, $600,000 was slated for think tanks, including Citizens for a Sound Economy, the Cato Institute, the Manhattan Institute, and the Hudson Institute. The firm budgeted hundreds of thousands of dollars for lobbying coalitions in nearly every state, ranging from $50,000 for Arizona to $478,000 for Mississippi, to $600,000 for California. The budget for media buys alone was $7.5 million for a single year.

In a January 1995 memo, Keith Teel, one of the industry lawyers at Covington & Burling, said the mission of the tort reform PR involvement was to help with legislative efforts, to put the plaintiff lawyers on the defensive, and possibly even to elect pro–tort reform officials. Stealth, however, was a critical component of the entire program. Teel noted, "Because these media activities, to be effective, must not be linked to the tobacco industry, we hope that significant industry funding encourages other groups to make similar contributions to support such activities."

Unfortunately for Teel and the other tobacco execs, just as the CALAs were proving immensely successful, their cover was blown. In 1994 Cohen had appeared at a meeting of the Public Affairs Council, the professional organization for public-affairs executives, and gave a talk about his role in setting up Astroturf groups to lobby for tort reform. To explain APCO's techniques in this burgeoning field, Cohen used Mississippi where APCO had set up a CALA-type group called Mississippians for a Fair Legal System (M-Fair) as a case study.

"Let me tell you about a problem that a client came to me with," he said. "It was December 1992, and they said, 'We want to pass a bill in Mississippi, and we've got a problem: If the legislators know we're the only industry that wants this bill, it's an automatic killer. And just to make it a little more difficult, we've joined up with one other industry to fund this effort, and they are worse than us. People dislike them more intensely, and, in fact, they don't even have any facilities in the state of Mississippi, not to mention the product they manufacture.' Then they said, 'The session ends in March. OK? So you've only got sixty days or so to do this. The issue is tort reform.'"

Cohen tackled the obvious problem first: the language. "*Tort* to the average person is dessert, it isn't a legal principle," he said. The second problem, he noted, was the opposition, namely trial lawyers, who were major political donors. Because his client—the tobacco industry—couldn't be tied directly to the campaign for the tort reform bill, Cohen explained that it put the industry at a competitive disadvantage in the campaign contribution department. His solution? Polling to find messages that average people would relate to—the famous "lawsuit abuse" slogans—much of it focused on demonizing trial lawyers so that candidates wouldn't want to take their money.

Cohen also stressed the need to build a coalition of other interest groups that would mask the involvement of the original client, or at least give the message more credibility. "In a tort reform battle, if State Farm is the leader of the coalition, you're not going to pass the bill. It is not credible. OK? Because it's so self-serving."

Many of the tactics APCO used in Mississippi were derived from traditional political campaign tool boxes, he explained to the council audience. "Things like polls, academic research, TV ads—anything to get the media's attention. The media took our side, and [the trial lawyers'] money became radioactive," Cohen said.

At that point, he showed the audience a clip of a local Mississippi news broadcast that recited the M-Fair spiel on "cleaning up the legal system" almost chapter and verse, and then gave out the group's 800 number in case any viewers wanted to get involved and give money. The clip had the audience of PR executives rolling in the aisles.

The speech was taped by the Public Affairs Council and sold to the public, and the PR watchdog group at the Center for Media and Democracy (CMD) in Wisconsin got hold of the tape. In 1996 investigative reporter Ken Silverstein publicized the tape in a study for the consumer group Public Citizen on the tobacco industry's role in the tort-reform movement. The study got picked up by the *New York Times,* which ran a few excerpts of Cohen's speech. The ensuing bad press prompted APCO to shut down the Mississippi group.

Even in the *Times* article, Cohen never divulged the name of his clients, and the tobacco industry got little mention in the article. The full extent of its role in funding and creating the CALA groups wouldn't become public until 2000, when Carl Deal and Joanne Doroshow published a study of the litigation documents through Public Citizen and the nonprofit Center for Justice and Democracy. Cohen's outing didn't put an end to the tobacco industry's stealth marketing of tort reform, either. Many of the CALA groups continued to prosper and continued with intense advertising campaigns in critical states like Ohio, where they also influenced judicial elections. In Mississippi, M-Fair just reconstituted itself under a different name and kept going as before.

Part of the reason the tobacco industry couldn't scrap its investment in the Astroturf groups was that 1995 was a huge year for tort reform. Republicans had taken control of both houses of Congress and had made lawsuit restrictions part of the Contract with America. GOP leaders vowed to pass legislation limiting products-liability and shareholder lawsuits, but President Bill Clinton was threatening to veto the products-liability bills. (He would eventually sign the shareholder bill, a major piece of tort reform legislation during his administration.) Rumors were also flying around Washington that the trial lawyers were planning on spending $20 million on a media buy to defeat the legislation, a rumor that proved to be wildly unfounded.

The tobacco industry rallied its CALA chapters to the federal cause in 1995, enlisting them to provide grassroots lobbying. Other tobacco-funded think tanks, including Citizens for a Sound Economy and ATRA, joined that year with the U.S. Chamber of Commerce and other business groups to hire APCO to produce the now-famous "firefighters ad" that ran nationally on CNN and stations in eleven states. The ad purported to show firemen who'd just rescued someone shortly before sitting down to complain about their fear of lawsuits. "I didn't take this job to sit around and worry about getting sued," says one. If lawsuit abuse doesn't stop, he says, "I might not be able to do my job. And my job just might be to save your life."

The ad was quickly denounced by the nation's firefighters, whose international association called for it to be pulled off the air. Vincent Bollon, general secretary-treasurer of the International Association of Firefighters, said, "America's citizens deserve to know that firefighters are absolutely not, as your ad suggests, afraid to save lives because of liability concerns."

Likewise, the money tobacco companies spent in 1995 and 1996 on federal legislation proved to be a bit of a bust. Congress did pass its favored products-liability law limiting smokers' lawsuits, but President Clinton vetoed the bill, and congressional Republicans were unable to override it. But the entire campaign would create a lasting legacy. The tobacco industry had demonstrated how the traditional tools of a political campaign could be applied to market an unpopular idea and make it part of the accepted conventional wisdom. The money it invested in its tort reform project also created a self-sustaining, permanent lobbying infrastructure that would turn what had been an occasional special interest into a recurring agenda item up there with education and Social Security.

CHAPTER THREE

Mess with Texas: George W. Bush
and the Texas Tort Moguls

Carol Ernst met her husband Robert in 1997 at a Texas gym where Robert was working as an instructor. A former smoker, Robert had spent the previous twenty years running marathons, competing in triathlons, and working out. They dated for several years before getting married in 2000. On May 6, 2001, Carol awoke to her husband's irregular breathing and realized he was in trouble. Two hours later, the fifty-nine-year-old man was declared dead at a local hospital. His heart had stopped.

In her quest to discover why her triathlete husband had died so suddenly, Carol read his autopsy and started to wonder whether the painkillers he'd been taking for the six months before he died might have been a factor. Robert's doctor had written him a prescription for Vioxx for pain in his hands. After reading more about the drug, which was pulled off the market in September 2004, she called a lawyer.

In 2005, Ernst's case ultimately became the first of nearly 16,000 Vioxx lawsuits in the nation to go to trial. The litigation shone an unpleasant spotlight on Merck, the manufacturer. Company documents revealed that as far back as 1997, Merck scientists were concerned about the increased risks of cardiovascular problems stemming from the drug's use. A large clinical study in 2000 confirmed the earlier fears, yet documents produced during litigation showed that Merck officials vigorously fought the Food and Drug Administration's attempts to add a warning about the risks to the Vioxx label. Other documents showed that Merck coached its drug-sales reps to play "dodgeball" with doctors who raised concerns about the heart risks.

Merck officials claimed during the Ernst trial that they didn't believe Vioxx posed heart risks until the company did another study in 2004. Texas jurors, though, didn't buy it. On August 19, 2005, the jury awarded Carol Ernst $24.5 million to compensate for economic losses and the mental anguish she suffered after having her husband suddenly snatched away from her. The jury then decided to punish Merck for recklessly marketing a drug it knew was dangerous. It awarded $229 million in punitive damages, the amount Merck had estimated in 2001 it could earn by heading off an FDA warning about the painkiller's heart risks.

When the Ernst case went to trial, Merck was a bit battered, but it was still a $70-billion company. The Texas jury verdict didn't amount to even 1 percent of Merck's market value. Nonetheless, conservative pundits immediately set to work decrying the verdict as a symptom of an out-of-control legal system.

On August 23, 2005, in the *Boston Globe*, two economists from Harvard and Stanford law schools wrote, "there is cause for concern about the size of the Texas award and about many similar judgments imposed on corporations in this country. The concern is that when corporations have to pay large damage awards, three things happen that may be disadvantageous to us as consumers." Steven Shavell and A. Mitchell Polinsky fretted that the verdict would drive up the cost of prescription drugs, and, anyway, Carol Ernst didn't need $253 million to compensate for her losses. A few million would have done the job. The authors also said that such verdicts cause drugs not to be developed or to be withdrawn from the market, and that they might result in "excessive producer caution," such as the practice of defensive medicine.

As with nearly all the postverdict news commentary, the economists' column assumed that Merck would actually pay $253 million. They failed to mention that, thanks to former Texas governor George W. Bush, Merck would never pay anything near $253 million, and the odds that it would ever pay Carol Ernst a dime were slim to none.

One of Bush's first legislative acts upon becoming governor of Texas in 1995 was to sign a law that would automatically reduce any punitive-damage award by a fixed formula, making it easier for companies to calculate, essentially, the most it would cost to kill someone. The law limited punitive damages to twice the economic damages awarded by a jury—that is, lost income and other earnings—plus noneconomic damages such as pain and suffering and mental-anguish awards up to $750,000.

Robert Ernst didn't make a lot of money. At the time of his death, he worked at Wal-Mart, making $22,000 a year, meaning that the income his wife lost from his premature death was a relatively small amount: about $450,000 for the rest of his working life. Clearly recognizing Wal-Mart's cheapness, the jury also awarded Carol Ernst $24 million for her mental anguish. In calculating the punitive damages, the judge could only count $750,000 of that $24 million plus the $450,000 in economic damages. That meant Bush's handiwork a decade earlier saved Merck about $227 million right out of the gate, as the judge reduced the punitive award to $1.6 million, chump change for the pharmaceutical giant, and hardly enough to create an incentive for Merck or other drugmakers to be more careful in marketing their products—as the jurors had hoped.

Merck is unlikely to have to pay even that reduced amount, however. Another one of Bush's 1995 reforms requires that any punitive-damage award undergo mandatory judicial review, meaning that the verdict will have to survive a trip to the vigorously antiplaintiff Texas Supreme Court, which in the 2004–2005 session overturned nearly 80 percent of the verdicts in favor of individual consumers, according to a study by the nonprofit consumer group Texas Watch. "It's very likely that once it gets through the judicial process, the Texas Supreme Court is likely to vacate the judgment all together," says Texas Watch Executive Director Alex Winslow. "Merck is going to walk away scot-free."

It's not just consumer groups that see long odds for the Texas Vioxx verdict. John H. Martin, a Dallas defense attorney who was not part of the Merck case and is a vice president of the Defense Research Institute, says, "I think given the size of the award, it's likely to be reduced or overturned on appeal."

W. Mark Lanier, the lawyer for Carol Ernst, is more sanguine about the odds of the verdict surviving, which he puts at "65–35 in my favor."

Regardless of how it turns out, the Vioxx verdict may be among the last of its kind in Texas, thanks to more recent reforms in the state. Under Texas laws passed in 2003, drug companies will largely be immune from lawsuits like Ernst's so long as their products were approved for sale by a government agency. So while the Texas Vioxx verdict brought cries of foul from columnists, the state is in fact a model that tort reformers—and George Bush in particular—have been trying to re-create in the rest of the country. Under the guise of reining in frivolous lawsuits, greedy trial lawyers, and Robin Hood juries, big corporations have all but eviscerated the civil justice system in Texas. While paying lip service to the idea that everyone should have his day in court, business-funded tort reform groups and their political surrogates have made getting into court in Texas harder than ever—and for many people, simply impossible, even when they have a legitimate claim. When injured people do finally get a jury trial, the law in Texas now ensures that those juries have less power than ever before.

No other state has gone so far so fast in overhauling its civil justice system. None of it would have been possible without Bush, who revolutionized the use of lawyer bashing and tort reform as a successful Republican campaign strategy, and has repaid his early backers by working to impose the Texas model on the rest of the country as president.

★ ★ ★

In all likelihood, George W. Bush would never have been elected governor of Texas without the early linguistic groundwork done by the tobacco industry and other Texas tort reform groups. Campaigning on products-liability law and appeal-bond reform is hardly the stuff of a winning candidate, regardless of how much the corporate world wants those things. The hard work of turning tort reform into an issue the general public could understand started in the late 1980s, but it was further tested and refined in 1992, when the right-wing Texas Public Policy Foundation hired the GOP pollster Jan van Lohuizen to test the lawsuit-abuse message among residents of the Rio Grande Valley in South Texas, where the first CALA started. The results were striking: 67 percent of residents responded favorably. Such good numbers were a rarity in politics, and tobacco companies leaped at the opportunity to exploit the issue in campaigns to elect pro-tort reform candidates.

Based on the polling data, Philip Morris made two ads sponsored by the American Tort Reform Association to test the impact of tort reform issues in Texas state senate elections and the possibility of using them in swing elections. The ads were used in the 1992 Democratic primary between challenger Juan Hinojosa and incumbent Eddie Lucio Jr. in Weslaco, who ran on a tort reform platform. After a bruising campaign, Lucio won, and his margin of victory was higher in Weslaco, where CALA-sponsored antilawsuit publicity was high.

The tobacco industry believed that the election helped the following year when the legislature passed its favored products-liability law, as it made Democrats wary of siding too much with trial lawyers. The election ads in Texas, in fact, were so successful that the industry planned to expand its campaign work into other states and to push it further in Texas.

By 1993, when Bush was gearing up to run for governor, the tobacco industry wasn't the only party looking to make tort reform a major political issue in Texas. Business groups in the state had loosely organized a few years earlier to push medical-malpractice and workers'-compensation issues, but the state supreme court had overturned the limits on medical malpractice as unconstitutional. Several influential businessmen were agitating for more.

David Weekley Homes is one of the biggest private home builders in the country. In the late 1980s and early 1990s, the company was building feverishly in Texas, keeping up the housing stock for the state's rapidly growing population. In its expansion quest, Weekley had bought some land near Houston on the cheap, discounted because the soil was too unstable to hold the foundation of a house without considerable prep work. Another home builder had already tried and failed to develop the site, but Weekley plowed ahead anyway and built a new subdivision called Cypresswood. It wasn't long before the foundations of many of the homes started to fail, including the model home used to sell buyers on the development.

The crumbling houses—and Weekley's failure to come clean with the home buyers and to fix the problems adequately—prompted a rash of lawsuits from home owners who were stuck in falling-apart houses they couldn't get fixed and couldn't sell. More than a dozen home owners in Cypresswood sued the company, alleging that it had engaged in deceptive business practices.

The lawsuits apparently did little to reform the company's practices. In 1996 the federal Occupational Safety and Health Administration (OSHA) fined the firm $221,500 for health and safety violations at a building site in Denver, at the time the largest fine ever levied against a Colorado home builder. But the Houston cases did spur one of Weekley's principals to mount a formidable challenge to the Texas consumer-protection and other tort laws that allowed those home owners to bring suit in the first place.

Richard Weekley, a cofounder of the company, joined with three other men, and in 1994, with $15,000 in seed money from the tobacco industry, launched Texans for Lawsuit Reform as a new political force in the state.

At its kickoff, Weekley proclaimed that lawsuit abuse was "the number one threat to Texas's economic future." Like most other tort reform offensives, TLR's seized on a populist notion with adherents from coast to coast: namely, that lawyers are ruining America by bankrupting corporations with outrageous claims. Yet, like Weekley, some of TLR's founding members may have been motivated, at least in part, by their own experiences. A sampling:

· The late Enron CEO Ken Lay gave $25,000 in start-up funds for TLR. Lay had written to Bush in 1994 that if Texas didn't do something about its "permissive" legal climate, Enron might just have to leave the state. Today, after more than four thousand Enron employees have lost their jobs and their retirement funds invested in the company, and Lay has been convicted of conspiracy and fraud charges related to his management of the company, Lay's reasons for having wanted legal immunity seem pretty obvious. But back then, he had more pedestrian concerns about Enron's gas and energy operations. In 1994 one of the company's methanol gas plants exploded in Pasadena, Texas, injuring several people working nearby. A neighboring chemical corporation sued Enron to block the plant from coming back on line, arguing that it had a long history of flagrant safety violations that were endangering workers.

· Dr. James Leininger, founder of the Texas Public Policy Foundation, heads up Kinetic Concepts, a company that makes high-tech hospital beds that have prompted a rash of lawsuits from patients and nurses alleging that the rotating beds dropped or crushed patients.

· Jim "Mattress Mac" McIngvale, another TLR funder, is a furniture-store owner who got sued after a three-hundred-pound African lion kept at his Texas Flea Market mauled an eight-year-old girl, tearing off part of her skull in 1987. The girl required extensive reconstructive surgery and faced the prospect of permanent brain damage. Her parents, who had no health insurance, sued McIngvale for allowing the lion on the premises. It was the lion's second offense; elsewhere, it had attacked three-year-old twins a year earlier.

· Bob Perry is CEO of Perry Homes, a Texas home-building firm that was sued more than sixty times between 1988 and 2003, including one suit that involved homes built on a toxic-waste dump near Houston. Perry Homes was one of many defendants involved in a $200-million insurance settlement of the case in 1992. Perry would later gain national fame for underwriting Swift Boat Veterans for Truth in its savage media campaign against John Kerry in the 2004 presidential race.

Whether or not the suits were successful, they certainly influenced the attitude of the founders about litigation. Their history as frequent defendants also hindered the founders' legislative agenda. Most of the leading funders of the burgeoning Texas tort reform movement, in fact, provided case studies in why the right to sue is such an important one. Given these image problems, TLR needed a spokesperson, a front man with influence, who, most importantly, didn't scare people into thinking that tort reform would deprive them of their constitutional rights.

George W. Bush was the obvious candidate. His father had raised tort reform briefly in his campaign against Bill Clinton in 1992, to good effect. And because of his family ties, the younger Bush already knew many of the leading players, particularly in the tobacco industry. Craig Fuller, Philip Morris's vice president, had been Bush senior's chief of staff in the White House. Thomas Collamore, an assistant secretary of commerce during the first Bush administration, was Philip Morris's VP of corporate affairs and point person for the company's political donations. Of course, the name recognition couldn't hurt.

The former Yale cheerleader was the friendly face business groups needed to make lawsuit restrictions palatable to the public. Austin consumer attorney David Bragg says, "In the same way that Reagan legitimized the Christian right, Bush legitimized tort reform in Texas."

Bush also had political aspirations of his own. He'd been considering a run for the governor's office since 1990 but decided to wait until he'd actually done something memorable, like run a baseball team. Philip Morris consultant Karl Rove recruited Bush to run in 1994. (Rove would continue to work for the tobacco giant until 1996, even as he worked for Governor Bush.)

Without any public service record to speak of, much less a serious employment history, the younger Bush needed to create an issue to call his own, but one that wasn't too complicated or required in-depth policy discussions. Helpfully, Rove pushed him to adopt the tobacco industry's pet cause—tort reform—as one of his three primary campaign issues. As Rove told Wayne Slater and James Moore in their book *Bush's Brain,* "I sort of talked him into that one."

With its poll-tested messages and simplistic anecdotes about old ladies and spilled coffee, tort reform was ready-made for Bush, providing an answer for virtually any policy question. The Bush health care policy? Restricting medical malpractice lawsuits, of course. Bush's jobs program? Tort reform worked for that too. Perhaps the real genius of linking Bush to tort reform, though, was that it was a brilliant wedge issue, one that appealed to both conservatives and liberals in the way that welfare reform had once done. And that was important, because starting in 1992, Bill Clinton had begun to co-opt welfare reform as an issue for Democrats, depriving the GOP of a reliable campaign issue. By 1996, it was a dead horse.

Like welfare reform, tort reform offered many of the same subtle messages. A candidate like Bush could advocate limits on lawsuits as a form of restoring "personal responsibility" to a declining culture by cracking down on the malingerers who tried to use the legal system to blame others for their problems. The famous urban lawsuit myths and the McDonald's coffee case made perfect stump speeches. Tort reform tapped all the Calvinist notions of American culture about the nature of misfortune, and it separated those who believed in "traditional" values from those who saw the legal system as a mechanism for changes liberals couldn't accomplish through legislative measures.

Then, of course, there was race. Bush could use tort reform as a way of pandering to the reactionary wing of the GOP without scaring off swing voters. Simply going to the Rio Grande Valley and talking about frivolous lawsuits was enough to conjure up the image of "wetbacks" crossing the river to make a lawsuit out of slipping on a banana peel in the store of some hardworking small businessman. The same went for the attacks on juries, where the alleged runaway jury was almost always Latino—the implication being that poor minorities were using the legal system as a way of redistributing wealth.

The best part about campaigning on tort reform was that, like welfare mothers before them, the people most likely to object—that is, the victims of refinery explosions or medical malpractice—were too few, too broke, and too politically impotent to protest much. Sure, there were the trial lawyers. But they provided the perfect foil in the debate: the greedy parasites fighting off tort reform simply to continue lining their pockets with the ill-gotten gains of the "lawsuit lottery."

Tort reform offered practical political dividends as well by helping Republicans pick off influential segments of the Democratic Party, namely small-business owners and doctors. In the past, says former political consultant Richard Jenson, "Small businesses in Texas were absolutely a part of the Democratic Party. They had no where else to go." But with tort reform as a campaign issue, small businessmen who worried about getting sued and being crushed by liability insurance premiums suddenly found themselves courted by Republicans espousing a war on frivolous lawsuits and promising that tort reform would reduce their insurance premiums. While the small-business economic interests were often at odds with those of the big businesses that dominated the GOP, tort reform also put the smaller businesses at odds with their former allies in the Democratic Party, who were heavily indebted to trial lawyers. They eventually sided with the tort reformers.

A similar situation existed with the doctors, who had been part of a coalition that Rove created to elect Republican judges to the Texas Supreme Court back in 1988. And while the Republicans were eager to draw the doctors and small businesses into their camp, the tort reformers were equally thrilled to have them fronting for the less sympathetic big-business interests that were really the driving force behind, and the biggest beneficiaries of, the tort reform movement. "They were a good and necessary addition to tort reform movement and they needed to put them out front," says Jenson, who now does jury consulting work, mostly for plaintiff lawyers.

When Bush lined up behind tort reform, the money started flowing his way. People and groups associated with tort reform donated more than $4 million to his statewide campaigns, more than any other interest category other than the oil and gas contributions. In addition, the year of Bush's first gubernatorial campaign, the tobacco industry set aside $100,000 to underwrite a PR campaign in Texas heralding the epidemic of "lawsuit abuse" in the state, which certainly didn't hurt his cause. As Rove explained to the *Washington Post* in 2000, once Bush declared war on "junk lawsuits," "business groups flocked to us."

Indeed, not only were business groups willing to ante up, tort reform was an issue they could all agree on, even businesses that historically didn't share the same interests, like the more liberal high-tech companies and the older, dirty industrial giants in oil and manufacturing. They might not see eye to eye on environmental issues, but they had a mutual interest in seeing limits on shareholder lawsuits. Thanks to the support of the tobacco industry and the Texas tort moguls, Bush squeaked past Governor Ann Richards in 1994 with barely half the vote.

In January 1995, just a few days after taking office, Bush set to work. He met with members of a CALA group at a salsa factory outside Austin. Declaring a legislative emergency on out-of-control lawsuits, Bush said,

"Tort reform is the most constructive and positive and meaningful economic development plan Texas can adopt." Calling the laws a "job creation package," Bush went on to sign a series of measures that severely restricted citizens' ability to seek civil justice.

The measures gutted the state's once-progressive deceptive-trade-practices law, which allowed consumers to challenge sleazy used-car dealers or check-cashing joints over rip-offs large and small. Not only did Bush's new law cap punitive damages, but it raised the evidentiary standards to make it even harder to win them at all. The new laws barred plaintiffs from recovering any money if they were more than 50 percent responsible for an injury—meaning smokers were pretty much screwed. They also restricted where plaintiffs could bring their cases. Taken together, the package helped tilt the legal playing field firmly to the side of "chronic defendants" who routinely ended up on the receiving end of lawsuits.

Tort filings in Texas had already been declining before Bush signed the bill, but his favored measures encouraged the trend. Between 1993 and 2002, the rate of personal injury lawsuits filed in Texas plummeted 40 percent. Consumer lawsuits against shoddy mobile-home dealers and other crooked businesses have become almost nonexistent. Stephen Daniels, a research fellow at the American Bar Foundation, says lawyers simply can't afford to take cases that don't hold the possibility of punitive damages or awards for mental anguish, because the actual amount of money involved in such cases is often so small. "Whether it was intended to or not, it may have the effect of cutting off the access to the courts. If [lawyers] don't want to take your case, you don't get into court," says Daniels.

Aside from the policy implications, though, Bush proved conclusively that tort reform was a winning issue for a new breed of Republican candidates. The strategy was so successful that business groups packaged the model and exported it to other states, particularly in the South.

The coup de grace for the tort reform movement, of course, came in 2000, when its leading lights helped elect Bush president. Indeed, many of the key players in Bush's 2000 presidential campaign were die-hard tort reformers from Texas: Alan "Bud" Shivers, a spokesman for Texans for Lawsuit Reform, was the treasurer for Bush's second gubernatorial campaign, a major-league "pioneer" for Bush's presidential races, raising more than $100,000, and a cochair of the Bush-Cheney Recount Fund in 2000. Ralph Wayne, the head of the Texas Civil Justice League, was a cochair of Bush's 2000 presidential campaign. Of course, there was Ken Lay, an active member of TLR and active Bush funder in 2000. And Bush's pollster? The famous Jan van Lohuizen, the same man who helped craft the "lawsuit abuse" message for the CALA groups back in 1992.

With Bush, tort reformers finally achieved a complete merger between their wish list and the Republicans' political agenda. And by doing so, they helped break down the barriers to major restrictions on lawsuits. As lawyers in Texas like to say, Bush made it acceptable for people to be mean. He helped make once-radical proposals that hurt mostly victims of medical malpractice or horrible industrial accidents seem mainstream. "The bully pulpit makes a heck of a difference," says Jenson, who notes that before Bush's successes, tort reform groups he saw in other states were not nearly as organized as they are now. "It's a heck of a formula they have now. It's amazing how organized it is, how disciplined they are moving from state to state and how well they can sell the same formula even with the regional differences."

And there's no better place to see how well the investment has paid off in the business world than back in Bush's home state of Texas, where the revolution that Bush helped start has progressed beyond its founders' wildest dreams.

Most Texans aren't fully aware of what they've lost until they find they need a lawyer. That's what happened to Jacque Smith. In November 2003, Smith's eighty-five-year-old mother, an Alzheimer's patient, was living at the Heritage Duval Gardens Nursing Home in Austin. Late one night, a staffer entered Smith's mother's room and raped the elderly woman. Another employee witnessed the assault but apparently didn't bother to report it to anyone and went home after his shift finished. Smith learned about the assault only because the witness mentioned it to someone at the home during an unrelated conversation later the next day. After her mother was examined at a hospital, the assailant was arrested and charged with aggravated sexual assault. The man, Kevin Arceneaux, later confessed to the crime, and was sentenced to twenty-five years in prison.

Smith consulted a lawyer about filing suit against the nursing home. In the past, such a suit might have garnered a multimillion-dollar settlement or jury verdict for the victim. Texas has some of the worst nursing homes in the country. A 2002 study by the special-investigations division of the U.S. House Committee on Government Reform found that 40 percent of Texas nursing homes had violations of federal regulations that caused harm to nursing-home residents or placed them at risk of death or serious injury. More than 90 percent did not meet federal staffing standards. The poor conditions of Texas nursing homes led to a cottage industry in the legal profession, whose lawsuits posed much larger threats than any state sanctions.

A Harvard University study found that nearly nine out of ten nursing-home plaintiffs in Texas received compensation, a success rate that the study deemed "off the scale" in personal injury litigation, and a sign that the negligence as well as the severity of injuries in the cases was clear-cut. Rather than pledge to clean up its act, the nursing-home industry lobbied hard for the passage of legislation that would put the lawyers out of business.

The industry sought a cap of $250,000 on noneconomic damages like pain and suffering awards in negligence lawsuits. They were joined by doctors, who were loudly complaining about their medical malpractice insurance rates and demanding similar caps in medical malpractice lawsuits. The legislation, passed in September 2003, two months before Smith's mother was attacked, was something of a Trojan horse. Not only did it cap noneconomic damages in lawsuits against doctors and nursing homes, it capped wrongful death damages at $500,000. The new law made lawsuits against emergency-room doctors and nurses as well as other medical malpractice lawsuits much harder to bring by putting strict limits on discovery and the role of expert witnesses and raising the evidentiary standard for proving negligence. Any reports from state inspectors about inadequate care or other problems in nursing homes, and any fines assessed, are now barred as evidence in nursing home cases as well.

The losing party in litigation can now be forced to pay the winner's legal fees, another deterrent in medical malpractice cases where doctors generally win 70 percent of cases that go to trial. The new law changed the way lawyers' fees in class actions are calculated and made those cases harder to bring. The law immunizes manufacturers from lawsuits if they met federal safety standards, even if those standards are weak or meaningless. All told, the new law radically raised the bar for consumers and other individuals to bring lawsuits against wrongdoers.

While the legislation was all that TLR could have hoped for and more, tort reformers faced one big problem: the courts. "The old court threw out seven medical malpractice bills as unconstitutional," says the Texas Civil

Justice League's Ralph Wayne. The previous bills violated both the state and federal guarantees of equal protection and the open-courts guarantee of the state constitution.

So, to ensure that the bill would stick, tort reformers put a proposal on the ballot to simply amend the constitution to allow the state legislature to pass new caps. During the election, Texas residents probably didn't realize that they were voting to let substandard nursing homes off the hook in court. Nor did they realize that the new amendment didn't apply just to doctors and nursing homes. It applied to oil companies, insurance companies, drug companies, and any other defendant in a lawsuit that the legislature should later decide needed protection from lawsuits.

Instead, the measure was sold as a way of keeping doctors in the state and making health care more affordable. The ballot measure, too, was voted on in a special election in September 2003, outside the regular election season, to ensure that few people would actually show up to vote. After both sides spent more than $17 million on the campaign, it passed by a slim margin, with only 9 percent of the state's voters casting a ballot.

The new law has had the results desired by its backers. When Jacque Smith looked for an attorney, she discovered that her first hurdle might be simply finding one willing to take the case. The first attorney she called declined, as few lawyers in Texas will now handle such a complaint against a nursing home. Then she contacted consumer attorney David Bragg, who explained to her that the most her mother could win would be $250,000, because there were no economic damages involved. Smith's mother, after all, didn't have a job to lose, and she didn't incur significant medical bills. After taxes and legal fees, she would receive at most $100,000, which would make her ineligible for Medicaid; the money would ultimately go back to the nursing home industry that failed her in the first place.

As a result, Smith was unsure whether she would pursue legal action because she worried that any money that might result from it "would not be used to improve the quality of her [mother's] life." But she was frustrated by the prospect of simply dropping the case. "It feels like somebody should be held accountable," she says.

Finally, in late 2005, after her mother died, Smith decided to go ahead and pursue litigation. A new lawyer, Frank Ivy, filed the lawsuit in March 2006, and discovered that it would be even harder than they had originally thought. As it turned out, the nursing home was in receivership, meaning that it had been in financial trouble and creditors had appointed an outside firm to run the company. The receiver had failed to obtain malpractice insurance for the home, so even if Smith prevails on the merits of her lawsuit, it's very possible that the nursing home won't have the means to pay any judgment or settlement. But at the moment, Smith says, she intends to press on with the suit, if only in the hope that it might help clean up the Texas nursing home industry and so future elderly residents will be better cared for.

CHAPTER FOUR

We Wuz Robe'd:
Unseating Liberal Judges

Not content with influencing the outcomes of state races, the GOP-big business alliance found an even more powerful target: state supreme court judges, who are selected by voters rather than appointed by governors. Some of the earliest attempts by business groups to influence judicial elections had come in Texas in 1988. But in 2000, the U.S. Chamber of Commerce, the nation's most powerful business lobby, decided to step up the action and make state judicial elections a central focus of its work to change the nation's tort system.

Jim Wootton, then the executive director of the chamber's Institute for Legal Reform, told the *National Journal* that year that the group intended to spend $10 million on state judicial elections in a handful of states. "Business is now stepping up to the plate to respond to the new political influence of the trial lawyers in the wake of the tobacco settlement," he said.

Top on its list of targets was Mississippi, where business groups believed the state supreme court was biased against out-of-state corporations and beholden to trial lawyers. As evidence, they often pointed to the case of the Loewen Group, a Canadian funeral home company accused of trying to monopolize the local funeral home business. In 1995, a jury returned a $500 million verdict against the company.

Just to appeal the verdict under state law, the Loewen Group would have had to post a bond for $625 million, enough to put the company into bankruptcy. The company challenged the bond issue, but the state supreme court ruled that the bond was required, and Loewen eventually settled the case for $175 million and blamed the court for forcing it to settle. The ruling infuriated business groups, who already saw Mississippi's legal system as a problem.

Mississippi's supreme court had also committed the cardinal sin of invalidating part of a tort reform law designed to protect the tobacco industry from smokers' lawsuits passed the early 1990s. Former Mississippi Supreme Court Justice Chuck McRae, the judge most responsible for that decision, became the chamber's public enemy number one in Mississippi.

McRae was always an unconventional jurist. Before he was elected to the bench in 1990, McRae had been a successful plaintiff's attorney and president of the state trial-lawyers' association. Like many plaintiff's attorneys, McRae was a self-made man with humble roots and firsthand experience with the tragedy of random accidents, which made him something of a populist from the bench. McRae's mother choked to death on a piece of meat when he was twelve. His father, a shipyard electrician, died three years later of a sudden heart attack, leaving McRae orphaned and largely impoverished. He worked his way through college in Ohio, living in the attic of his frat house and relying on the generosity of girlfriends to smuggle him food from the cafeteria.

Rather than crush his spirit, the early struggles gave McRae an especially vibrant lust for life. He kicked off his seventh decade by running with the bulls in Pamplona and climbing Mount Kilimanjaro. A tall, striking figure with a windburned face and shock of white hair, McRae was known to show up at the courthouse wearing gold chains and a leather jacket that declared Never Legal on the back. Not so long ago, a business lobbyist told a local paper that he'd seen the sixty-something McRae swimming at the local reservoir in a Speedo thong. Throughout his thirteen-year tenure, McRae kept the courthouse abuzz with rumors of his late-night escapades and frequent sightings on the dance floor. McRae had raced sports cars as a young man while teaching school in Florida, and when he wasn't on the bench, he often swapped his black robe for black leather and rode cross-country to biker conventions, continuing his lifelong romance with Harley-Davidson.

Most state supreme court justices are lucky if members of the press even know who they are, but McRae had a way of making headlines—and usually it wasn't because of his jurisprudence. One night in 1995, police arrested McRae after he crashed his Camaro outside Jackson and refused to take a Breathalyzer test. He later pleaded no contest to a drunk-driving charge. A year later, *Reader's Digest* named him one of America's worst judges, observing that he'd once written a decision that said, "I cannot emphasize strongly enough my abhorrence for the all-too-common practice of driving under the influence of alcohol." In 1999 McRae was arrested again while speeding along I-55 in Jackson on his motorcycle. That time he contested the drunk-driving charge and was found innocent at trial, escaping with only a $136 speeding ticket.

It wasn't his driving habits or his wardrobe, though, that put McRae in the crosshairs of the business community. From his earliest days on the bench, McRae wrote decisions that nudged the state towards the gentler tort law that favored the working people he knew so well. His rulings helped overturn some of the corporations' favorite defenses against lawsuits, and he advocated for the liberal application of the state's workers'- compensation laws. McRae had further riled the local business community by writing a decision in the case *American Bankers v. Alexander,* which changed the court rules to allow mass tort lawsuits in Mississippi, continuing the flood of prescription drug litigation that was flowing into the state.

In 2002 McRae joined with the court majority in allowing family members who file a wrongful death suit over the loss of a loved one to win compensation for the loss of enjoyment of life that occurred as a result—making Mississippi one of only six states in the country to do so.

Despite all the news about his lifestyle, McRae was sharp as a tack, and the skills of persuasion that once served him so well before juries also worked with his colleagues on the bench, most of whom were not especially liberal. Many of the court's liberal decisions came because McRae succeeded in convincing four of the court's more conservative members to come around to his point of view—a fact that particularly galled corporate defendants, especially in 1994, when McRae helped plunge a knife through the heart of the state's new tort reform law. McRae's decision in the case was especially devastating to the tobacco industry, for which the law was specifically tailored to protect only a year earlier. After the decision, the American Tort Reform Association put McRae on the cover of its magazine, *Liability Week,* in an issue that urged ATRA's members to focus their attention on state judicial elections.

McRae was reelected in 1994 to an eight-year term, leaving the business groups without many options for immediate relief. But in 1995, after the Camaro crash, McRae says the business-friendly local prosecutors took the unprecedented move of presenting the misdemeanor charges to a grand jury in an attempt to get him indicted so that he'd be forced off the bench. In 1998, he says, before he was arrested for speeding, he was regularly followed by a state trooper looking to catch him doing something untoward behind the wheel.

McRae rebuffed calls for his resignation and held on until 2002, when he was up for reelection. That year, business groups brought out the big guns and aimed them squarely at McRae. In May 2002 the U.S. Chamber of Commerce held a national press conference in DC to announce that it was launching an all-out attack on the state of Mississippi's legal system. Not only did the chamber plan an extensive get-out-the-vote initiative for the state's upcoming judicial elections, but it also bought $100,000 in newspaper ads throughout the state labeling Mississippi's court system a drag on the state's economy. "It's a sad day in America when an institution like the U.S. Chamber of Commerce has no choice but to shine a spotlight on the state's legal environment," said Thomas J. Donohue, the chamber's president.

Using a study it commissioned from DC tobacco industry lawyer Bert Rein, the chamber claimed that Mississippi was losing more than 7,500 jobs a year thanks to its lax tort laws, and that its failure to cap damages in lawsuits cost the average resident $264 a year. These numbers would be repeated like a mantra for the next several years as the chamber and its allies pushed tort reform legislation in the state. Armed with millions of dollars and dubious facts, the chamber also set about to radically change the makeup of the Mississippi Supreme Court, primarily by ousting McRae.

The business groups' interest in McRae and his state court brethren nationally was fairly straightforward. Even though the groups had won all sorts of legislation protecting them from lawsuits, by 2000 almost one hundred bills had been overturned by the courts. Some of the most brilliant minds in the plaintiffs' bar had mounted serious constitutional challenges to the new laws, and as a result, sweeping judicial decisions in Illinois, Ohio, Arizona, and Alabama had struck down entire pieces of legislation as unlawful restrictions on citizens' access to justice.

The way the business groups saw it, judges, and their "unholy alliance" with the plaintiff lawyers, had set the tort reform movement back considerably.

"It was deemed to be judicial nullification," says James Wootton, who was head of the U.S. Chamber's Institute for Legal Reform at the time of the group's entry into judicial elections. "That made the role of the judiciary crucial to whether or not you could ever sustain legal reform at the state level. If you didn't change who was on the supreme court, the supreme court could use doctrines that were plastic enough that they could be shaped to invalidate tort reform measures. It was hard to believe that you could really change the legal system of a state without addressing that."

The strategy of electing pro–tort reform judges offered the corporate world other advantages as well. Jury verdicts are extremely fragile flowers, especially those in favor of plaintiffs and involving large sums of money. To survive, the verdicts must endure the scrutiny of judges, who have the authority to not only reduce the damage awards but to throw out the verdicts entirely. Electing judges who were ideologically hostile to juries in the first place would help tilt the playing field in favor of corporate defendants who had trouble when forced to appear before twelve average Americans. And these judges could make sure that any legislation passed to restrict lawsuits would sail through without any interference from the Constitution.

Buying a new court was also far cheaper than changing the direction of fifty state legislatures. For instance, the Mississippi Supreme Court had only nine members, and judicial races historically had aroused so little public interest that in 1990, winning candidates ran on less than $35,000.

The chamber poured money into judicial elections in states where supreme courts had either overturned tort reform legislation or seemed likely to, including Ohio, Michigan, Illinois, and the two leading southern "tort meccas," Alabama and Mississippi. In 2000 the chamber spent about $1 million on ads in Mississippi backing four probusiness judicial candidates. The chamber eluded state campaign finance laws by claiming that the ads were about issues, not direct candidate advocacy, and therefore were exempt from public-disclosure laws. The move allowed giant companies to route hundreds of thousands of dollars through the chamber rather than the candidate's campaign committee, where they would face statutory limits and have to be disclosed.

Several of the Mississippi candidates on the receiving end of nasty chamber-sponsored TV ads, as well as the state itself, went to federal court and asked for restraining orders against the chamber to take the ads off the air, arguing that they were violations of state campaign finance laws. The chamber ultimately prevailed, after a federal appellate court ruled that the ads were an expression of free speech. But the voters didn't take kindly to the out-of-state business activism, and only two of the chamber's four favored candidates won. After those mixed results, the chamber and its business allies tried a different tactic for the next election.

In 2002, even though the chamber had held a DC press conference to announce its plans to meddle in Mississippi's judicial elections, it kept a relatively low profile in the state. Instead, in the closing weeks of the campaign, an obscure Virginia-based nonprofit group called the Law Enforcement Alliance of America (LEAA) started running ads against McRae in Mississippi.

The National Rifle Association (NRA) had set up LEAA more than a decade earlier to counter law-enforcement groups that supported gun control. In 2002 still-unidentified benefactors funneled $4.5 million into LEAA's coffers. The money was then used in elections around the country, including in Mississippi. In the weeks leading up to the 2002 judicial election, LEAA spent nearly $500,000 on TV ads—51 percent of all the ads run in the entire race—attacking McRae, even though McRae was actually a member of the NRA and, like LEAA, opposed gun control and supported the death penalty. The LEAA ads recycled the ten-year-old *Reader's Digest* story naming McRae one of America's worst judges and hammered him for "being the only judge to vote to reverse the conviction of the murderer of a three-year-old girl."

LEAA also ran ads supporting McRae's opponent, lawyer Jess Dickinson. As it turned out, Dickinson didn't need the boost. He raised more than $1 million, mostly from corporate sources. In one TV ad, Dickinson leaned into the camera to say, "Frivolous lawsuits are costing us our health care and our jobs. Mississippi is suffering while a few lawyers are becoming multimillionaires." McRae raised about $633,000, mostly from trial lawyers, and received little assistance from the kinds of outside groups that were spending money on Dickinson's behalf.

Dickinson also got a boost from the nation's leading tort reform champion, President George W. Bush, who paid a visit to Mississippi in August 2002 and gave a speech urging limits on lawsuits. Battered on every front, McRae's campaign faced an uphill battle. But perhaps the final nail in his coffin came from an unexpected source: the FBI, which began investigating trial lawyer contributions to state supreme court judges.

"The government leaked that I was being investigated by the feds during the election," says McRae, who acknowledges that even without the investigation, he was facing a tough campaign. "Because of my lifestyle, I gave them a lot of material," he says wryly over a Sprite at Hal & Mal's, a favorite Jackson watering hole. Even though he was never implicated in the judicial bribery investigation, he was roundly defeated in November 2002.

The new court quickly worked to undo McRae's legacy. Charlie Ross, a Mississippi state senator whose law firm had represented the Loewen Group in its Mississippi litigation, bragged in the *Wall Street Journal* in the fall of 2005 that the state supreme court had "virtually eliminated the mass tort industry in Mississippi."

Rick Patt, a plaintiff's lawyer and former administrator for the state courts, has collected some anecdotal evidence on the change in the supreme court. He says that for about two years after McRae was defeated, the Mississippi Supreme Court did not uphold a single plaintiff's verdict in its entirety. The record ended in 2005 when a business owner successfully sued the city of Jackson for flood damage to his home, and the court upheld the verdict.

"You can really see the change," says Patt. The court in the late nineties, he says, was far more deferential to juries and lower-court judges. Tort reform champions mirror Patt's observations. "The defeat of Chuck McRae was unheard of for a sitting supreme court chief justice," says Jackson publisher Wyatt Emmerich, who considers himself the intellectual leader of Mississippi's tort reform movement. "That really changed everything. The court did an about-face after he was defeated."

Before McRae's defeat, the court had three reliably conservative votes, three somewhat liberal, including McRae, and three swing voters who were less predictable but who also became extremely conservative after the tort reform battles. The new court is a distinctly ideological bunch.

Jess Dickinson, who replaced McRae, spoke openly at an insurance industry forum in California in 2004 about the tort system. He said to the group, "Until we get fair judges in the court system, it doesn't matter what happens in the legislature in terms of tort reform. There was a time when judges in Alabama gave plaintiff attorneys tremendous leeway in civil cases. After a while, those judges were out, and the lawyers just moved on to filing cases in Mississippi."

The impact of Dickinson's ascension to the court was apparent almost immediately after he took office, and it's nowhere more striking than in the case of *Eckman v. Moore.* Jason Moore, twenty-seven, was an up-and-coming young executive at a local furniture company who went to the movies one night in 1999 and slipped and fell in the bathroom, injuring his head. He became disoriented and drove away from the theater. When his wife couldn't find him, she called him on his cell phone and persuaded him to go to a nearby emergency room. A CT scan showed that he had some bleeding in the frontal lobe of his brain. Neurologist Walter Eckman saw Moore the next morning and prescribed some pain medication. But Moore's condition worsened, and his blood pressure rose sharply. According to the complaint, the hospital twice alerted Eckman that Moore wasn't responding to treatment. Eckman ordered some more pain and blood-pressure medication over the phone and told the nurses to check Moore every few hours.

As it turned out, Moore was suffering from a subdural hematoma, which was dangerously compressing his brain. He had all the symptoms, but according to the plaintiffs, Eckman never saw him again until after Moore went into cardiac arrest and was left profoundly brain damaged. Had Eckman operated early on to relieve the swelling in the brain, experts later testified, Moore likely would have survived with no major trauma. (Eckman, however, maintained that had the hosptial checked on the patient's condition properly and reported it to him, the decline would have been caught and Moore would have had surgery.) Instead, Moore died in an Arkansas nursing home about a year later, leaving behind his wife and young child.

In 2000 Moore's wife filed a malpractice suit against Eckman and the hospital, and the case went to trial in Tupelo, a mostly white and very conservative part of the state not known for its sympathy to plaintiffs. Nonetheless, the jury hit Eckman and the hospital with a $5 million verdict, the largest in the county's history.

The verdict turned Eckman into something of a tort reform celebrity after *Forbes* magazine put him on the cover as yet another innocent victim of a tort system run amok. Eckman was an unusual choice for the cover. Not long after the malpractice verdict, in 2003, Eckman became a plaintiff in another lawsuit that revealed another side to his medical practice. Apparently Eckman performed a high number of expensive neurosurgeries on many of his workers'-compensation patients, enough to attract scrutiny from one of the employers in the program. The company sent two cases to outside reviewers to assess whether the company should pay for the surgeries Eckman had done on two of the company's employees.

The physicians who reviewed the medical records questioned whether the surgeries had been necessary, and one doctor wrote, "It is embarrassing to me that there are people in my profession which would resort to tactics like these and give the entire profession a bad name. To me, this borders on white-collar crime." Based on the review, the company declined to pay Eckman's bills. When Eckman got wind of the evaluation, he sued both the company and the reviewers for defamation and libel. The trial court threw out Eckman's suit, a decision the supreme court upheld. But the high court did have good news for him in his medical malpractice case.

In October 2003 the Mississippi Supreme Court had upheld the $5-million malpractice verdict against Eckman and the hospital by a 5–3 vote. But in March 2004, with McRae gone and Dickinson in his place, the court made the highly unusual move to take a second look at the Eckman case, even though Eckman had missed the deadline for filing a motion for a rehearing. The new court reversed the jury verdict and sent it back for a new trial on the grounds that there had been faulty jury instructions, improper closing arguments, and evidence that would have prejudiced the jury against the doctor (this apparently included that Moore's lawyers had shown the jury too many photos of the couple's wedding, a fact that the court had found harmless just six months earlier). It was an extraordinary reversal of fortune. At that point, Moore's wife and her lawyers threw in the towel.

Despite its activism, the new court has been thin-skinned in the face of criticism. In 2004 an attorney requested that Dickinson recuse himself from sitting on a case in which the defendant had donated $10,000 to Dickinson's campaign. Dickinson not only refused to withdraw from the case but later joined with the court in publicly reprimanding the lawyer, Dana Kelly, and fining him $1,000 for disrespecting the judiciary.

In 2004 the court threw out a $500,000 jury verdict awarded to the family of an elderly woman who fell in the parking lot of an adult day care center and subsequently suffered a stroke a few days later. The woman's lawyers filed a motion for rehearing, much the same way that Eckman had. Rather than grant their request, the court decided to sanction the lawyers.

The lawyers in this case were hardly raving liberal trial lawyers. One, Mark Baker, is a conservative Republican state representative, and the other, James Bobo, is the attorney for the city of Pearl. The lawyers had written that the Supreme Court's decision tossing out the jury verdict "does a disservice to the court and the parties and almost certainly will cause confusion and uncertainty among the bench and bar." They then wrote, "In an unscholarly fashion, the opinion appears to overturn long-established principles of law . . . It can be fairly stated that the opinion does violence to the 'letter and the spirit' of the Law." For that, the judges hauled them into court to explain why they should not be sanctioned for their behavior. In December 2005, the court declined to punish the lawyers other than to strike their motion from the public record.

Mississippi lawyers note that the new court doesn't show the same kind of hostility to juries when they want to kill somebody in a criminal case. After the U.S. Supreme Court vacated a Mississippi death sentence imposed on a seventeen-year-old boy, justices were outraged by the high court's refusal to defer to a jury, writing, "It is not the Constitution which is changing, but only some individual justices rearranging a shapeless concept to fit their personal whims and declaring that to be the law du jour,

without sufficient deference to the intent of the framers of the Constitution; the rule of law; legislative acts; and finally, the decision of a jury."

★ ★ ★

What's going on in Mississippi courts is hardly an anomaly. Judicial elections around the country have become slugfests as business groups have
poured money into the races. As we have seen, their involvement in these
efforts is not new.

After Texas, Alabama became a focal point in 1994 after the state court
upheld a number of large punitive damage awards against big out-of-state
corporations and overturned a 1987 tort reform law that would have capped
punitive damages at $250,000. In 1994 Karl Rove ran the campaign of the
first Republican elected to the Alabama high court in the twentieth century,
helping turn the once genteel judicial elections vitriolic. State politicos
dubbed 1996 "the year of the skunk" because of an ad run by an incumbent
supreme court justice that alluded to his opponent and featured pictures of a
skunk, accompanied by the caption "Some things you can smell a mile away."

With Rove's help, the Alabama Supreme Court went from a nine-
member Democratic majority in 1993 to an eight-to-one GOP majority by
2000. In 1999 the state legislature passed tort reform not so different from
the bills that had been struck down as unconstitutional in years past, and
the new court let it stand.

But the recent efforts by the U.S. Chamber of Commerce to systematically change the composition of a number of influential state courts all at
once is virtually unprecedented, both because of the sheer amount of
money involved and the maliciousness of its advertising campaigns. The
amount of money spent nationally on state judicial elections jumped by 61
percent in 2000 over the previous election cycle, an increase fueled almost
entirely by the U.S. Chamber. And the money went primarily to low-blow
attack ads on television. (Researchers at the nonpartisan Justice at Stake
Campaign concluded that in the judicial elections in Alabama, Mississippi,
and Ohio, the only interest groups spending money on TV ads were business groups.)

In 2000, the chamber targeted Ohio justice Alice Robie Resnick, who
wrote the majority decision in the 1999 case that overturned the state's tort

reform legislation as unconstitutional. The chamber contributed between $1 million and $2 million to Resnick's opponent. Funneling money through stealth groups like Citizens for a Strong Ohio and Americans for Job Security, business interests ran $4 million worth of "issue advocacy" ads against Resnick that brought cries of protest across the state about their tenor. In one radio ad, a woman said, "I thought Ohio was on the leading edge of reining in outrageous lawsuits." A man then replies, "We were—that is, until Alice Resnick fixed it for the trial lawyers and overturned real reforms proposed by the governor and the legislature."

(Resnick held on to her seat.)

The hot race of 2004 occurred in West Virginia, where the U.S. Chamber and business groups targeted Supreme Court Justice Warren McGraw. McGraw had riled businesses by authoring a 1999 decision that allowed people exposed to toxic chemicals to win damages to pay for years of medical testing to monitor for illnesses known to be caused by the chemicals.

Donald Blankenship, the CEO of Massey Energy, one of the state's biggest coal companies, plowed $1.7 million of his own money—"one dollar for every West Virginian," he claimed—into a PAC called And for the Sake of Kids. Blankenship's interest was tort reform—that is, money. His company was a defendant in several lawsuits over the impact of mountaintop-removal mining operations. But the TV ads sponsored by the PAC were about child molesters. One suggested that McGraw himself was the pedophile, with an announcer opening the ad by intoning ominously, "He sexually molested multiple West Virginia children. Liberal Judge Warren McGraw cast the deciding vote to set this reprehensible criminal free."

The truth was that McGraw was one of three judges in the majority who refused to revoke the probation of a young man who'd been sexually abused himself before going on to abuse a half brother at age fourteen. The man was released on probation when he was eighteen, and prosecutors wanted to send him to jail because he'd smoked some pot and drank booze. The justices had written, "Considering Mr. Arbaugh's tender age and extreme victimization, we cannot, we will not, surrender any opportunity to salvage his life and turn him into a productive member of society." The ad was effective. Republican Brent Benjamin defeated McGraw, a Democrat, 53 percent to 47 percent, to become the first nonincumbent Republican to win a state supreme court seat since the 1920s.

The dirty politics and explosion of money in judicial campaigns paid off for the chamber. In 2000 and 2002 chamber-backed candidates won twenty-one out of twenty-four targeted races, and in 2004 the chamber's candidates swept twelve of thirteen supreme court races it targeted. In 2004 business outspent lawyers almost two to one, investing $21.5 million in supreme court races nationally. Lawyers and labor, by comparison, chipped in $13.3 million.

Watchdog groups have tried to analyze whether donors to supreme court races get favorable treatment when they appear before the court. In 2003 the Institute on Money in State Politics compared Alabama's state supreme court's decisions to donations. It determined that contributors to a justice were involved in 63 percent of the cases heard by the court during the period it studied, and in about 30 percent of those, contributions had come from only the winners in the case. But the watchdogs are asking the wrong questions.

State supreme court decisions have tremendous impact on the way the tort system operates broadly, not just for the immediate parties that come before it. State supreme courts can change the rules. They can set high bars for actually using laws already on the books and set impossible standards for proving negligence or admitting expert witnesses. They can prevent good cases from ever being heard. And there's plenty of anecdotal evidence to suggest that the new business-friendly state courts are doing all of that, profoundly changing the average American's fortunes in the legal system.

As in Mississippi, these new judges are rapidly rewriting the rules of tort law, overturning established precedent at record speed and even further reducing the number of jury verdicts that survive on appeal. The results have been especially severe in Texas, where probusiness judges have dominated for more than a decade. No one understands that better than Donna Hall.

Over the twenty-nine years that Charlie Hall went to work at the Diamond Shamrock Refining Co. in Dumas, Texas, he would often tell his wife, Donna, "If anything ever happens to me out there, sue 'em." Hall, fifty-two, knew that the plant was a dangerous place to work, and his instructions to his wife proved prescient. In 1996 the refinery exploded, and a flash fire left Hall with burns over half his body. He lived for nine agonizing days before finally succumbing to his injuries. After he died, Donna did his bidding, got herself a lawyer, and proceeded to sue the oil company for failing to take simple safety precautions that would have saved her husband's life.

When the case went to trial, a San Antonio jury found that Diamond Shamrock had been grossly negligent and could have easily prevented Hall's death by spending a small amount of money on safety and maintenance on previously identified danger spots. The jury hit the company with a $42.5-million punitive-damage judgment, hoping to send a signal to Diamond Shamrock to clean up its act. Much to the surprise of the jurors, however, the judge slashed the award to $200,000—barely enough to pay Hall's legal fees—saying that legal changes Governor Bush had made in 1995 gave him no other choice.

Hall and Diamond Shamrock appealed various parts of the verdict. In 2001 an appellate court granted Hall a new trial, agreeing that the trial court had wrongly reduced the jury verdict. Diamond Shamrock, in turn, appealed the decision, and the case went up to the Texas Supreme Court. In 2005 the court issued a stunning decision. It didn't even bother to take up the issue of the award reduction. It simply said that Diamond Shamrock wasn't guilty of gross negligence and entered a judgment in favor of the oil company. After nine years of litigation, Hall got absolutely nothing, and the oil company got off scot-free.

The decision was extraordinary, both for the amount of money involved and because the state's highest court had decided to substitute its judgment for that of the jury. After all, it's the jurors who sit through the hours of testimony and all the arguments from both sides of a case. The jury, not the supreme court, was supposed to decide whether Diamond Shamrock was grossly negligent. Joe Lovell, one of Hall's attorneys, says that thanks to the Texas Supreme Court, "It's cheaper [for the refinery] to kill Charlie Hall than to make sure it doesn't happen again."

Hall's story is extreme, but it's representative of the conservative court, which has become famous for its hostility to both juries and individual plaintiffs. According to studies by the nonprofit group Texas Watch, in 1990 win rates for plaintiffs and defendants had run about fifty-fifty. By the 2004–2005 term, the ratio was 78–22 for the defense. The only time individual plaintiffs had a decent shot was when they sued a *lawyer* for malpractice. Insurance companies, the prime mover behind most tort reform enterprises, came away the clear winner. Another study by Texas Watch found that of 132 insurance cases the court decided between 1991 and 1999, insurance companies won 71 percent, and many of those cases came after Republicans took control of the court in 1994.

Those numbers, though, don't tell the whole story. Citing a study done by lawyers Jerry Galow and Amy Horowitz, Texas Watch notes that the Texas Supreme Court accepted just 7.5 percent of appeals filed by people who were policyholders or injured claimants trying to get their benefits paid properly. On the other hand, the court accepted one-third of appeals filed by the insurance companies.

The Texas Supreme Court is the modern template for business groups seeking to reshape other state high courts. The judges supported by the U.S. Chamber of Commerce are all cut from the same cloth as Priscilla Owen, the Texas Supreme Court justice nominated by Bush to the federal bench. While on the Texas court, Owen was assigned the case of Willie Searcy, a young man who'd been completely paralyzed from the neck down in a car accident when he was fourteen. A jury had awarded him $40 million in a lawsuit filed against the automaker for a defective seat belt that led to his catastrophic injury. A court of appeals had reduced the verdict to $30 million, and the carmaker appealed the case to the state supreme court.

Lawyers for both sides had asked for a speedy response; the family could not afford Searcy's round-the-clock medical care and desperately needed the money. Owen ignored the request and waited more than two years before finally writing an opinion in 1998 throwing out the verdict. She held that the plaintiffs had filed the suit in the wrong court, an issue that wasn't among those the court had agreed to hear when it accepted the case. The delay was so egregious that her conservative colleagues on the bench issued a one-paragraph order along with the opinion that said, "While members of this court disagree over whether our disposition in this case has been timely . . . we unanimously agree that the parties' request should have been granted."

The note was of little consolation for the Searcy family. While Searcy waited in vain for a new trial, his parents did their best to take care of him, scrimping together enough money to hire a nurse for a few hours at night so they could sleep. The nurse would stay until four in the morning. Searcy's mother would rise at five o'clock to take over. But one night in 2001, in that one hour when he went unattended, Searcy's respirator failed, and with no one there to notice, he died at the age of twenty-two.

Judges in the Owen mold have seized control of influential state courts around the country, most notably, perhaps, in Michigan, where the state supreme court was once a pioneer in progressive environmental law. In 1998, after a bruising and expensive election in which tort reform and other business groups poured money into the campaigns of conservative candidates, the court went from three Democrats, three Republicans, and one Independent, to five Republicans and two Democrats.

Mary Ellen Gurewitz, the general counsel of the Michigan AFL-CIO, studied the impact of the change in the term following the Republican takeover. In the first half of 1999, she found that in cases involving insurance companies, the court ruled against plaintiffs in nineteen out of twenty cases, compared to the previous year, when the court split twenty-three to twenty-two in similar cases. The court had also set to work overturning established case law at a record-breaking pace, overruling ten legal precedents in just the first half of 1999. In the past, such decisions had come about once a year.

Gurewitz wrote, "[T]he way to understand this Court's work, and to predict how it will decide cases in the future, is not to analyze or explain the law as lawyers are trained to do, but simply identify the litigants. . . . The principles which appeared to underlie the Court's decisions are these: unions lose, personal injury plaintiffs lose, civil rights plaintiffs lose, workers'-compensation claimants lose, criminal defendants lose, insurance companies win, corporations win, Republicans win."

Even business groups themselves have been shocked at how well their efforts to swing the courts have paid off. In West Virginia, the transformation happened almost overnight, after Warren McGraw's departure from the bench. The West Virginia Chamber of Commerce conducted a study of the court's decisions, comparing the fall 2004 session to spring 2005, and found that business fortunes had made a dramatic turnaround. In the fall of 2004, employers had won 42 workers'-compensation cases before the court, while claimants won 132. The following spring, employers won 254 workers'-comp cases while claimants won 181—a state record for business.

With conservative tort reformers now in control of courts in much of the South, big states like Michigan, and once-liberal states like West Virginia, the elections are likely to cool down—but the previous campaigns have left partisans on both sides calling for an end to judicial elections altogether. Tort reformers are big fans of appointed judges, particularly in states with conservative governors. Chuck McRae, for one, thinks this is a bad idea.

Even though he was defeated in 2002, a quirk in Mississippi law left McRae on the bench for another year, which he used to tweak his fellow justices for their tort reform stances. After finally leaving the bench in mid-2003, McRae took a trip around the world and then returned to Mississippi, where he took up life again as a plaintiff's attorney at his daughter's law firm. Looking back, he says he harbors no ill will toward the voters who threw him out of office. Despite all the rough-and-tumble world of the elections, he says he'd never advocate trading the democratic process for an appointed judiciary. His faith for change still lies with voters and juries. "I fought that fight for thirteen years, and I'm glad the people saw fit to give me my life back," he says.

CHAPTER FIVE

Cash Bar: The Campaign to Cut Attorney Fees

The Republican establishment in Texas has never held a great affection for attorney John O'Quinn. Over a career spanning more than three decades, many consider O'Quinn the Lone Star State's premier ambulance chaser (something he denies). He embodies the sort of entrepreneurship that has long infuriated tort reformers, not to mention Texas's guardians of lawyerly propriety. Twice, the Texas bar authorities have tried (unsuccessfully) to revoke his law license. In 1997, O'Quinn pleaded guilty to misdemeanor charges of practicing law in South Carolina without a license and paid $250,000 in fines after prosecutors alleged he had solicited clients there after a US Air crash in 1994. A drinking problem had led to at least one embarrassing run-in with local police while driving, though O'Quinn has since joined Alcoholics Anonymous.

And yet O'Quinn had made a fortune before Texas juries, particularly in breast-implant litigation but also representing injured workers and other average folks against big corporations. Once, he even won $8 million for a man whose prize bull was poisoned by pesticides. The establishment scorn for O'Quinn, though, grew exponentially after he became one of a handful of Texas lawyers hired by the state to take on the nation's tobacco industry.

In March 1996, O'Quinn and other prominent state lawyers—Walter Umphrey, Wayne Reaud, John Eddie Williams and Harold Nix—joined with the state attorney general, Dan Morales, in filing a lawsuit against the nation's largest tobacco companies to recoup Medicaid costs of treating sick smokers. Morales had recruited O'Quinn & Co. to bring the lawsuit because his office didn't have the resources to engage in what would likely be a protracted and costly gamble with long odds of success. That year, *American Lawyer* reported, the tobacco industry spent an estimated $600 million on legal fees fending off lawsuits, which it had effectively done nearly one thousand times since 1954. In 1996 tobacco companies employed some twenty-three law firms in Texas alone, according to the *Texas Observer,* and the industry was well known for its scorched-earth defense tactics.

The private lawyers Morales hired would work for the state on a contingency-fee basis, meaning that they would take on all of the risk and put up their own money for expenses. In exchange, they'd get 15 percent of whatever they won for the state. If they lost, they got nothing. At the time the Texas tobacco suit was filed, it was considered such a long shot that Governor George W. Bush wished Morales "all the best" in his battle. Bush never objected to the arrangement with the private attorneys, nor did anyone in the state legislature speak out against the state's contingency-fee agreement. Simply no one thought they'd win.

Initially, the tobacco companies resorted to their usual tactics of burying opponents in discovery requests. At one point, they demanded the medical records for every single Medicaid patient in Texas, according to the *Texas Observer.* But the plaintiff lawyers fought back, spending nearly $50 million of their own money on the case. Two years later, the nation's tobacco companies agreed to settle lawsuits with Texas and other states for $246 billion over twenty-five years. The state of Texas would get $17.3 billion. As part of the deal, some three hundred private plaintiff lawyers who'd represented the states stood to receive as much as $30 billion in fees for their services.

Suddenly, Bush and his corporate backers realized that the contingency-fee agreement with the state was about to award O'Quinn and those other four trial lawyers not just millions but billions of dollars for their work. Big corporations saw that just as asbestos and breast-implant litigation fees had funded the tobacco litigation, the tobacco fees would give some of the nation's most skilled plaintiff lawyers the financial wherewithal to mount risky, expensive, but potentially lucrative lawsuits against other of the nation's biggest—and until then untouchable—industries, including gun manufacturers and booze producers. Even McDonald's might be at risk.

The fee wars were on.

Several states went to court to challenge the fees awarded to the lawyers they hired, including Texas. Tort reform groups also launched a media campaign to characterize the fees as obscene and unethical. In Texas, the battles were particularly nasty. A new advocacy organization, Texans for Reasonable Legal Fees, founded by Hugh Rice Kelly, general counsel to Reliant Energy in Houston, organized direct-mail campaigns to "educate" the state's business leaders about the travesty of the legal fees, lest they fail to grasp why a valid contract should not be honored or why businessmen should be prevented from charging market rate for their work.

Not long after Morales announced the Texas settlement, Bush and seven state legislators filed suit to reduce the lawyers' fees, even though any reduction would have gone back to the tobacco companies, not the state. "I will never understand and never agree that five private law firms should collect more than $3.3 billion for working less than two years on a case that was settled before it went to trial," Bush said. "The fee seems totally out of proportion for the work performed." The argument, though, failed to persuade a federal judge who reviewed the lawyers' work and found that it justified the fees.

Some of the corporate bigwigs behind the Texas tort reform movement were pretty well compensated themselves—think Enron's Ken Lay—and they'd never complained that, say, obscene CEO pay was shortchanging shareholders. But the specter of lawyers like O'Quinn accessing a billion dollars in fees drove the tort reform groups, and their political supporters, to distraction. After all, if O'Quinn could make hay over a cow, just think of what he could do with all the new tobacco money?

In 1999 John Cornyn, a tort reformer and state supreme court judge, ousted Morales as attorney general and immediately set to work launching a criminal investigation into the state's selection of Umphrey, O'Quinn, and the others to handle the tobacco litigation. None of the lawyers was ever charged with a crime or ethics violations, and in the end, after three years of litigation solely over the fees, the original five lawyers walked away with $3.3 billion. The only casualty was Morales, who had attempted to cut in a friend on the fees. This particular lawyer really didn't do any work on the litigation, and Morales got sentenced to four years in prison after pleading guilty to mail fraud and tax evasion.

Cornyn, though, took his crusade with him when he was elected to the U.S. Senate in 2002. There he joined with Arizona senator John Kyl in pushing legislation that would impose a 200 percent tax penalty on "excessive" legal fees in lawsuits that resulted in settlements or judgments of more than $100 million. The law would apply to fees awarded before the bill even took effect. The proposed legislation would also have required the Internal Revenue Service to regulate contingency fees, a move that even libertarians thought was a little extreme, especially given that regulating legal fees was traditionally a state, not federal, function. The bill didn't get far, but Kyl and Cornyn have vowed to keep trying.

In the end, the tobacco litigation was sui generis. Many of the issues that it raised simply didn't apply anywhere else. Nonetheless, the lawyers' fees energized the tort reform movement like never before. They provided new fodder for an old campaign by Republicans and tort reform groups to hobble plaintiff lawyers by attacking the way most of them get paid. After the tobacco settlement, tort reform proponents launched a blizzard of new proposals to restrict plaintiff lawyers' contingency fees. In 2003, for instance, the tort reform group Common Good petitioned twelve state supreme courts to restrict contingency fees on the grounds that the fees were unethical and needed to be better regulated by the judiciary—to protect consumers, of course. "The American legal system is supposed to serve the public, not the lawyers," said Common Good Chair Philip K. Howard, announcing the initiative. "Where there is little or no litigation risk, far more of the proceeds should go to the victim, not provide a windfall for lawyers." (All the petitions were rejected as clearly biased in favor of defense attorneys, whose fees wouldn't be affected by the proposal.)

Many states included restrictions on plaintiff lawyers' fees in medical malpractice reform legislation, and the Bush administration even used its regulatory authority to restrict legal fees in the federal radiation workers'-compensation program making it difficult for victims of nuclear testing exposure to get benefits. Other federal legislation was introduced to eliminate the right of plaintiff lawyers to recoup legal fees in civil rights cases and to radically restrict fees in asbestos litigation.

Proponents of such laws argue they would give more money to clients and less to their lawyers. Who could oppose that? Of course, that's not how contingency fees really work. Contingency-fee law practice is essentially a form of gambling, as the tobacco lawyers showed so well. Plaintiff lawyers generally use the proceeds of their winning cases to subsidize the losers, whose costs they have to eat entirely. Restrictions on their fees make it harder for lawyers to take many cases. And without lawyers willing to front the costs of a lawsuit, most injured people would have no access to the courts, regardless of the merits of their cases, because they simply couldn't afford it. From a political standpoint, though, pitching limits on lawyers' fees got a lot easier after a few of them made billions from the to-bacco litigation.

Lawyers working on contingency fees have been giving corporate America fits for at least a century. In the early 1900s, when the Industrial Revolution was producing an epidemic of workplace accidents, injuries, and deaths, tort law changed to respond to the bloodshed, and a new breed of personal injury lawyers popped up to give the new laws teeth. Unlike those from the silk-stocking firms that were the exclusive bastion of WASP privilege, these new lawyers tended to be immigrants and Jews who worked their way through law school at night and made their practices in personal injury law using the contingency fee. Their clients were the great unwashed masses generally shunned by the elite bar members.

The contingency fee, with its boom-or-bust nature of payment, encour-aged personal injury lawyers to generate high-volume practices in order to round up enough winning cases to compensate for the losing ones. Lawyers had to hustle, and to that end, they resorted to all the free-market tech-niques available to them: advertising, ambulance chasing, cultivating sources in police departments and hospitals to refer cases—all the unique features long associated with the dregs of personal injury law. Contingency-fee prac-tice was—and is—highly entrepreneurial, with its best practitioners con-stantly seeking out new and potentially profitable areas of litigation. That's why critics have regularly accused contingency-fee lawyers of stirring up lit-igation and eventually causing an "explosion" in lawsuits.

In the early twentieth century, however sleazy they seemed to the es-tablished bar, many of these lawyers were quite successful (as they are today), costing "the trusts" and big insurance companies some serious cash. It wasn't long before organized business campaigned to discredit the lawyers and drive them out of practice. One of the earliest examples came in 1905, when the country's major insurance and railroad companies cre-ated an organization called the Alliance Against Accident Frauds, which was purportedly designed to wage war on people who faked accidents and filed bogus insurance claims. When the group opened its first Chicago branch in 1907, the *Chicago Tribune* reported that it would seek the prosecution of "shyster lawyers who endeavor to mullet employers and other concerns." C. S. S. Miller of the Casualty Company of America, of New York, declared, "The people we are after are first the fake claimants, second the shyster lawyers, the ambulance chasers who make a business of bringing these suits even where no damages have been sustained. We will endeavor to secure the disbarment of lawyers lending themselves to these frauds and to the revocation of the licenses of the doctors who assist them."

The group appealed to bar associations to enforce stricter ethics codes against the plaintiff lawyers. At the time, bar associations were dominated by corporate lawyers from the railroads and insurance companies and were happy to lend a hand. In 1908 the American Bar Association issued its Canons of Professional Ethics, which, for the first time, barred lawyer advertising and soliciting clients, making violations of the canon grounds for disbarment. Shut out of the cozy networking environments of private clubs and golf courses, where the corporate lawyers did all their soliciting unimpeded by bar officials, the new personal injury lawyers, according to the ethics code, were supposed to hang out a shingle and demurely wait for clients to walk in the door. It was a recipe for starvation, so naturally there were plenty of violations.

Armed with the canons, the Chicago Bar Association announced in June 1912 that it was launching a massive investigation into the "classes of attorneys who resort to doubtful methods in carrying on the practice of their profession." According to the Chicago Tribune, these "trouble hunting pluggers" included defense attorneys who represented indigent criminals, lawyers who helped paupers in bankruptcy cases, and, of course, the "ambulance chasers," whose frivolous lawsuits were preventing people with meritorious cases from getting speedy trials and justice.

Many of these bar association investigations were openly anti-Semitic and xenophobic. In Philadelphia in 1928, for instance, during one of the many "investigations" into ambulance chasers in the early twentieth century, one of the bar's esteemed ethics experts, Henry Drinker, complained about the "Russian Jew boys" who "came up out of the gutter," conducting their law practices by "merely following the methods their fathers had been using in selling shoe-strings and other merchandise."

In New York City, the bar association persuaded the New York State Supreme Court to hold public hearings that would help rid the profession of the scourge of personal injury lawyers working on contingency fees. The bar hired a former prosecutor, Isidor Kresel, who determined from his research that personal injury lawyers were "men who have no background, no character, not sufficient preliminary education, no idea of the ethics of the profession, and no distinction in their minds between business and profession; men who consider these cases as business, treat them as business, just as if they were selling shoes or clothes."

In the wake of the hearings, in 1929, New York state legislators introduced several of the nation's first tort reform bills, designed to tamp down the plaintiff lawyers. Among other things, the bills would have limited attorney compensation in negligence cases to 33⅓ percent of any award, including any court expenses. They would have prevented injured victims from retaining a lawyer for fifteen days after an accident, banned the hiring of runners, and forced the court to approve the settlement of all personal injury cases.

Despite a host of media coverage and support from Governor Teddy Roosevelt, the bills were killed off by upstate Republicans who suspected heavy involvement of the insurance companies and saw the regulation of personal injury lawyers' compensation as bordering on unconstitutional. Assemblyman Horace Stone said at the time, "There is no doubt that these bills came from the insurance companies, and probably if the insurance companies had as much influence here as they have elsewhere, the measure would have been passed." He said the bills put the legal profession on the same plane as pawnbrokers. He criticized their supporters for trying to "tell us how much we can charge for our services. The governor doesn't dare do this with any other profession."

Eventually, plaintiff lawyers fought back against these sorts of attacks. In the 1970s, they won important victories in the U.S. Supreme Court upholding their free-speech rights to advertise and, to some extent, solicit clients. Legal activists led by Ralph Nader also began to champion the contingency fee as a democratic institution that gave Americans liberal access to the courts. But the contingency fee remained controversial, and establishment disdain for lawyers who relied on it persisted.

Manhattan Institute scholar Walter Olson devotes a whole chapter of his 1991 book, *The Litigation Explosion,* to the evils of the contingency fee, writing that the system is corrupting (unlike, say, the $800-an-hour jobs in corporate law firms). Olson writes, "Few occupations offer such chances for dishonest persons to become very rich. A job that offers enormous returns to unscrupulousness will attract many unscrupulous persons and corrupt many persons of ordinary character."

Attacks on contingency fees tend to come hand in hand with attacks on the lawyers personally, usually over their alleged greed, poor breeding, ostentatious displays of wealth, and bad taste. In 1989, when the modern tort reform movement was just kicking into high gear, *Forbes* magazine ran a feature called "The Best Paid Lawyers in America," which focused only on plaintiff lawyers. It may mark the only time that the free-market cheerleader ever devoted a cover to bashing people for making money. A chart accompanying the article listed all the top lawyers—along with the law schools they graduated from, to support its contention that plaintiff lawyers are really drawn from the bottom of the barrel. (Not too many Harvard types made the list.)

With echoes of Isidor Kresel, Olson complains in his book, "These men (very few are women) seldom seem to favor sober, understated ways of spending their newfound wealth. One has turned lawsuits against doctors into a villa in the south of France and a $2-million Paris apartment. A list of their known holdings is spangled with the ranches, jets, and very fancy cars that befit tycoons riding a cash wave with no end in sight. And indeed, no end is in sight."

Criticizing anyone in America for making and spending money seems, well, un-American. Even Congress lost its enthusiasm for limiting the fees of the tobacco lawyers in 1998 after hearing testimony from lawyers representing cigarette makers who admitted earning well over $500 an hour. Most self-respecting Republicans couldn't plausibly argue for restrictions on the plaintiffs' lawyers when the defense lawyers were pulling in that kind of cash. The only reason the tort reformers can plausibly argue for regulating plaintiff lawyers' pay is that unlike most other professions, lawyers' conduct and licensing are governed by the courts in conjunction with bar associations and their ethics codes. Those codes require "reasonable" legal fees. So tort reformers have set out to convince judges and the public that most contingency fees are unreasonable and therefore should be either banned outright or restricted—always, of course, in the name of the consumer, who, as legal-ethics expert Professor Monroe Freedman likes to say, clearly needs to be protected from his lawyer more than he needs money for his injuries.

To make their case, tort reformers needed an expert, someone to give their arguments an intellectual veneer. They found him in Cardozo Law School professor Lester Brickman.

Brickman's expertise is in the area of legal ethics. His ascent as a media star began in 1989, after he published a dense article in the *UCLA Law Review* arguing that contingency fees paid to plaintiff lawyers are frequently invalid as a matter of ethics, policy, and law because the cases involve little risk—the central element of the "contingency."

Brickman lamented that judges were turning a blind eye to massive abuses as lawyers received windfall fees from doing little work on cases that were easy wins. Case in point, he said, was a medical malpractice lawsuit in Kansas, *Walters v. Hitchcock,* in which a jury awarded $2 million to a young woman whose surgeon had accidentally removed part of her esophagus while taking out her thyroid. The woman required further surgery in which her esophagus was repaired with part of her colon, resulting in horrible pain and suffering and an inability to eat.

Brickman claimed in the article that there was never any doubt that the woman would get paid, meaning the lawyers faced little risk in taking it on. He also claimed that the lawyers likely earned in excess of $3,000 per hour. That eyepopping figure was enough to land him in the *New York Times,* where Brickman said that such outrageous fees violated the lawyers' code of ethics as "illegal or clearly excessive," but that nothing was being done about it because the fees "are so much a part of the culture that people have stopped questioning them."

Neither the *Times* nor the *Review* ever questioned how Brickman arrived at such a staggering number in the Walters case. A footnote in the UCLA piece simply says that Brickman assumed the lawyer would spend three hundred hours getting the case through trial and take half of the $2-million trial verdict.

The lawsuit in question began in 1979 and didn't get through the final appeal to the Kansas Supreme Court until 1985. By Brickman's calculations, Walters's lawyer would have devoted less than one hour a week to the case over six years, a preposterous notion given the complex nature of medical malpractice litigation, especially in a case that involved a trial and several appeals. In response to questions, Brickman said that he obtained filings in the case and showed them to the "med mal lawyers" who provided estimates of the time required and that he erred on the high side to be conservative.

In the Walters case, there were two attorneys, Gloria Vusich and Felix Kancel, both now retired. Here's what Vusich, now seventy-one, recalls about the Walters case: despite Brickman's claim that the case was a slam dunk, Vusich says the prominent area doctor fought them tooth and nail to the very end. Vusich says that she worked on the case for six years without getting paid. "We didn't make anything until they finally capitulated. It went all the way to the [Kansas] supreme court. I spent hours and hours, millions of hours on that case. It dragged on forever."

She says they made very little money on the case because their client had been a friend of Kancel's, and they represented her as a favor. The client had young children, and the lawyers wanted to make sure she got most of the award. "I'd a betcha we didn't even get ten percent," Vusich says, noting that they also didn't get the fee in a lump sum but rather in dribs and drabs as the client was able to pay it. Vusich says she's never heard of Brickman and is certain that she never spoke to him for his article. When I told her that he claimed in the *New York Times* that she'd collected in excess of $3,000 an hour on the Walters case, she said, "I'd like to get my gun."

Nonetheless, Brickman's career as a critic of contingency fees flourished. He went on to make more and more proclamations about the "windfall" fees supposedly earned by personal injury lawyers who take little risk. In 1994 he was telling the *New York Times* about a case in which he calculated that each plaintiff lawyer earned a fee as high as $25,000 an hour for routine legal services, a claim that was recycled endlessly in other media outlets. He also estimated that the hourly return on contingency fee cases was at that time five to eight times higher than a quarter-century earlier.

Brickman's activism, though, didn't end with the media. He is the leading architect of several proposals to restrict plaintiff lawyers' pay. In 1994 Brickman coauthored a Manhattan Institute treatise called "Rethinking Contingency Fees," which stated, "Many cases exist in which liability is not contested, where the effective hourly rates of compensation obtained by contingency-fee lawyers range from $1,000 to $5,000 to $10,000 to as high as $25,000 to $30,000 per hour."

Brickman and his coauthors, Michael Horowitz and Jeffrey O'Connell, offered no empirical data to support this assertion—indeed, a footnote referred readers to Brickman's 1989 *UCLA Law Review* article, another article written by him on asbestos litigation, and a couple of newspaper articles noting that lawyers in some cases had received high fees. Nor were the figures compared to the fees earned by the lawyers working for corporate defendants.

Based on his conclusions, Brickman proposed that the nation radically restructure the way plaintiff lawyers do business, by limiting contingency fees. The Manhattan Institute delivered the proposal in pamphlet form to every state supreme court judge in the country, with a request that the courts restrict contingency fees. None did, and the American Bar Association has twice rejected similar requests as biased in favor of defendants. (The proposal resurfaced in 2003 in Common Good's state court petitions.)

Brickman then took his plan directly to the people. In 1996 he was a primary drafter of Proposition 202 in California, a ballot initiative that would have capped contingency fees in personal injury cases at 15 percent when a defendant offers a settlement early in the case. Similar measures were introduced in Michigan and Texas. The California initiative was backed by tech companies facing securities lawsuits, the insurance industry, and Intel cofounder and millionaire Tom Proulx, who funded a series of TV ads that portrayed plaintiff lawyers as fat cats living in the lap of luxury. Actor Charlton Heston did some voice-overs. The measure lost by a slim margin, perhaps because, around the same time Proulx was bashing rich lawyers, he was spending $4.5 million to buy up three of the houses adjoining his hilltop home in Palo Alto, California, so he could tear them down and build a seven-acre custom-designed private golf course.

In a written response to questions about his proposals, Brickman said his proposals all arise from his legal ethics perspective, and that the proposals "seek to protect consumers from [contingency-fee] lawyers' fee-gouging practices."

But history wasn't on Brickman's side; similar ballot measures had been rejected twice before in California, and his failed as well. But Brickman had the good fortune of picking the right issue at the right time. When the tobacco litigation headed toward settlement, and the lawyers' fees became headline news, Brickman was suddenly in demand, both as a commentator and an expert for those seeking to challenge the fees. Then-Governor George W. Bush hired him to help with his lawsuit over the Texas tobacco lawyers' fees. (During the 2000 presidential campaign, Bush, the antitax candidate, promised to pass a retroactive tax on the "windfall" legal fees of plaintiff lawyers, another idea that Brickman has advocated.)

In a statement to the federal judge supervising the tobacco case in Texas, Brickman argued that the lawyers should have reduced their fees because they really didn't face as big a risk as they let on. Brickman suggested that the lawyers must have had some incriminating information about the tobacco companies that they didn't share with the attorney general before signing the contingency-fee contract. Otherwise, why would they have taken on such a risky venture? (Brickman was apparently referring to documents that had been stolen from a tobacco company by a legal assistant and widely publicized long before the Texas lawyers inked their contract with Dan Morales.) He also suggested that the attorney general and all the lawyers in his office had been duped by the ever-devious plaintiff lawyers into signing on to a raw deal—one, incidentally, that provided for significantly lower contingency fees than lawyers in other states and in other personal injury suits, where the standard fee is usually one-third of any settlement or verdict. The Texas lawyers' contract gave them only 15 percent.

Based on that supposition, Brickman argued that the lawyers should have reduced their fee to reflect the reduced risk in the case. Bush's lawsuit failed, but the tobacco fees continued to generate an immense amount of media coverage, for which Brickman stood at the ready to supply pithy quotes about the obscene earnings of the "Sultans of Brunei Club" of plaintiff lawyers.

Interestingly, Brickman actually used the services of a plaintiff's lawyer back in 1988. Brickman was the plaintiff in a derivative lawsuit against Tyco Toys, as well as in a class action on behalf of other shareholders in the company, alleging a variety of fraud and self-dealing on the part of those running the company. Through information obtained in discovery, his derivative suit was successful in dislodging one of the company's principals, and Tyco's market value increased by $30 million almost overnight even as the rest of the stock market went into the tank. A few months after the change in management spurred by the lawsuit, Tyco's shares were trading at more than $10 higher than before the suit was filed, meaning that Brickman would have netted a tidy profit on whatever shares he held before the suit.

Plaintiff attorney Edward Labaton represented Brickman in the case on a contingency-fee basis. "Lester was delighted with the results," says Labaton, who still marvels about Brickman's later career bashing lawyers—the same ones who helped file his suit. "Every time I see his work, I find it kind of ironic. When his own investments were at stake, he was more than happy to be a derivative-suit plaintiff on a contingency fee." Labaton says that Brickman wouldn't have been able to bring the case paying for it on an hourly basis. "We had over $600,000 in time on that case. Academics don't make that kind of money." Not only was Brickman pleased with his results, but he apparently supported his attorney's request for $850,000 in fees, which was granted. (Brickman says his Tyco lawsuit was a share-holder derivative action, not a tort claim of the sort his work focuses upon.)

A few academics who specialize in empirical research have turned a skepti-cal eye to Brickman's research on contingency fees. These academics have been toiling away in obscurity, crunching numbers and collecting real data to create a portrait of what contingency-fee legal practice really looks like. Their work conflicts substantially with Brickman's frothy pronouncements about trial lawyers' windfalls. One of the most prominent among them is a professor at the University of Wisconsin named Herbert Kritzer.

Kritzer is a social scientist who specializes in empirical research on the legal system. As with many academics in this area, including Brickman, Kritzer says he has been retained in various legal cases as a consultant based on his work, both for defense and plaintiff lawyers. "I'm not a virgin," he says with a laugh. But he says that he has tried to put enough data out there for others to verify it independently regardless of what his perceived biases may be. Kritzer's work was funded by the National Science Foundation and has spanned more than a decade—much of it inspired by Brickman, who he says "doesn't understand how to do social science. He's never done any re-search. He's not trained to do it, and there's no evidence he's ever done it." (Brickman denies this, noting that his training includes a summer-long course in social science research methodology and a several-week institute at Dartmouth on statistical analysis.)

Kritzer was moved by Brickman's 1994 proposal to undertake a mas-sive study on contingency-fee legal practice to find out if the assumptions underlying Brickman's proposals were, in fact, accurate. As part of his re-search, he spent a month each with three different plaintiff lawyers in Wis-consin, following them around every day and studying their work, clocking the time they spent on various activities and how much they billed. He studied the way they screened cases and the way they negotiated settle-ments, all firsthand.

Kritzer supplemented his own reporting with a battery of surveys, dozens of interviews with both defense and plaintiff lawyers, insurance claims adjustors, and other analyses of legal fees. The results were compiled in his recent book, *Risks, Reputations, and Rewards: Contingency Fee Legal Practice in the United States.*

A Civil Action this isn't. Watching the law at work is akin to watching grass grow, and Kritzer paints a surprisingly dull portrait of the life of a variety of plaintiff attorneys. The lawyers he studied spend large amounts of time haggling over small amounts of money with low-level insurance claims adjustors. They spend a lot of time on the phone. They hunch over the computer and research scientific articles. They turn down almost every potential medical malpractice client that comes in the door. They hardly ever go to trial. But most importantly, Kritzer found, they don't make nearly as much money as Brickman claims.

A small percentage of Kritzer's sample did indeed command the high hourly rate that Brickman has so criticized. About 1 percent of the lawyers in the over eight hundred cases he studied made more than $2,000 in an hour. But the lawyers in the study were also two and half times more likely to have lost money on a case than to hit the jackpot of $1,000 an hour or more. Eleven percent of the cases had a return of either zero or a negative number, including one poor soul whose effective hourly rate on a case was −$2,617. But the average Wisconsin contingency-fee lawyer made about $132 an hour, which was about the same as any other lawyer who billed by the hour. But the variations in the numbers were more extreme than for those who billed by the hour, reflecting the risks involved in this kind of legal practice. As one attorney told Kritzer, he made most of his money on ten or twelve cases a year, while on the rest he was lucky just to cover the costs of running his practice.

Brickman has claimed that personal injury lawyers are engaged in what amounts to price fixing by enforcing a standard contingency fee of one-third in all their cases, regardless of the risk involved. Yet Kritzer discovered that the fees lawyers charged varied considerably depending upon the client's situation and the limits of the defendant's insurance policy, as well as the nature of the case. In only about 60 percent of cases did the lawyers in his study charge a flat 33⅓ percent fee. In the others, the fees dipped as low as 5 percent in a case where there was clear liability, severe injury, and a small insurance policy involved. Other lawyers reported charging up to 50 percent if the case went to trial. In nearly 20 percent of the cases, the lawyers reported that the final fee was less than what they could have taken based on their contract with the client.

Brickman has criticized Kritzer's work, complaining primarily that Kritzer left out the Sultans of Brunei Club from his survey. But Kritzer has noted that out of the sixty thousand or so plaintiff lawyers in the country, very few could be considered those types of heavy hitters. For instance, he identified only eleven out of sixteen hundred members of the Illinois Trial Lawyers Association in the Chicago area who could command such extremely high fees. And he says he did include such lawyers in the study, but because there were so few of them, their impact on the results were not significant.

Other researchers, though, have examined some of those in the sultan club, studying the fees claimed in class actions, which because of their size have made some lawyers quite rich. Among those is Professor Theodore Eisenberg of Cornell Law School. Like Kritzer, Eisenberg, together with NYU law professor Geoffrey Miller, found that contingency fees are highly variable. The percentages tend to go down as awards go up, meaning that the better the lawyers do for their clients, the smaller their fees are. In the cases Eisenberg and Miller studied, the average fee was about 22 percent—a small cry from the 50 percent windfall Brickman has cited. Kritzer's and Eisenberg and Miller's work squares with earlier research done by the Rand Corporation and by National Economic Research Associates, an economic consulting firm. In 1996 the latter published an extensive study on securities class actions and found that the fees averaged roughly 30 percent to 33 percent of the recovery.

Given that the recovery in an average personal injury lawsuit is relatively small—in Kritzer's study it was about $30,000—it's clear from a host of empirical research that most personal injury lawyers aren't commanding very high rates. Typically, though, that research has not dampened the media's enthusiasm for Brickman. Brickman is a one-man quote machine. The *New York Times* quoted or published him more than three dozen times between February 1994 and February 2005. The number of times the *Times* quoted or published Kritzer during that same time? Zero.

Reporters also never mention that Brickman is not simply an ivory tower observer in such matters. He has a side business as an expert witness and consultant for defendants and their insurance companies in lawsuits, particularly asbestos companies, which have long been interested in limiting plaintiff lawyers' fees. In a CV he submitted in one bankruptcy proceeding and a subsequent deposition, Brickman noted that he'd worked as a consultant for the Keene Corporation, GAF Materials Corporation, and Raymark Industries, all major asbestos companies. (He's also been retained by the American Tort Reform Association to write amicus briefs on behalf of asbestos companies appealing various lawsuits.) While he doesn't make out as well as the sultans he so often criticizes, Brickman charges a hefty fee for his services. In an expert-witness report he submitted in 2003 while working for lawyers for the Hartford Accident and Indemnity Company, Brickman disclosed that his customary fee was $650 an hour.

In a deposition in the same case, he noted that he had devoted sixty or more hours to preparing his report, and that was before the many hours of deposition. At that rate, Brickman would be collecting some $26,000 for a regular forty-hour work week—a pretty good gig that dwarfs that of most of the plaintiff lawyers he likes to bash.

All this is not to say that there aren't abuses of contingency fees. The business of law is no different from any other business, and as the white-collar crime scandals of the past few years have shown, access to big pots of money often brings out the worst in people. Brickman is right that in some cases lawyers make out like bandits. The contingency fee does create an incentive for lawyers to do as little work as necessary to claim the largest award. But lawsuits don't happen in a vacuum. Defense lawyers work by the hour, which gives them an equally strong incentive to drag out litigation as long as possible—a practice known as "churning"—to try to run up their own bills; this provides a sort of perverse counterweight to the incentives on the other side. And when problems do arise, judges are already empowered to review and challenge fees to ensure they're fair to the clients, in a process that doesn't infringe on everyone else's access to the courts.

For many tort reformers and their political allies, the real problem with contingency fees isn't one of fairness to consumers but, rather, what the lawyers do with the money. Brickman summed it up neatly in testimony before the Senate Judiciary Committee in 1996, when he said, "The contingency fee has been called the key to the courthouse for the injured plaintiff—and, indeed, that is undeniable. But it is also the key to enormous and untold riches. It yields plaintiff lawyers well in excess of $15 billion annually—wealth which is redistributed throughout the political and judicial process to purchase protection from public scrutiny."

It wasn't until the early 1990s that the Republican Party firmly grasped just how much trial lawyers were contributing to the liberal establishment.

And that's when restrictions on lawsuits and lawyers' fees shot up on their list of priorities, right up there with lower taxes and smaller government. Since then, demonizing trial lawyers has no longer been just about keeping them away from potential clients or making it harder for them to sue. It's been about limiting the influence of their money in Democratic politics.

CHAPTER SIX

Shock and Law:
The War on Lawyers

The man who, more than anyone else, had the foresight to see tort "reform" as a potent issue for the Republican Party was a figure who in future years would become known as a political mastermind: Karl Rove.

In the late 1980s, Rove was working on the campaign of Texas Supreme Court Justice Tom Phillips, who was running for reelection. As the campaign heated up in late 1987, *60 Minutes* broadcast a segment about the Texas judiciary called "Justice for Sale." The episode featured Houston lawyer Joe Jamail hobnobbing with state court judges, all while wearing a hidden mike. One of the richest lawyers in Texas, Jamail represented the oil giant Pennzoil in a legal battle against Texaco over its alleged interference with a merger between Pennzoil and Getty Oil. A jury awarded Jamail's client $10.3 billion, a giant verdict that the Texas Supreme Court refused to review or reduce the year of the broadcast. After the footage of his chummy relations with the judges Jamail appeared before, *60 Minutes* reported the then-shocking news that Jamail had contributed generously to the campaigns of several of the judges on the court that upheld his verdict.

The broadcast caused a national stir and proved to be the opening salvo in the 1988 state judicial elections, which marked the beginning of Rove's campaign to create a long-term Republican majority in the state. Phillips used the *60 Minutes* footage in TV ads to bash his rival, Justice Ted Z. Robinson, accusing him of taking millions in contributions from plaintiff lawyers. Six seats on the court were up for grabs, and Phillips ran as the "reform" candidate, pledging to bring a clean slate to the courts. He linked arms with several other Republican candidates backed by defense lawyers working for big businesses and the state medical association looking to crack down on medical malpractice lawsuits.

It was the first time that a political candidate had made trial lawyers' political contributions a major factor in a modern election, and Rove used it to good effect. The Phillips race showed just how potent the issue could be. It worked so well that Phillips pulled out the *60 Minutes* report again for his 1990 race. Rove went on to fine-tune the lawyer-bashing rhetoric in other judicial elections in Texas and Alabama, highlighting his opponents' financial ties to the plaintiffs' bar. He created a model that has now become a staple of Republican campaign strategy.

But Rove can't take all the credit for discovering trial lawyers as a campaign issue. Indeed, if there's one person who deserves the lion's share of the credit for launching the current wave of trial-lawyer bashing, it's former vice president Dan Quayle.

Throughout his term, Quayle had struggled to find an issue he could call his own. He finally found it in August 1991, when he gave a speech in front of the annual meeting of the American Bar Association to lay out the first Bush administration's plan for reforming the nation's legal system. Drafted with help from then-solicitor general Kenneth W. Starr, the civil-justice-reform proposal was a recycled mishmash of tort reform proposals such as a loser-pays rule for attorneys' fees, caps on punitive damages, and limits on expert testimony. But Quayle gave them a new spin: he made legal reform about lawyers.

"Does America really need seventy percent of the world's lawyers? Is it healthy for our economy to have eighteen million new lawsuits coursing through the system annually?" he asked the lawyers. He claimed that litigation cost $300 billion a year in "self-inflicted competitive disadvantage" in the global economy. As soon as Quayle finished his speech, ABA President John Curtin Jr. jumped up and criticized the vice president for blaming lawyers for all the country's problems. Quayle, never known for thinking on his feet, shot back and defended his proposals, and called for lawyers to challenge the status quo for a "better legal system in America."

Quayle's impromptu debate with the ABA president became headline news. In an even bigger surprise, Quayle reported that fan mail was pouring in, with supporters running fifty to one. The administration's political advisors were ecstatic. Quayle had proved that by deploying a handful of simple phrases, even the dimmest bulb in the Republican Party could score enormous political points bashing lawyers.

The response to Quayle's speech was so positive that George H. W. Bush reframed his election rhetoric when running against Bill Clinton the next year. Where he had once been moderate on the issue of civil justice reform, a few months after Quayle's speech Bush was blaming "ambulance-chasing lawyers" for forcing doctors out of practice and scaring parents out of coaching Little League. GOP focus groups indicated that the issue was a clear winner for Bush.

In his nomination speech at the GOP convention in August 1992, Bush charged that Clinton was backed "by every trial lawyer who ever wore a tasseled loafer," his biggest applause line of the evening. In campaign appearances, Bush read from a fund-raising letter written by the president of the Arkansas Trial Lawyers Association urging lawyers to "dig down deep and give to Bill Clinton," who had never "failed to do the right thing where we trial lawyers were concerned." When Clinton campaigned in Texas, Bush took out newspaper ads that read, "Stop the Trial Lawyer Takeover of the White House."

The campaign wasn't quite enough to get Bush reelected, but it convinced Republicans at the federal level that lawyer bashing was a winning issue for them. In 1994 Congressman Newt Gingrich of Georgia put an antilawyer plank in the Contract with America as part of his plan for creating a GOP majority in Congress. More importantly, though, Republican activists began to talk openly about attacking lawyers because of their pivotal role in funding Democratic politics. They thought organized labor was in a death spiral and was rapidly losing its influence in politics; as a result, the Democratic Party, especially at the state level, was heavily dependent upon contributions from personal injury lawyers.

In 1994, Grover Norquist, the president of Americans for Tax Reform, wrote an article in the conservative magazine *American Spectator* that laid out explicitly why attacks on trial lawyers were imperative. In Texas, he reported, trial lawyers were the "single largest source of campaign funds" for then-governor Ann Richards and the state's Democratic Party, where the trial-lawyer lobby was "second only to the teachers unions" in power at the state level.

Norquist advocated legislative proposals that would specifically deprive left-leaning lawyers of significant income. Top on his list was a plan for no-fault auto insurance in the states. He estimated that such a move would deprive personal injury lawyers of about $5 billion annually. "The political implications of defunding the trial lawyers would be staggering," wrote Norquist. He recognized that many of the proposals to limit the lawyers' earnings faced steep odds in legislative bodies, so he suggested an alternate course: reframing the issue to isolate trial lawyers and their self-interest. In other words, Republicans needed to make the lawyer money radioactive, so that candidates who took it would suffer in the polls once their funding sources were revealed.

The question was how to do it. Norquist cited polling done by the American Tort Reform Association that was designed to "instruct candidates and consultants on how to turn the trial lawyers' financial power against them." As with much of the tort reform message, the antilawyer questions in the surveys polled off the charts. In Alabama, Norquist wrote, a 1993 poll showed that 80 percent of those surveyed would be more likely to vote against a candidate who took lots of plaintiff lawyer money. Seventy percent would find a trial-lawyer endorsement enough to vote against a candidate. Polls done in Louisiana, Mississippi, and Texas produced similar results.

Norquist recognized that the Democrats couldn't triangulate out of this issue: they couldn't afford to be moderate on tort reform because they desperately needed the lawyers' money. And that, he predicted, would be their undoing.

Coached by pollster Frank Luntz, who gleefully observed in 1997, "It's almost impossible to go too far when it comes to demonizing lawyers," the GOP made carefully articulated lawyer bashing part of their regular public rhetoric. Meanwhile, big corporations underwriting the nation's tort reform groups poured money into new efforts to publicize the lawyers' political contributions and to push legislation that would hurt them in the pocketbook. It was the perfect synergy of political opportunism and corporate special interests. The tactic paid off beautifully. In 1999, all but one of the ten candidates for the Louisiana state legislature that were attacked as trial lawyers lost.

One difficulty with focusing the public on plaintiff lawyers' campaign contributions, though, was that the donations were difficult to track. Many trial lawyers are solo practitioners who donate as individuals. There was no publicly available list of the nation's best plaintiff lawyers to check against the donation records, and the impact of their giving was most profound at the state level, where public-disclosure records are spotty at best. Tallying up all the gifts would be labor intensive, not to mention expensive. There was also the issue of relativity: the trial lawyers' donations would pale in comparison to those companies interested in bashing them. But that was merely a PR problem that could be overcome with the right spin and enough money, which the tobacco industry had in spades.

In 1996, Philip Morris created a nonprofit "money and politics" watch-dog group whose sole mission was to serve up studies to reporters on the campaign contributions of plaintiff lawyers. The group, called Contributions Watch, was launched by the State Affairs Company, a Reston, Virginia, PR firm run by former executives from PR giants Burson-Marsteller and Hill & Knowlton.

Conceived with a healthy understanding of the media, Contributions Watch made its debut with a study on state campaign finance offices to help establish its credentials as a legitimate nonprofit group before launching the attacks on lawyers. The PR gurus coached the group's executive director, a former staffer from the Federal Election Commission, to target "opinion leader" magazines, including the *National Journal,* the *New Republic, Congressional Quarterly,* and the *Washington Monthly,* and the media quickly picked up the report. Contributions Watch staff happily reported back to their bosses that even National Public Radio was covering it. The relationship between tobacco, the PR firms, and Contributions Watch were all carefully disguised, as the project was calculatedly top secret. But the principals involved made one small mistake: they hired a temp.

Tom Wheeler was a young hipster in the Washington area who played in a band and knew something about computers. He agreed to take a temp job that, as he understood it, would involve working for the tobacco industry. He was hired to create the donations database for Contributions Watch. While working at night building the database, Wheeler also started running the photocopier, and he eventually leaked a juicy trove of documents to PR-group watchdogs Sheldon Rampton and John Stauber, who then wrote about it in their newsletter *PR Watch.*

Leaked memos from the group's executive director showed that Contributions Watch was laying the groundwork for more media coverage of its second report, which would focus on the plaintiff lawyers. The group was providing information to the *Wall Street Journal's* Glenn Simpson, who they felt would be sympathetic and eager for the "exclusive." Simpson in July 1996 wrote an expose of the trial lawyers' giving habits, noting that the Contributions Watch report was "the most comprehensive examination of trial lawyer giving to date." According to Simpson and the study, trial lawyers had donated more than $11 million in federal elections between January 1995 and April 1996. Apparently, when the article was written,

Simpson wasn't aware of the tobacco industry's support for the project, which for just one month of Contribution Watch research totaled more than $65,000.

The PR firm behind Contributions Watch, the State Affairs Company, didn't limit its work to political contributions, either. It also solicited contracts from other business groups that might be interested in portraying consumer and environmental groups as shills for trial lawyers. A State Affairs memo to Philip Morris suggested that the firm target fifteen different public-interest groups, including Consumers Union, Public Citizen, and Center for Science in the Public Interest, and later, the Sierra Club, Greenpeace, and the Environmental Defense Fund.

State Affairs staff proposed to report monthly to Philip Morris on these groups' activities, providing document packages including their IRS forms, financial statements, annual reports, research on the board of directors, and so on. Seeing a growth industry, the PR company offered similar services to Monsanto, Texaco, W.R. Grace, and Blue Cross/Blue Shield, the latter of which was trying to convert to for-profit status but running up against opposition from Consumers Union. (Blue Cross apparently got its money's worth. State Affairs planted a story in the *Wall Street Journal* bashing Consumers Union as "GUARDIAN OF THE LAWYERS' HONEY POT.")

All the research and its dissemination to the media was part of a larger plan to influence the upcoming judicial elections in many states. The tobacco industry had been heavily involved in state judicial elections since at least 1990. By the time Contributions Watch was up and running in 1996, the tobacco industry alone was devoting nearly $1 million to judicial elections in Texas, Alabama, and Louisiana.

After Wheeler, Rampton, and Stauber exposed Contributions Watch as a tobacco-industry creation, it quickly disbanded. But its legacy lingered. The data had clearly proved what Norquist had observed anecdotally in 1994, particularly at the state level. The Democrats were highly vulnerable to attacks on trial lawyer funding. One Contributions Watch study focused on Mississippi and the attorneys who brought the state's tobacco lawsuit. The group found that Mississippi had fewer than 600 plaintiff lawyers, but they accounted for a large share of the state Democrats' campaign contributions. And of those 600, only 125 gave more than $200 at a time. Today those findings could be replicated all across the country. Despite the revolution in fund-raising brought on by Howard Dean and the internet, in many states the only large campaign contributors to the state Democratic Party are trial lawyers.

Take Pennsylvania, a hotly contested swing state in the 2000 and 2004 presidential elections. Of the five top contributors to state party entities tracked by the entities' nonprofit nonpartisan research group Center for Public Integrity for the 2003–2004 election cycle, only one gave to the Democrats: Richard Schiffrin, a Pennsylvania class action attorney who donated $50,000. By comparison, the other four donated a total of $564,050 to the Republicans. The Association of Trial Lawyers of America (ATLA)* contributed $191,520 to the state party affiliates, making it the third-largest organizational donor, behind John Kerry's campaign group and a PAC run by Governor Ed Rendell, both of which also got trial-lawyer money.

In 2002, when Texas Republicans swept all statewide offices, including the governor's office, a Senate seat, and control of both chambers of the legislature, for the first time since Reconstruction, the single biggest donor to the state Democratic Party was the Texas Trial Lawyers Association, which gave $2.3 million. The only other big institutional donors were five law firms, mostly those that had won large fees in the tobacco litigation. John O'Quinn alone gave the state party $550,000. That small handful of people accounted for 15 percent of the money raised by the state Democratic Party, and nearly 30 percent of the money Democrats raised from within the state. The national Democratic Party, by contrast, gave only about $1 million to its Texas affiliate for state races, leaving Democratic state legislators to fend for themselves.

These figures help explain the Republicans' obsession with tort reform over the past few years. Limiting lawsuits may not be one of the top three concerns for the average voter, but nearly all of the measures on tort reformers' wish lists promise to gut funding for the Democratic Party and other liberal groups. Caps on punitive damages, restrictions on class actions, limits on contingency fees—nearly all would cut into the earnings of plaintiff lawyers, and many of the specifics in current tort reform legislation recently passed or introduced are actually designed to achieve maximum pain for the lawyers.

Take, for instance, the movement to cap noneconomic damages in medical malpractice cases at $250,000. Medical malpractice lawsuits make up a tiny portion of the nation's legal docket—only about 5 percent in state courts—but they account for some of the largest verdicts. According to data from the U.S. Department of Justice's Bureau of Justice Statistics, in 2001 (the most recent year for which data is available), plaintiffs won only 27

*In June 2006 the organization changed its name to the American Association for Justice. It is still using the acronym ATLA as of press time.

percent of malpractice trials in state courts. But when they did win, about
30 percent won more than $1 million, and more than 60 percent won more
than $250,000 (although BJS doesn't say how much of these awards is for
pain and suffering).

The few lawyers who can command the best cases and persuade juries
to award significant sums of money in these cases are people like John Edwards, or Jack Olender, the reigning king of medical malpractice lawyers in
Washington, DC. Olender and his wife gave nearly $120,000 to the Demo-
cratic candidates and party entities between 1994 and 2004. Caps on damages would cut into Olender's firm's business, as well as make it harder for
anyone to succeed him on the throne. The $250,000 cap on pain-and-
suffering awards has wiped out entire law firms. One such law passed in
Texas in 2003 prompted at least one large law firm that specialized in nursing home litigation to simply close up shop.

Given that Republicans have openly declared war on trial lawyers,
many of their supporters have puzzled over why the lawyers don't do a
better job of fighting back. Among them is consumer activist Ralph
Nader. Nader's relationship with the lawyers has deteriorated since his
2000 presidential race, when many Democrats blamed him for Al Gore's
loss. But Nader's analysis of why Republicans and the tort reform groups
have gained the upper hand in the debate over the civil justice system is
insightful.

Sitting at a library table in his cramped Dupont Circle office in DC one
day in the fall of 2005, Nader shakes his head and says, "It's really the fault
of the plaintiffs' side that they didn't argue the case in time. They didn't go
into other forums of public opinion in time. They hunkered down. When
was the last time you saw the president or executive director of ATLA on
TV? You see the executive director of all these right-wing think tanks, all
these trade groups—Cato, Heritage [Foundation]—they're always on TV.
But when's the last time you saw [former ATLA head Tom] Henderson on
TV? They're all hunkered down as if they're ashamed of what they're
doing. So that's part of the problem." He also notes that the lawyers are
"lone rangers," and that they don't work in large organizations of the sort
that run effective public policy advocacy programs. They focus intensely on
the cases in front of them, not the bigger picture, he says. "They'll bend
your ear on their deposition from yesterday, but it's very narrow, very technical. They almost never return calls," Nader complains.

Hunkering down, though, may stem from experience. In-house polling
done by ATLA dating back to the mid-1950s found that most of the group's

PR efforts to rehabilitate the image of trial lawyers had flopped. In 1969 John Lyons, the dean of the University of Arizona Law School wrote an article in ATLA's magazine, *Trial,* observing that no amount of PR would change the public's view of lawyers. "The relationship between the public and the legal profession has always been a strange, complex, and completely illogical phenomenon . . . on one hand, society loads lawyers with public and private responsibilities far beyond that of other citizens; on the other, it professes to be convinced that lawyers as a class are venal, self-seeking, and pettifogging."

Despite the talk of their wealth and power, when it comes to challenging the tort reform movement in the court of public opinion as well as in legislative bodies, the trial lawyers are badly overmatched. Aside from a couple of consumer groups, ATLA is the only institutional voice supporting the tort system against attacks from the entire Republican establishment, all of the nation's biggest companies, and dozens of right-wing think tanks devoted to "civil justice reform." When Congress was considering a bill to restrict class-action lawsuits over the past several years, the business world devoted so many lobbyists to the bill that there was nearly one lobbyist for every member of Congress. By contrast, ATLA had five.

As one veteran observer in Mississippi observes, the fight comes down to this: "On one side, you've got trial lawyers who can't work together because they're mostly competitors," says Ayers Haxton, a trial lawyer and former Mississippi state legislator. Then, he says, they simply have the wrong set of skills for the political battle. "Up until recently, we never even advertised, yet we're competing against people who sell soap . . . Trial lawyers don't think about putting aside money to advertise to protect the civil justice system. It doesn't seem like you should have to, since it's part of our system of government."

Efforts by trial lawyers to combat limits on lawsuits or restrictions on their ability to practice have been focused mostly on overturning legislation through the courts, where they do their best work and where they have a more level playing field. Relying heavily on the Constitution, the trial lawyers have succeeded in overturning a host of tort reform legislation in state courts. But working the courts has lately proved insufficient, as the courts have been stacked with Republican ideologues hostile to the interests of most individual plaintiffs.

As the trial lawyers have floundered, Democrats have bobbed and weaved and in some cases *supported* those very measures specifically and openly designed to hobble them as an opposition party.

In 2004 trial lawyers gave $36 million to the national Democratic Party and a whopping $123 million to individual Democratic candidates—$22 million of which went to John Kerry's presidential campaign, according to the Center for Responsive Politics. In return, Kerry endorsed tort reform on national TV.

Kerry is not alone among Democrats in caving in to attacks on their trial-lawyer connections. In February 2005, eighteen Democratic senators voted in favor of a sweeping bill to restrict consumer class actions against large corporations, including the party's new all-star, Illinois senator Barack Obama, and former presidential candidate Joe Lieberman. (Despite Kerry's declaration during the debate, he voted against the bill.) Thirty-two Democrats in the House also voted in favor of restricting class actions. Democratic governors in conservative states like West Virginia, Mississippi, and Alabama have signed tort reform legislation in recent years as well after coming under attack for taking money from plaintiff lawyers.

There's little sign that the Democrats fully understand just how intertwined the tort reform campaign is with the Republicans' political goal of solidifying its majority. Their stance on lawsuits has left many political observers scratching their heads. "Call me naive, but you have to believe they're voting out of conscience," says Republican political consultant John Weaver, who worked on Kerry's campaign. "And if they really believe in limiting victims' rights, then that's how they should vote."

Indeed, when Democrats buck the trial lawyers and support tort reform, they may very well be taking a principled stand against their own donors. Sadly, though, the more likely truth is that they're simply pandering to their other funders—like the insurance industry, which gives vastly more money than the trial lawyers. The biggest tort reformers among the Democrats get significant campaign contributions from insurance companies, key beneficiaries of restrictions on lawsuits. Senator Ben Nelson of Nebraska, for instance, is a conservative Democrat and a tort reform supporter whose largest donors are companies such as AIG, Allstate, AFLAC, and Mutual of Omaha. Likewise, Connecticut senator Christopher Dodd voted with his donors on the class action bill. Metropolitan Life, a life-insurance company that recently settled a class action for $120 million for overcharging African-American policyholders, has showered Dodd with its largesse. Dodd was also an original cosponsor of the Private Securities Litigation Reform Act of 1995, which restricted shareholder lawsuits, and worked to override Bill Clinton's veto of the bill.

Politicians, like the rest of the general public, have heard the story of the McDonald's coffee lawsuit. "It's the result of thirty years and hundreds of millions of dollars by the business community to convince people that tort reform is right," says Pamela Gilbert, a Washington attorney who served as the executive director of the U.S. Consumer Product Safety Commission during the Clinton administration and has lobbied for consumer groups against tort reform. "The public is beginning to believe that we have too many lawsuits and the people to blame are the ones suing, not the wrongdoers. The Democrats who vote for tort reform should know better."

In the end, though, the real explanation for the Democrats' position on tort reform may go back to Grover Norquist's predictions more than a decade ago. By focusing on tort reform, Republicans have put Democrats in something of a pickle. If they defend the lawyers, they risk losing at the polls amid charges of supporting frivolous lawsuits and greedy opportunists. If they embrace tort reform, they lose a critical funding base. Either way, they are in big trouble. If the Democrats want to peer into the crystal ball and see the future of the party without plaintiff lawyers, they need look no further than Mississippi.

In August 1997 Biloxi lawyer Paul Minor did not look like the usual bargain shopper at the Kmart superstore off Interstate 55 in north Jackson, Mississippi. Accompanied by two U.S. marshals and a gaggle of news cameras and reporters, Minor marched into the store and attempted to collect a judgment against the store he had won a few days earlier on behalf of a woman and her daughter who in 1992 had been abducted from the Kmart parking lot. Two teenagers brutally raped the mother at gunpoint in front of her fourteen-year-old child, and a jury had found Kmart negligent for failing to provide security in the parking lot. It awarded the family $3.4 million.

Inside the store, Minor blasted Kmart for refusing to pay the award. He charged that his clients had been victimized twice by Kmart, once by being abducted there and again when the company refused to pay the jury award.

A federal judge intervened before Minor could make off with any of the cash from the store vault, as he'd been threatening to do, and Kmart asked the court to sanction him for improper behavior. (The company, did, however, finally post a bond securing the award payment.) The court later ordered Minor to reimburse Kmart $8,000 for its legal fees, stating that Minor "was seeking to embarrass [Kmart] and call attention to himself as a tireless laborer of the bar attempting to obtain justice for his client when, in fact, there was no basis whatsoever in fact or in law for the actions taken."

Jackson jurors, though, seemed to have a higher opinion of the Vietnam veteran turned personal injury lawyer. After Kmart asked the court to reduce the jury award, in 1999 the case went back to a second jury to reconsider the damages. In that second trial, Kmart lawyers argued that the uninsured woman and her daughter could afford to get counseling on their own and didn't need the money the original jury thought was warranted. Minor told the jury, "Kmart wants you to do their dirty work. They want you to treat the dignity and the quality and the serenity of their lives and the losses that they have incurred like a blue-light special."

The jury came back with a $5-million verdict in favor of Minor's clients: $1.6 million more than the original award.

Flamboyant, a bit arrogant, and masterful with the media, Minor was the embodiment of all that tort reformers love to hate about trial lawyers. The son of a prominent Mississippi journalist and civil rights champion, a cofounder of South Mississippi Legal Services Corp., and a former president of the state's trial lawyers association, Minor is something of a celebrity in Mississippi. His fame stems not just from the Kmart episode or even his 60 Minutes appearance exposing the dangers of Firestone tires on the rollover-prone Ford Explorer. Minor's most notable resume entry is the $71.5 million his firm earned in legal fees awarded as part of the state's historic settlement with the nation's tobacco companies.

Minor generously redistributed his wealth to political causes, giving a half-million dollars to Democratic Party entities and candidates between 1996 and 2003. Minor's prominence as a local fund-raiser and donor to Democratic candidates in the state was such that he was known as "the judge maker"—the go-to guy for candidates seeking election to seats on the state bench. But his role in politics also made him a prime target of Republican business interests who were often on the receiving end of jury verdicts he won and of politicians who lost to the Democrats he financed.

In 2001 President George W. Bush appointed one of those losing candidates as U.S. Attorney of Mississippi. Dunn Lampton was a twice-failed Republican congressional candidate and local district attorney whose campaigns had been financed by many of the very companies Minor had successfully sued. In July 2003 Lampton unveiled a grand-jury indictment against Minor and three state judges on a long list of racketeering and bribery charges. The bribes, in this case, were actually campaign contributions and loans, but the indictment alleged that Minor engaged in an elaborate scheme to bribe state judges to secure favorable rulings for his cases before them.

The press made the case sound like just another crooked-lawyer story, something out of a John Grisham novel. But whether or not Minor was guilty really didn't matter, as the prosecution alone succeeded where other tort reform efforts had failed: it put Minor out of business, both legally and politically. It helped elect Mississippi's second Republican governor since Reconstruction, persuaded the state legislature to pass massive restrictions on lawsuits, and it may have permanently disabled the state's Democratic Party.

Minor's trouble really all started in 2000, when the U.S. Chamber of Commerce decided to go after the Mississippi Supreme Court. As part of its campaign to unseat several judges and install new "profairness" candidates on the bench who favored tort reform, the chamber made the unprecedented move of spending about $1 million on ads in Mississippi backing four probusiness judicial candidates. The infusion of out-of-state money started something of an arms race in state judicial elections.

A primary target of the campaign was Oliver Diaz Jr., a handsome former appellate court judge appointed to a supreme court vacancy by Governor Ronnie Musgrove, a Democrat. Diaz had actually served in the state legislature as a Republican, but business groups opposed him because he was a trial lawyer. The chamber ads attacked Diaz for taking more than $100,000 in trial-lawyer donations for the race. Diaz's opponent, Keith Starrett, raised $375,000 from the state manufacturing association, big insurance companies, the National Federation of Independent Business, oil and gas companies, and the lawyers who defended them. With the chamber's help, he outspent Diaz by more than $500,000.

It was the most expensive judicial race in state history. In the end, Diaz beat Starrett, but his campaign committee ended up deeply in debt, with tens of thousands of dollars in loans needing repayment once he took the bench, and no obvious means of paying them back. His only source of funding came from the same trial lawyers who helped elect him—and whose cases were pending in his courtroom. Minor played an active role in helping Diaz retire the debt.

Paying the judges' campaign debts was not as easy as it sounds. The lawyers did have money, which they were actively putting into politics, particularly through their own political action committee, the Institute for Consumers and the Environment Political Action Committee (ICE PAC), the second-largest PAC in the state next to the Republican National State Elections Committee.

Yet Mississippi's handful of rich plaintiff lawyers were severely constrained by campaign finance laws in how much they could give. And for candidates like Diaz, there simply wasn't anyone else to turn to.

Former state legislator and current Democratic fund-raiser Ayers Haxton says that in Mississippi, "nobody else with any progressive blood in their veins has any money except the trial lawyers." He estimates that until 2003, about half of the state's Democratic Party money came from trial lawyers. In Ronnie Musgrove's 1999 race for governor, just ten Mississippi trial lawyers donated as much to his campaign as the Democratic National Committee, contributing $379,500, of which $112,000 came solely from Minor.

The fund-raising problem became especially acute in the judicial elections. Mississippi judicial elections are nonpartisan, so progressive candidates couldn't rely on any help from the national or local Democratic Party. National liberal-interest groups were largely indifferent to the races, failing to grasp just how much the elections could affect their causes on everything from labor issues, to drug safety, to the environment. When they did weigh in, it was often to *tsk-tsk* the trial lawyers' contributions as much as the business groups'. As a result, judges were in the awkward position of having to beg for money from the very people who appeared in their courts every day.

The cozy relations between the trial bar and some of the state's judiciary had existed for years, but as the tort reform battles in the state heated up, business groups were looking for any opening to skewer the lawyers. In June 2002 they found a good one.

That year, the state trial-lawyers association had held its annual meeting in Biloxi. After the meeting, there was a party at a local bed-and-breakfast for outgoing president Shane Langston. Hard-partying trial lawyers made so much noise that the B and B's neighbors complained to city officials. A quick investigation by the *Biloxi Sun Herald* revealed that among the revelers at the party were representatives of the state's judiciary, including Diaz, whose ex-wife owned the B and B.

A few weeks later, the FBI paid a visit to Langston's law firm bearing copies of checks the firm had written for the party. The agents suggested that lawyers in the firm had dummied up invoices for the party to launder money through the B and B as a way of paying off Diaz's campaign loans in exchange for favorable rulings. The FBI continued to visit most of the state's leading plaintiff attorneys and interrogate them about their various donations to judicial races.

The investigation was well timed, coming right in the middle of an-other competitive judicial election. Almost overnight, the trial-lawyers' campaign contributions dried up, as the lawyers feared attracting more law-enforcement attention. Even if they had been giving, many candidates didn't want their money. Trial-lawyer money in Mississippi had become ra-dioactive.

While news about the FBI investigation leaked out in October 2002, just in time for the judicial election, prosecutors didn't bring a single indict-ment in the case for almost another full year. It wasn't until late July 2003 that Lampton's office unsealed a series of indictments against Minor, Diaz, and two other judges, charging them with various counts of bribery, extor-tion, and racketeering under a law normally used to prosecute gangsters and Mafia leaders.

From the beginning, the federal prosecutors had a pretty weak case. They alleged that Minor had paid off campaign loans for Diaz in exchange for favorable rulings, but Diaz had recused himself from Minor's cases when they came to his court. Another one of the judges wasn't even on the bench when Minor arranged to pay off his campaign loan.

Nonetheless, the indictments came at a critical time in Mississippi pol-itics. Incumbent governor Ronnie Musgrove, a Democrat, was fighting for his political life in a race against Washington über-lobbyist Haley Barbour, who made Musgrove's ties to the trial lawyers a central theme of the cam-paign. The Mississippi Republican Party mailed out full-color ads to state voters highlighting the charges against Minor and noting that he'd given Musgrove's previous campaign $112,000. The ads, combined with Barbour's $10 million war chest (compared to Musgrove's $8 million) worked like a charm, and in November 2003 he became only the second Republican gov-ernor in Mississippi since Reconstruction, winning 53 percent of the vote. The indictments also accomplished what the election in 2000 had not: get-ting Diaz off the bench. He was suspended pending the outcome of his trial, leaving the court with a 6–2 probusiness majority.

The disappearance of the trial-lawyer money all but wiped out the De-mocratic Party in Mississippi. In the 2003–2004 election cycle, the Missis-sippi Democratic State Party raised only $450,000, according to the Center for Public Integrity. The Republican State Party committee raised $4 million.

The federal investigation also put an end to the trial lawyers' fledgling PAC. Whereas ICE PAC had donated $370,000 in the 1999 campaign, in 2003, its last election, ICE PAC gave just $97,000. The PAC died for good in early 2005. "I don't see how the Democratic Party is going to reconstitute it-self after this," says Jackson newspaper publisher Wyatt Emmerich. "I'm afraid it's going to be a one-party state again."

Meanwhile, supporters of lawsuit restrictions got nearly every item on their wish list. In 2004, newly installed Governor Barbour called yet an-other special session on tort reform, and the state legislature passed bills wiping out mass torts such as asbestos and prescription drug cases like Vioxx. They capped noneconomic and punitive damages in most tort cases and made it more difficult for successful plaintiffs to recover money in court.

As for Paul Minor, Diaz, and the others, in early 2005 they finally got their day in court, in a grueling three-month trial. The jury ultimately found Diaz innocent on all charges. Minor was acquitted on four counts of mail fraud and one count each of bribery and extortion. The jury failed to reach a verdict on several other charges against Minor and the other judges, and they walked away free men.

The posttrial euphoria didn't last long. As soon as the verdict was an-nounced, Lampton unsealed a new indictment against Diaz for tax evasion and later announced his intention to retry Minor on bribery charges. Diaz was acquitted in an April 2006 trial on the tax charges, and he returned to the bench.

But the years of pending bribery charges—along with Mother Nature—took their toll on Minor. In August 2005, Hurricane Katrina wiped out his famous Frank Lloyd Wright house in Biloxi. He moved to New Orleans, where a tree fell on his new house, which was then looted. His wife was di-agnosed with breast cancer. Minor decamped again to Baton Rouge, where in late 2005 he was arrested for drunk driving while he was still out on bond pending the second bribery trial. A judge ordered him to undergo sub-stance abuse treatment as condition of staying out of jail. But in March 2006, two law enforcement officers spotted Minor in a Jackson bar and re-ported to the judge that he was drunk. The judge sent Minor to jail for a week for violating his probation, and then ordered him to stay in a residen-tial treatment facility to await the bribery trial, set for late October 2006.

CHAPTER SEVEN

Millions Served: Jackpot Justice and the Jefferson County Juries

In November 2002 viewers of the TV news magazine *60 Minutes* learned that Jefferson County, Mississippi, was the nation's capital of "jackpot justice," and that "plaintiff lawyers have found that juries in rural, impoverished places can be mighty sympathetic when one of their own goes up against a big, rich, multinational corporation."

Exhibit A for *60 Minutes* was a 1999 verdict in a case against American Home Products, the maker of the infamous diet drug fen-phen, which has killed several hundred people and injured an estimated 45,000 others. That year, twelve Jefferson County jurors slapped AHP with a $150-million judgment for injuries that its diet drug caused to five Mississippi residents. Correspondent Morley Safer set up the broadcast asking, "What's behind these generous awards?"

What followed weren't interviews with some of the jurors who actually sat through the trial. Nor were viewers treated to an airing of the corporate conduct that led to the lawsuits in the first place. Instead, the veteran broadcaster sought an opinion from a local florist who supposedly had received a multimillion-dollar settlement in a different fen-phen lawsuit. The florist, unnamed in the broadcast and hidden behind a screen during the interview, made some startling allegations. He claimed that trial lawyers were bribing jurors to give big awards.

"The jury awarded these people this money because they felt as if they were going to get a cut off of it," he told Safer. Beyond that anonymous comment, the show that bills itself as TV journalism's most respected news organization offered no other evidence about payoffs to jurors.

Safer did offer up Wyatt Emmerich, the publisher of a Jackson newspaper, who told me in an interview that he has never even driven through Jefferson County. Emmerich offered this explanation for the generous awards: "Look at the jurors. These are disenfranchised people. These are people who've been left out of the system, who feel like, 'Hey, stick it to the Yankee companies. Stick it to the insurance companies. Stick it to the pharmaceutical companies.' The African-Americans feel like it's payback for disenfranchisement. And the rednecks, shall we say, it's like, 'Hey, you know, get back at' revenge for the Civil War. So there's a lot of resentment, a lot of class anger, a lot of racial anger. And it's very easy to weave this racial conflict and this class conflict into a big pot of money for the attorneys."

The *60 Minutes* broadcast was just the latest media attack on Mississippi juries, which had been under siege since the mid-1990s by national business groups because of the perception that plaintiff lawyers were relying on them to win huge sums of money from deep-pocketed corporations. Safer noted in the broadcast, "The situation's gotten so bad that for the first time in its ninety-year history, the U.S. Chamber of Commerce warned companies about the risk of doing business in Mississippi."

What he didn't say was that at the time of that announcement, the U.S. Chamber of Commerce was spending $100,000 on an advertising campaign in Mississippi to push for a cap on damages in lawsuits against corporations and that it had pumped thousands of dollars into local judicial elections to help elect pro-tort reform judges to the state supreme court. Nationally, the chamber's Institute for Legal Reform had committed to spend $60 million lobbying for restrictions on citizens' rights to sue, a fact Safer also left out of his reporting on Mississippi.

Despite the hype about the county's "generous jurors," at the time of the broadcast, Jefferson County had only had three truly large verdicts, ever: a $48.5 million one in a 1998 asbestos case, the 1999 fen-phen trial, and a $13-million verdict in 2001 in a case against a shoddy home builder (later reduced by the judge to $335,000). It was hardly the only place in the country where a large lawsuit had produced a large verdict. Even other parts of Mississippi had rendered more big verdicts. But Jefferson County made the perfect media horror story. The image of an all-black mostly poor jury deciding the economic fate of huge, multinational corporations was a powerful inducement for tort reform to rally the troops, particularly the elected ones.

Like much of the national news coverage of Jefferson County, the *60 Minutes* broadcast played like a PR package ginned up by tort reform advocates. In fact, the most scandalous of all the allegations in the segment proved to be fiction. The florist who charged that Jefferson County jurors were on the take later retracted his comments, saying, "I just said it as a joking statement." CBS spokesman Kevin Tedesco said the network could not comment on the segment because several jurors had sued CBS for libel (suits that were later dismissed). But the network never issued a retraction, and the damage was done.

The day after the program aired, the Mississippi legislature passed new restrictions on lawsuits, and shortly afterward the FBI launched an investigation into the charges of jury corruption that was still ongoing three years later without a single charge filed against a juror.

The story of Mississippi's Robin Hood juries was an easy sell for tort reformers, as it played into racial stereotypes that have plagued news coverage of the jury system for years. 60 Minutes bought into the old canard that poor and minority jurors are overly generous to plaintiffs, a phenomenon often called the "Bronx effect." The term was coined back in 1987 by author Tom Wolfe in his novel The Bonfire of the Vanities. Wolfe described a plaintiff lawyer who files malpractice claims in the Bronx rather than in Westchester County because he believes that the poor minority Bronx juries were a "vehicle for redistributing the wealth."

The legend of a Bronx effect has lived on, even making its way into a 2000 litigation handbook that recommends that defendants unlucky enough to get sued in the Bronx should try to change venues. Allegedly proplaintiff venues tend to change with the political winds. After the Bronx, there was "the Bank," a courthouse in a heavily minority area of Los Angeles County. Then there was Hale County, Alabama, where in 1999 jurors hit the Whirlpool Financial National Bank (now Transamerica Bank) with a $581 million verdict for a scheme to defraud elderly and illiterate people through satellite-dish sales. That case prompted Alabama to pass tort reform that same year, so the torch passed to Mississippi, which moved into the spotlight as the favorite plaintiffs' paradise, particularly Jefferson County, which has more black residents and the highest unemployment rate in the state.

Legend notwithstanding, there's not much empirical evidence that poor minority jurisdictions routinely dole out big awards to plaintiffs. Cornell professors Theodore Eisenberg and Martin Wells did an empirical study to see whether, in fact, demographics actually corresponded to jury verdicts. In 2002 they found that large black populations actually correlated negatively with award levels; in other words, jury awards were lower in areas with lots of African-Americans. Neil Vidmar, a professor at Duke Law

School, and Mary R. Rose, a professor of law and sociology at the University of Texas, did a similar study in the Bronx and found no statistically significant evidence that jurors were more generous or more proplaintiff than in neighboring jurisdictions. They actually found that Wolfe was off a little in tagging Westchester County jurors as stingy. Westchester had very high median awards in medical malpractice cases, although that was mostly because there were so few of them.

Nonetheless, the idea that poor minority jurisdictions are hostile to business is actively encouraged by groups like the U.S. Chamber of Commerce and the American Tort Reform Association, which regularly put out "studies" showing that various jurisdictions are "judicial hellholes" because they are too proplaintiff. Among the 2003 hellholes identified by the tort reform association were all the heavily African-American counties in Mississippi, two mostly Latino counties in Texas, the heavily Latino Miami-Dade County in Florida, and the mostly black Orleans Parish in Louisiana.

In 2004 the Center for Justice and Democracy (CJD), the nation's only antitort reform advocacy group, compared the twelve jurisdictions in the ATRA 2003 hellholes report to census data. Of the twelve, nine were in predominantly minority areas, and all but one were areas that have larger minority populations than the rest of the state they are located in. The U.S. Chamber of Commerce has likewise released an annual survey on state litigation climates and of the eighteen jurisdictions identified as problematic in 2003, fifteen were predominantly minority—including Mississippi's Jefferson County.

Despite the obvious racial undertones to the hellholes study, it has been cited authoritatively over the past several years by the *Chicago Tribune,* the *St. Louis Post-Dispatch* (which put it on the front page), the *L.A. Times,* the Philadelphia *Daily News,* the New Orleans *Times-Picayune,* the *Dallas Morning News, Forbes, Business Week,* the *Wall Street Journal,* the *Washington Times,* and *USA Today.* (None, incidentally, covered the CJD report.) The stories, especially those in smaller news outlets, tend to quote civic leaders wringing their hands over their standing on the list and demanding that the legislature take action by passing restrictions on lawsuits.

A close look at what happened in Jefferson County shows why subtle racist attacks on juries are such an effective political tool for big corporations looking to deflect attention from their own wrongdoing and insulate themselves from future accountability. The technique is particularly effective in southern states, where tort reform frequently is as much about race as it is about the law.

Mississippi attorney William Liston Sr. says he saw the effect firsthand when he and a group of plaintiff attorneys arranged a meeting with the Mississippi Economic Council to see if they could find a compromise on tort reform legislation pending in the state. Liston says, "They said they wouldn't agree to any deals because, as one man said—and I won't name names—but he said, 'I could get sued and hauled into Jefferson County, and my company could go bankrupt just because it's'—well, he used the *n* word—on those juries."

★ ★ ★

One thing *60 Minutes* did get right about Jefferson County, Mississippi, is that it is one of the poorest places in the country. It's also the blackest. Eighty-five percent of its residents are African-American, the highest proportion of black residents anyplace in the entire country, according to the 2000 census. More than 36 percent of those residents fall below the federal poverty line, and 15 percent are unemployed. The per capita income is about $9,000. Barely half the population has a high school degree. During Jefferson County's fifteen minutes of fame as the capital of "jackpot justice," attorney Jeff Varis in neighboring Claiborne County says that business groups frequently claimed that no one wanted to do business there because of the legal climate. But, he says, "Nobody's ever done business in Jefferson County."

With fewer than ten thousand residents, the rural county lies ninety miles southwest of Jackson and borders the Mississippi River between Vicksburg and Natchez. The sparsely populated rural landscape is dotted with tin-roof tenant houses, squat brick "Jim Walter" homes, and the ubiquitous mobile home.

The only visible evidence of Jefferson County's prominence in the "litigation industry" is a smattering of "fen-phen houses," the huge brick-and-column McMansions that pop up in unlikely places—one overlooks a trailer park—and reflect wealth vastly out of proportion with the rest of the county. The largest sits on about forty acres on Highway 61, the road to Natchez. It's owned by one of the five plaintiffs in the 1999 fen-phen trial and is worth about $600,000, according to county property records—hardly a millionaire's mansion by East or West Coast real estate standards, but in an area where the median home value is less than $50,000, it's a traffic stopper.

Despite the handful of big houses and the occasional Jaguar on Main Street, the influx of lawsuit wealth has not trickled down to the rest of the county. There's not a chain restaurant or 7-Eleven to be found. In the country, shacks by the side of the road are home to mom-and-pop grocery stores that fill the void. The major employer in the county is the government, including the Jefferson-Franklin Correctional Facility.

Fayette, the county seat, has a tiny and dilapidated Main Street dominated by the Jefferson County Courthouse, Bankston Drugstore, a bank, and DJ's Chicken House, a carry-out shack shaded by an overhang of broken green fiberglass that's about the same size as the local police station down the road. Shabby storefronts are either boarded up or filled with renters who sell plastic-flower arrangements for funerals or distribute oxygen tanks and other supplies to the county's sickly residents. At the time of the fen-phen trial, Jefferson County claimed just twenty-two retail businesses.

Before the Civil War, Jefferson was a plantation county, a legacy that meant whites were always a minority, but they held all the power and all the political positions because most of the population couldn't vote. But in the 1960s, Jefferson County became the first area in the state where African-Americans took control of government for themselves. After civil rights legend Medgar Evers was assassinated in 1963, his older brother, Charles, returned to Mississippi from Chicago and took over his brother's leadership post with the state NAACP. In 1969, Charles Evers made history by winning the mayorship of Fayette, becoming the first black to hold elected office in the state since Reconstruction. He reigned over the town until 1981 and again from 1985 to 1989.

Evers's preparation for controlling the levers of government was eclectic, to say the least. In the '40s and '50s, Evers had been a civil rights organizer with his famous martyred brother, but he was run out of Philadelphia, Mississippi, by angry whites and went to Chicago, where by his own admission, Evers worked as a pimp and a numbers runner.

Evers's election helped speed the exodus of white residents—Fayette is now 97 percent black—and left African-American residents in control of their own destiny for the first time very suddenly. Today Jefferson County has the largest number of black elected officials of any place in the country, even if they only get to preside over a dwindling tax base and shrinking population. (Evers, meanwhile, has become a popular Mississippi radio host—and a Republican.)

The transition to black self-governance engendered a fair amount of resentment among the state's white population that is still palpable today. One day when I was visiting Fayette, I stopped in to look around the abandoned Masonic Temple that sits across Main Street from the courthouse. Inside, a couple of older white Masons were doing some work getting ready to tear the building down. A man named Wayne explained that the lodge was dying off; its members weren't being replaced, because "all the niggers came in here and messed things up."

★ ★ ★

The demographic changes in Jefferson County are an extreme example, but what happened to the jury pool there mirrors changes that have swept through the country over the past forty years to make juries more inclusive and representative of a cross section of their communities. While attacks on jury competence are as old as the institution itself, it's no coincidence that the tort reform movement really began to gather steam just as minorities finally started to achieve a significant role in the legal system.

"In the legal literature, much of this hubbub over juries has been since this shift in demographics," says Steven Landsman, a law professor at DePaul University, who serves on the American Bar Association's American Jury Initiative Project.

In the early years of the country, eligibility to serve on juries was severely limited by the "key man" system, in which appointed jury commissioners chose "key men" from the community to serve on juries—upstanding men, generally white property owners, thought to have good judgment worthy of a juror. That system persisted well into the 1980s in some places. But the civil rights movement chipped away at the old rules and gradually allowed minorities a place in the jury box.

Burnell Harris, the Jefferson County circuit court clerk, says that before he started his job in 1984, there weren't many blacks on juries in Jefferson County. Historically, appointed jury commissioners handpicked jurors from the voter registration rolls, and blacks weren't allowed to vote in Mississippi until 1965. Even then, it took years before blacks were adequately represented on Mississippi juries, even in majority-black areas like Jefferson

County. Harris says, "Prior to the '80s, they either weren't selected, or they were afraid to serve."

Even being called for jury duty didn't mean that blacks actually sat on trials, because lawyers could dismiss them in peremptory strikes. It wasn't until 1986 that the U.S. Supreme Court, in *Batson v. Kentucky,* ruled that jurors in criminal cases could not be stricken from a panel solely on the basis of race. It was another five years before the court would hold that the same was true for civil trials, in the 1991 case *Edmunson v. Leesville Concrete Co.*

G. Thomas Munsterman, who heads the Center for Jury Studies at the nonprofit, nonpartisan National Center for State Courts, says, "The jury was really unchanged until the sixties. It wasn't until 1975 that the Supreme Court said you can't exempt women just because they're women." He says that technology has changed so that jurors are no longer picked from manual lists. Now, in most states, jurors are chosen from a much larger pool, including driver's license records, tax rolls, voter registration lists, even welfare rolls. But Munsterman says the last state to get rid of the "key man" was West Virginia, in 1986, so the democratization of the American jury is a relatively new phenomenon. "All of this is very recent," he says.

Race, though, wasn't the only reason that Jefferson County became known as the capital of jackpot justice. For a few years, it really was something of a hotbed of mass tort litigation. A number of factors combined to make the county an easy target for tort reformers looking to bolster their case for restrictions on lawsuits. Some of it had to do with the vexing problem of how to effectively use the legal system to compensate large numbers of people who've been injured by a consumer product, like a prescription drug. As other states swallowed the tort reform poison, Mississippi became a haven for those shut out of court elsewhere. Other factors were simply quirks of history.

Executives of Fortune 500 companies subjected to litigation in Jefferson County like to blame trial lawyers for their fate, but they really ought to blame Hoss and Little Joe Cartwright for their troubles. Guthrie Abbott, a retired professor of civil procedure from the University of Mississippi School of Law, says that in 1964, the *Bonanza* boys were slated to perform at the Mississippi State Fair. But when they learned that they'd be playing before a segregated audience, actors Dan Blocker and Michael Landon canceled their appearance. Before then, state law didn't provide a mechanism for local residents to sue out-of-state entities in state court unless they were actually doing business in Mississippi. The state legislature was incensed by the snub and changed the state long-arm statute so that the contract could be enforced in state court, and the *Bonanza* boys could be sued for not showing up.

"There wasn't anything that unusual about the way the cases ended up in Jefferson County," explains Jackson plaintiff attorney John Griffin Jones. "All of the reasons that Mississippi law was so liberal for plaintiffs was xenophobia. Anyone who messed with us, we wanted to haul them into our local court, mostly the railroads. We didn't ever want to have to go to Washington State or, God forbid, New York, to file a lawsuit."

The same law that allowed racist legislators to punish the *Bonanza* boys would provide a mechanism thirty-five years later for injured Mississippi residents to hold multinational corporations accountable for their behavior right there on the same block as DJ's Chicken House.

In one sense, Mississippi's legal system was also rather conservative, in that its civil justice system lacked a class action rule that would allow large numbers of claims to be consolidated into a single lawsuit the way they are in other states. Instead, when presented with lots of similar asbestos or financial-fraud cases, state court judges linked similar cases together for efficiency purposes under Rule 20 of the civil procedure rules, or the "joinder" rule, which, as often interpreted by some of the state's judges, turned out to be far more liberal than a class action rule would be. Mississippi also had a generous six-year statute of limitations for personal injury cases and a "good as to one, good as to all" rule, which meant that a lawyer needs only a single plaintiff or defendant to bring a lawsuit in a particular county before piling on other plaintiffs from out of the area. Along with all of that, the state's judges rigorously enforced a ninety-day limit on discovery, which kept a lid on one of defense lawyers' favorite delay tactics of dragging out discovery to force plaintiffs' lawyers to spend more money.

All these factors, along with the state's speedy trial rules, served to bring a host of lawsuits to smaller Mississippi courthouses, where plaintiff lawyers could gain an edge by getting cases to trial quickly. One or two big verdicts were enough to give lawyers some leverage in trying to get companies to settle hundreds of cases rather than risk going to trial in a hostile venue.

Even so, plaintiff lawyers still needed a friendly judge willing to agree to join all those cases together, and they seemed to find one in Circuit Court Judge Lamar Pickard, who managed the docket in the Twenty-second Judicial District, which included Jefferson, Claiborne, and Copiah counties. Pickard made headlines in 1998, when Jefferson County became the forum for a major asbestos trial. The case, known as *David Cosey et al. v. E. D. Bullard et al.,* had seventeen hundred coplaintiffs and five defendants. The first group of plaintiffs went to trial in May 1998. There were twelve, two of whom had already died. A jury returned a $48.5-million verdict in actual damages.

Pickard, a former plaintiff attorney himself, earned the enduring scorn of corporate America after he allegedly phoned the defendants and advised them to settle the remaining cases within thirty days, lest he send the remaining claims back to the same jury to decide damages for all of them. Pickard also apparently warned that the defendants would have difficulty appealing his decision because Mississippi law at that time required the defendant to post a bond worth 125 percent of the amount of the verdict before filing an appeal. Although he was acting within his authority, Pickard's comments were widely publicized and used to bash him as a proplaintiff judge.

The following year, Jefferson County was awash in mass torts, including the notorious fen-phen case, which was filed in April 1999. Walter Johnson, a lawyer who has defended drug companies in the county, says that Jefferson County had already started to get a reputation as a "tort hell," but he says, "Fen-phen is the thing that catapulted everything."

Even with the friendliest of judges and juries, Jefferson County would never have made national news if it weren't for the misbehavior of the drug companies hauled into court there. Most empirical research done on jury decision making has all come to the same conclusion: that jurors, regardless of race, class, or gender, make their decisions based on the evidence before them. In the fen-phen trial, the evidence was particularly bad, which is why the drug ultimately led to the largest products-liability settlement of all time.

Six million people took the diet drug Pondimin (fenfluramine) or its chemical cousin, Redux (dexfenfluramine), before they were pulled off the market in 1997 after researchers linked the drugs to rare and potentially fatal heart and lung disease. In the months following the drug recall, 500,000 people were represented in class action cases against the manufacturer, American Home Products (now Wyeth). All the lawsuits alleged that AHP had known about the dangers but aggressively marketed the drug anyway, without providing adequate warnings to patients or doctors. More damaging, discovery during the litigation revealed that AHP had withheld reports of the drugs' adverse effects from the FDA in order to secure approval for Redux in 1996.

The Mississippi lawsuit was only the second fen-phen case in the country to go to trial. The first was in July that same year, when a Texas jury returned a $23.4 million verdict for a woman named Debbie Lovett, who had allegedly developed heart-valve leaks from taking the drugs. The Jefferson County trial involved five of more than eight hundred plaintiffs represented by veteran Houston plaintiff attorney Michael Gallagher and Jackson attorney Dennis Sweet.

In the Mississippi fen-phen trial, Kenya Tenner was the only plaintiff from Jefferson County, and she was also the youngest, having first taken the diet drug when she was just eighteen. Four of the plaintiffs claimed to have pulmonary hypertension, and another had heart damage. Most also suffered from a myriad of health problems related to obesity, as several of them weighed over three hundred pounds, a condition that likely resonated with Jefferson County jurors. The county recently made fame as the fattest place in the country. Fully 26 percent of the county residents are officially obese, according to government researchers, which is also one reason why so many area residents had taken fen-phen.

Nonetheless, defense handicappers were focused on the race of the jury, not their waistlines. AHP hired former Mississippi congressman Mike Espy, who had only a few months earlier been acquitted on corruption charges stemming from his tenure as U.S. secretary of agriculture. "He was kind of rusty," says Jerry Scott Sr., a juror. Robert Johnson III, a former state senator from the area, teamed up with Espy as cocounsel. But the jurors were well aware of why the men were in the courtroom. "The only reason the company picked Johnson and Espy is because they were black," says Scott.

AHP might have done just as well hiring a fat white woman to try the case. As juror Jesse Jackson notes, Espy was a pretty good speaker, but the problem was that "he didn't show no evidence that the drug wasn't hurting people. They had all these doctors out of New York, New Jersey, and AHP could never prove that the drug didn't hurt people . . . Every day AHP would bring in files and files, stacked up in huge piles in the back of the courtroom. But I was waiting for one of them to come and say which stack was the one that showed how many people the drug had saved, and they never did that."

Instead, mountains of documents and testimony from company employ-ees showed conclusively that AHP clearly knew of the risks of its diet drugs but didn't warn doctors or patients that they might be at risk of devel-oping heart-valve damage or primary pulmonary hypertension, an often fatal lung condition. By the time the Jefferson County case went to trial, AHP was already trying to settle all the potential heart-valve injury cases nation-ally for $4 billion. The Mississippi plaintiffs had opted out of the settlement, thinking they could do better at trial.

It was a smart gamble. Plaintiffs' attorney Dennis Sweet has famously joked that the big news would have been if he'd lost this case, because since 1999, AHP has lost almost every single fen-phen case that's ever gone to trial, including one in 2004 in which savvy Texas lawyer John O'Quinn eluded the state's cap on punitive damages by proving that AHP engaged in criminal behavior. The jury came back with a $1-billion verdict in favor of a single plaintiff.

AHP's behavior in the fen-phen debacle had simply proved mostly in-defensible. In Mississippi, plaintiff attorneys produced damning correspon-dence, like an email from Kay Anderson, a company administrator to Dr. Patty Acri, AHP's product labeling director, who wrote, "Can I look for-ward to my waning years signing checks to fat people who are a little afraid of some silly lung problem?" Other documents showed that AHP estimated that it would lose $800 million if the FDA forced it to put a "black box" warning on the drug label to adequately inform users of the danger of heart and lung disease; so it decided to fight the warning and withhold reports of adverse effects of the drug from the government—a display of greed that didn't sit well with many jurors.

AHP's only hope was to attack the plaintiffs themselves. Attorney Robert Johnson III did an admirable job of arguing that the plaintiffs weren't, in fact, sick, and that their health problems predated their fen-phen use. But in showing that the plaintiffs had other health problems, AHP only ended up further emphasizing its lack of concern for the people who took its products. One juror, Patricia Gamble, says, "The drug company brought up a lady's hysterectomy. I thought that was inappropriate."

In the end, Sweet brought in an economist who outlined the expected future medical costs and lost income that the plaintiffs could expect to suffer as a result of their drug-related injuries. He asked the jury to award actual damages of $25 million each to four of the plaintiffs, and $30 million to Tenner because of her longer life expectancy. And then the issue went to the jury.

Since the jury in Jefferson County has been pilloried for its biases and backwardness, it might be useful to meet a few of its members. Sitting around the kitchen table at her mother's house on a glorious spring day in 2005, Patricia Gamble, thirty-nine, recalls her experience. At the time she was called to serve as a juror in the Jefferson County fen-phen case, she wasn't employed, but she resents the implications from the media that she's uneducated. She graduated from high school and attended some community college before quitting for a job. A Baptist and one of seven children, Gamble has worked most of her life in a place that doesn't offer a lot of options for a good paycheck. She's done child care, worked outages at the nuclear power plant in Port Gibson, cleaning up the plant during scheduled shutdowns, and now she works nights at the prison. As she talks about her background, her sister, who is mute, occasionally comes over and reaches a hand over Gamble's shoulder. Gamble responds with a gentle squeeze back.

She says that the fen-phen trial was her first experience serving as a juror. The trial lasted several weeks, and she says they often sat there from 8:00 A.M. to 8:00 P.M. listening to all the testimony. After such an education, she can lecture at length about FDA drug-labeling procedures, the black box warning system, the symptoms and causes of primary pulmonary hypertension. She developed opinions about the testimony of the drug company executives. "The company only seemed interested in money," she says.

During their deliberations about the award, Gamble says that she urged her fellow jurors to give equal amounts to all the plaintiffs. "I thought we should be fair," she says. So after much debate, instead of giving Tenner $30 million and the rest $25 million, they decided all five plaintiffs should get $30 million each, for a grand total of $150 million. The numbers were not out of line with the award in Texas, nor were they much different from verdicts handed down around the country in similar trials in years to come.

The verdict was not a forgone conclusion. Jerry Scott Sr. says the panel split nine to three, and because they used anonymous ballots to vote, he doesn't know who the holdouts were.

Like Gamble, Scott is livid about the 60 *Minutes* broadcast and media characterization of the jurors as illiterate and uneducated. The forty-six-year-old father of three, says, "I only have a twelfth-grade education, but I have about an associate's degree worth of experience in the military." Scott lives on the hill across the road from Gamble's mother's house in a dilapidated silver trailer surrounded by dead cars, live dogs, and a smattering of broken glass on the front steps that made it look desolate and abandoned when I first went there. It was a striking contrast to the home of Kenya Tenner, the local plaintiff whose mansion comes courtesy of Scott's jury service.

When I finally met him at the county library, Scott was waiting for me, wearing a camouflage jacket, jeans, and a blue work shirt encircled with a money belt full of documents and business cards that he slowly produced as exhibits for his story. He is trim, with close-cropped hair and gold-rimmed bifocals that look military issued. Scott is direct and answered my questions as precisely as possible. "I try to stick to the facts. You get in trouble when you try to speculate about things you don't know," he says.

In some ways, Scott was probably as close to a dream juror for AHP as it was going to find in Jefferson County because after leaving the military, Scott once worked for a drug company in Missouri, collecting ragweed for allergy medication.

When Scott first showed up for jury service in 1999, he says he didn't know what kind of case he was getting called for. But he took his service so seriously that during the trial he put an outgoing message on his answering machine telling people he couldn't talk to anyone while he was on jury duty. "I didn't want to compromise the case," he explains.

Initially, he says, "It was hard for me to believe that the company would put something on the market that was dangerous." But as the trial wore on, he says, "We got to review autopsies of all the people who had died. I learned about echocardiograms, mitral valves." The evidence, he says, was convincing.

Along with all the anatomy lessons, Scott says that the jury got to see "sheer lying by corporate executives. It was clear that AHP lied to the FDA that the drug was safe. That was the main reason that we made the ruling that we did."

Once they settled on liability, Scott says, "There was a lot of bickering in the jury about what kind of award the plaintiffs should receive. Mr. Sweet had asked for X dollars for Kenya [Tenner], and we looked at it like, you cannot discriminate against anyone. All the rest of the plaintiffs deserve the same thing. But at the same time, we cannot put this company out of business." The jury had some parameters to work with. "We learned from an economist that Dennis Sweet had that AHP's net worth was something like $87 billion, more than the net worth of some third world countries."

Also weighing on their minds during the deliberations, he says, were the six million other people who took Redux and Pondimin, and whether there should eventually be punitive damages that would reflect that fact as well. "We argued a long time about that," he says.

Once they decided on the $150 million, Gamble says that Scott turned to them and said, "'One day this is going to come back to haunt us,' and he was right."

After the verdict, the jurors were never given a chance to impose punitive damages, as AHP that night offered to settle not just all of Sweet and Gallagher's cases but those of several other Mississippi lawyers to the tune of about $400 million. AHP was desperate to settle the case before the punitive award was issued. At that time, to appeal a jury verdict, a defendant was required to post an appeal bond worth 125 percent of the verdict, so if the jury had come back with punitive damages that were three time the compensatory award, as lawyers generally request, AHP was facing the prospect of posting a bond worth more than a half billion dollars if it wanted to get the verdict knocked down or overturned.

AHP had other worries too. At the time of the verdict, the company was trying to merge with Warner-Lambert Co., which was the target of a hostile takeover bid by Pfizer, another pharmaceutical giant. AHP was anxious to put a lid on its fen-phen liability to keep its stock price high enough to make the merger go through. A settlement in Mississippi was also critical to preserving the proposed $4.83 billion national settlement AHP was attempting to negotiate. Big verdicts were an incentive for injured people to drop out of the national settlement and pursue individual lawsuits in the hopes of getting a better deal. (Eventually, some sixty thousand former fen-phen users would opt out of the settlement to try to pursue their cases individually.)

Because it had such potentially large liability, AHP had an incentive to put as many former fen-phen users as possible into the settlement so that they wouldn't sue. To do this, the company offered to pay anyone who had actually taken the drug, whether they were currently sick or not. But the strategy backfired, and by 2004 the company had set aside $21 billion to pay claims of those injured by its product—five times its original estimate.

The fen-phen verdict and the ensuing settlement caught the attention of plaintiff lawyers from all over the country, but the media frenzy over Jefferson County didn't kick off until two years later. (60 Minutes didn't show up for three years after the verdict.) What really landed Jefferson County in the spotlight were the problems of the pharmaceutical industry. In the two years after the fen-phen trial, the FDA forced the recall of four widely prescribed drugs, setting off a tidal wave of national drug litigation against several of the nation's largest pharmaceutical companies. According to a study by the pro—tort reform Manhattan Institute, the number of mass actions filed against out-of-state defendants in Jefferson County jumped from seventeen in 1999 to seventy-three in 2000, and the vast majority of the plaintiffs weren't residents of the county.

Residents of Jefferson County, who had only twenty years earlier begun to regularly serve on juries at all, suddenly found themselves called up for jury service that would vest them with tremendous economic power over one of the largest industries in the world.

Wyatt Emmerich, the newspaper publisher featured on 60 Minutes, sums up the business community's sentiment about the situation when he says, "The idea of a jury in Jefferson County deciding whether Rezulin should be on the market, that's crazy."

Sitting on the arm of an old couch on the sagging porch of his family home in Fayette, Jesse Jackson at first glance seems like the kind of juror Wyatt Emmerich must have had in mind when he pictured a Jefferson County juror. Jackson's white clapboard tenant house has a sloped tin roof and a corrugated metal addition chock full of birdbaths, broken flowerpots, and kids' toys.

Jackson mumbles a bit, simply answering yes and no to questions about his jury experience. But as he warms up, he becomes more animated, and it becomes clear that he may have been one of the most attentive people on the fen-phen jury. He took detailed notes throughout the trial and probably got called up for jury service because he never fails to vote in an election. For his service, he has not only been humiliated by a national news broadcast, but he and the other jurors have been targets of a federal investigation.

Built like Pavarotti and a regular churchgoer who sings in the county's nationally renowned community church choir, Jackson, too, has a high school diploma. After high school, he worked for about four years as a logger until a tree fell on him, leaving him disabled. Now forty-two, Jackson says that at the time of the trial he was married, but not long ago, his wife walked out on him, and he is now a single parent trying to raise four kids. Since the trial, he's been visited by the FBI "about seven times," he recalls.

The first time they approached him at a service station. Agents apparently had been following him. Jackson dodged them by claiming to be someone else, but eventually the FBI cornered him at his house. They wanted to know about the fen-phen trial. "They wanted to know how we came by that decision," he says. "I told them, 'it's mostly the evidence.'" Apparently, though, that answer seemed too far-fetched for the G-Men, and they continued to press him about whether he'd gotten paid by anyone or whether he knew the jurors before he was on the panel with them. "They really pushed me," he says. "Nobody offered me anything. I told them, 'You see the way I'm living. This house passed to me from my dad after he died. I've been trying to fix it up and fix it up. Don't you think that I'd get it fixed up if I had some money?'"

According to three of the jurors, the FBI only asked about the plaintiffs' lawyers, specifically, Dennis Sweet, even though it was clear from the beginning that if anyone needed to bribe the jury, it was AHP. It's also well known down here that big companies, particularly tobacco firms, have for years been paying local residents to be "jury consultants," where they supposedly help defense lawyers vet jury lists before trials. Plaintiff lawyers believe this is simply a form of salting the jury pool should a case get to trial for one of these companies. Either way, rumors of jury tampering by big business aren't just local folklore. In 1988 a Mississippi smoker's lawsuit ended in a mistrial after serious allegations of jury tampering by the tobacco company in a case that became John Grisham's model for the book *The Run-away Jury.*

Jurors say that the only money they were offered in connection to their jury service came from a man named Arnold Clark Sr., a local private investigator who worked for AHP's lawyers. Gamble says that Clark invited her and the others to go down to the Eola Hotel in Natchez to answer some questions after the trial. "He offered me one hundred dollars to come meet with them. I think they thought one hundred dollars was tempting," she says with a laugh. "No one that I know of went." (Clark says that several jurors did go to the meeting, however.)

Jurors have also been interviewed by investigators from the U.S. Attorney's Office, and Scott and Jackson say they were also visited in the fall of 2004 by a man named George Steel, whose business card identified him only as a "civil and criminal investigator" in Washington, DC. Steel was asking questions about Dennis Sweet. (Using the information on the card, I tried to contact Steel, but he never responded to my calls and emails, and I could never determine who he worked for.)

The FBI investigation has continued. All the jurors were called down to the county sheriff's office in late 2004 for a meeting yet again with the FBI. "They wanted to know if we'd been bribed," says Scott. "They said they'd been through all our bank accounts. I told 'em I had twelve dollars at that time," he says with a laugh.

The federal investigation did finally net some fish, but none of them was a juror. Instead, investigators turned up a scheme in which Fayette residents had fraudulently made claims to the $400 million fen-phen settlement fund AHP set up after the 1999 trial. By February 2006, fourteen people had pleaded guilty to charges related to making bogus claims to the fund, which gave them each $250,000 despite the fact that they'd never taken the drug.

For the jurors, the fallout from their three weeks of jury service in 1999 has been bewildering. They say that they've been permanently affected by the negative publicity and the charges of corruption, which they've never been able to publicly refute. Several retained lawyers and filed libel suits against CBS, *60 Minutes,* and the florist, but the cases were thrown out.

The jurors' lawsuits only brought more ridicule, as tort reform groups circulated the tales as further evidence that Jefferson County was indeed the home of jackpot justice. Despite all the problems, though, the jurors are steadfast in their belief that not only did they honorably fulfill their civic duty but that in rendering the verdict, they were doing the right thing.

"I wouldn't say that I regret being on the jury. Back then," says Gamble, "who would have thought that all these people would invade on this? I don't regret giving the money. It was the right thing to do. [AHP] knew all along this drug was bad, and they didn't care."

CHAPTER EIGHT

Crackpot Justice: The Myth of the Frivolous Lawsuit

In all the media brouhaha over Jefferson County, Mississippi, tort reform advocates have decried the onslaught of frivolous lawsuits allegedly coming into the rural county. They've pointed fingers at the big-time plaintiff lawyers like Dennis Sweet, who have won hundreds of millions of dollars in jury verdicts there and elsewhere as the source of the scourge. But strictly speaking, most of those cases weren't frivolous by legal standards. After all, they survived a trip to a jury and the many procedural hurdles necessary to get there. That's not to say, though, that Jefferson County hasn't had its share of frivolous lawsuits. Many of them were filed by the same lawyer, but his law practice is a far cry from that of Sweet and his colleagues.

On Medgar Evers Boulevard in Fayette, Mississippi, on a grassy lot without sidewalks, sits a neat mobile home with a banner draped across the front: Law Offices of Kevin Muhammad and Associates. Muhammad is the official lawyer for the New Nation of Islam—an offshoot of the old Nation of Islam—founded by spiritual leader and "Son of Man" Marvin Muhammad, a slender African-American man who tools up and down Main Street in a purple Corvette. The group has set up a compound in the county and runs several businesses in Fayette, including the auto body shop next to the law office and a bakery on Main Street that sells donuts and presweetened cappuccinos.

Kevin Muhammad is one of only about three lawyers practicing in the county, and over the past several years he has produced a steady stream of litigation in Mississippi courts. Rather than sue big drug companies,

Muhammad found a niche suing some of the plaintiff lawyers who sue drug companies, particularly those involved in Jefferson County's big fen-phen lawsuit. In several lawsuits, Muhammad represented people who claimed they'd worked as the attorneys' "runners," rounding up clients, and then gotten stiffed on payment.

The allegations were salacious, since running clients for lawyers is illegal, but Muhammad's filings were also, well, unconventional. In one brief, Muhammad quoted the entire lyrics from the song "One Tin Soldier (The Legend of Billy Jack)." He wrote that his client's work on behalf of the fen-phen lawyers "could be characterized as that of a happy black slave singing 'Dixie' in the defendants [sic] tort fields, feverishly pick'in clients with no idea that his masters and whipping boy had no intention of giving him that kind of money to buy his freedom."

"I would not deny that my legal pleadings are creative," concedes Muhammad in an interview.

Creative or not, the cases were dismissed for various legal deficiencies. Undeterred, Muhammad would refile them in federal court, also naming the judges who'd dismissed the original cases. Muhammad filed so many baseless lawsuits that he ran up $100,000 in civil contempt fines, and in March 2004 a state-court judge threw him in jail for thirty days for ignoring his order to stop suing the fen-phen lawyers.

Despite the sheer volume of Muhammad's enterprising lawsuits, the state's major tort reform proponents have never said a word about him. To the contrary, many were privately gloating about the bad publicity that the suits brought to some of the state's leading plaintiff lawyers. Perhaps the main reason that Muhammad didn't become the poster boy for tort reform, though, was that none of the major lawsuit reforms passed in the state, or peddled nationally, would have affected him. As one plaintiff lawyer says, for tort reform to affect Muhammad's cases, "He'd have to win one."

Therein lies the disconnect between business groups' rhetoric about the epidemic of frivolous lawsuits and their policy agenda that claims to clamp down on those suits. As any good trial lawyer knows, the very definition of a frivolous lawsuit is one that isn't worth anything. With its focus on capping damages and restricting lawyers' fees, tort reform most affects good cases worth serious money while doing nothing to weed out nuisance suits like Muhammad's. Tort reform's focus on frivolous lawsuits is a red herring, designed to distract people from the real impact of the agenda, which is to keep legitimate cases out of court and away from juries.

President George W. Bush has made the frivolous lawsuit a staple of his stump speeches. When he took the podium at the Republican National Convention in New York City in 2004, Bush intoned, "We must protect small-business owners and workers from the explosion of frivolous lawsuits that threaten jobs across America." In his 2005 State of the Union address, Bush recycled a favorite campaign line, saying, "No one has ever been healed by a frivolous lawsuit."

Bush was implying, of course, that frivolous lawsuits are an easy way for unscrupulous people to make money off deep-pocketed defendants and their insurance companies, who would rather settle cheaply for a few thousand dollars than spend more money defending a baseless claim. But as Muhammad learned, frivolous lawsuits aren't a very reliable income generator for most people. Anyone who's ever tried to file a simple *legitimate* claim with an insurance company will know that getting insurance companies to hand over money is no easy task.

Serious researchers have proved as much, mostly by studying the closed claim files of medical malpractice insurers available in a couple of states. By looking at the insurers' own files to see what their settlement practices actually look like, how often they pay out, and how much money they pay in relation to the injuries alleged, researchers have found pretty consistently that insurance companies not only do not pay frivolous claims, but they also tend to fight off legitimate ones as well.

In 1992 a team of doctors published a study of closed insurance-claim files from a large New Jersey malpractice insurer. The doctors concluded after reviewing eight thousand files that payments for frivolous claims, where no malpractice had occurred, "are uncommon." (And these were doctors, mind you, studying the claims files.) They found that in cases where the malpractice was simply indefensible, the insurer paid about 91 percent of the time; where the issue was muddier, 59 percent of the claims; and it paid 21 percent of claims that were deemed defensible, meaning the doctor's conduct probably didn't violate any standards of care that would warrant a payout.

Even then, though, the doctors didn't find that those paid defensible cases were frivolous. To the contrary, they suggested a classification problem at work. Doctor-reviewers may have jumped the gun in deeming many claims defensible early on in the process. But when more information became available, evidence of substandard care by the treating physicians may have led the insurance company to settle. The researchers also noted that the number of claims deemed "defensible" may have been too high to begin with, the result of an insurance-company practice of initially calling every claim defensible as a way of avoiding unnecessary payments.

When insurance companies do pay people without a fight, it's generally not because their claim was frivolous but because the malpractice is so egregious, the injuries so severe, and everyone agrees on what happened. Duke law professor Neil Vidmar, in his ongoing study of Florida's closed-claim database, found that more than 10 percent of the million-dollar settlements in the files were paid by the insurance companies in cases where no one even filed a lawsuit.

The list of cases in which these types of settlements occurred shows just what it takes to get an "easy" payment from an insurance company. Here's a sampling:

· A fourteen-year-old boy goes to the hospital with a broken lower leg. Doctors put a cast on too tight. The leg has to be amputated. The insurance company awards $1 million.

· A fifty-six-year-old man goes to the hospital for stitches to a bad cut on his right index finger. He's given an IV sedative and is poorly monitored by nurses who weren't trained for the job. They notice he's dead only after removing the surgical drapes. His family receives $1 million.

· A man goes to the doctor suffering from chest pain. The doctor prescribes antacids. The man dies from a heart attack. The insurance company offers $10 million.

· A baby boy is taken to the hospital after a fall. The hospital fails to diagnose bacterial meningitis, stomach problems, and a 105.6 degree temperature. He's sent home without tests, returns to the ER again, and is again sent home. The boy ends up with severe brain damage, blindness, deafness, and immobility. The insurance company pays $1 million.

· A seven-year-old boy goes in for surgery to clear a blockage in his ear stemming from repeated infections. After a medication error, the boy dies, and the family is given $1.25 million.

The list of tragedies goes on for pages, suggesting that something really, really bad has to happen before an insurance company will just willingly hand over big money without a fight. That's not to say that small settlements in marginal cases don't happen, or that defendants who are only peripherally involved in an accident don't get sued. That's one reason why the political rhetoric about frivolous lawsuits resonates so well with doctors and small-business owners. But even in those cases that sound at first like classic frivolous cases often turn out to be much less black and white. Indeed, the definition of *frivolous* generally varies depending on which side you talk to.

Herbert Kritzer, a political science and law professor at the University of Wisconsin, has been studying the law practices of insurance-company lawyers. Kritzer says it's common for a defendant or its insurance company to bring other smaller parties into litigation as part of their defense. "It's a lot of finger-pointing," he explains. For example, in Minnesota, where he's been conducting research, there's been a big string of construction-defect litigation over water getting into houses during the 1990s, causing mold and horrible rot in the walls.

In these cases, the home owners are bringing claims against the general contractor who built the house, who then, as part of his defense, brings in the window maker, the stucco manufacturer—everybody he can think of who might share responsibility for the damage and thus relieve some of the contractor's financial burden. The problem, Kritzer says, is that even when it's clear there is an actionable injury suffered by the plaintiff, "It's not always clear who's responsible. By bringing in everybody—and it's the insurance companies that are doing this—you encourage them to make contributions to avoid the cost of litigation." Procedural rules of the courts, too, he says, actually require litigants to bring in anyone who is even remotely a possible defendant, ensuring that a few small fish will accidentally get caught in the net.

These rules, says Kritzer, are part of the American legal and social system that is based on the notion of individual, rather than social, responsibility. Other countries have national health care, which eliminates a lot of the costs that are sought in the American legal system. In America, he says, "You design a system like we do that's designed on personal responsibility, then you have to figure out who's responsible" for causing someone's injury, a job that's not always very clear-cut.

On January 16, 2003, Bush traveled to Scranton, Pennsylvania, where surgeons at Mercy Hospital had been threatening to walk off the job en masse to protest rising malpractice-insurance costs. Bush met privately with the doctors, hearing their complaints about large jury verdicts in lawsuits and the stress of working in a hostile legal environment. During the meeting, a doctor complained about a recent $7-million settlement in a malpractice case against the hospital's affiliate in nearby Wilkes-Barre.

After the meeting, the president gave a major policy speech, kicking off his push to enact federal caps on punitive-damage awards in medical malpractice suits, saying that the medical liability system is "broken" and driving away doctors, making health care unsafe. Bush railed against lawyers and "junk lawsuits" and "excessive jury awards," referring to the $7 million Wilkes-Barre case (which was actually a settlement, not a jury award). The "junk lawsuit" that Bush was referring to, though, was a classic example of a case where money was not the motivation behind its filing. The family in Wilkes-Barre filed suit to get answers.

In August 2000 doctors at Mercy Hospital were preparing to anesthetize seventy-two-year-old Frank Thornton before a scheduled surgery. While connecting him to a ventilator, Dr. Esther McKenzie, an anesthesiologist, mistakenly put the breathing tube down his esophagus rather than his windpipe. Neither McKenzie nor the surgeon, Dr. Walter Boris, were able to verify that the tube was in the correct position, which it wasn't, and Thornton was deprived of oxygen for six to ten minutes. A retired welder, veteran, and church deacon, Thornton suffered irreversible brain damage and never regained consciousness. He died a few weeks later.

Doctors told Thornton's wife of fifty-three years, Dorothy, almost nothing to explain what happened to Frank. According to her attorney, the surgeon refused to meet with her after the mishap in the operating room, and other hospital doctors who briefed her on her husband's condition also refused to talk about what went on in the operating room that fateful day. Brokenhearted, Dorothy sued to find out what happened to her husband.

When her lawyers deposed Boris, he claimed he could not recall any of the events that took place that day and also said he never told anyone he thought there had been an error in the OR, according to Michelle Quinn, one of Thornton's attorneys. But a few days later, lawyers deposed the hospital's risk manager, who said that Boris had come into the office within hours of the incident and said he thought the breathing tube had been misplaced. Two nurses also testified that they saw clear signs that Thornton's breathing tube was misplaced and had alerted other people in the operating room. Only three days into the trial, the hospital offered to settle. The CEO of the hospital, James May, issued an apology, saying, "I believe this legal action by the Thornton family represents a legitimate and sincere attempt to learn the truth."

Learning the truth is frequently the prime motivator for people filing lawsuits, particularly in cases of medical malpractice, and it's also one reason why the wrong people occasionally get named in those lawsuits, doctors in particular. Several researchers have noted, in fact, that filing a lawsuit is often the only way that a patient who has a bad health care outcome can find out exactly what went wrong, because the health care system practically demands that patients file a suit to access their own or a loved one's medical records.

This doesn't mean their cases are frivolous. Two economists, Henry Farber and Michelle White, studied medical malpractice claims brought against an unnamed hospital. They found that most malpractice cases brought against the hospital were totally reasonable based on what the plaintiffs knew at the time they filed it. But the information was frequently insufficient to help them figure out whether or not their injuries were the result of crappy care or just bad luck. The only way to answer the question, wrote Farber and White, was to "file a lawsuit and proceed with the discovery process," which would force the hospital to disclose further medical records and allow the plaintiffs to depose the doctors and other professionals involved in the case.

Once plaintiffs do get this information, many of them drop their suits upon learning that the injuries weren't the result of negligence, which helps explain why some 50 percent of all malpractice lawsuits are closed without payment. Doctors and nurses who turn out not to have been involved in the chain of events that caused the injuries in dispute also tend to get dropped during discovery. That doesn't make them any happier about having been sued, however, as any doctor will tell you.

Tom Baker, a University of Connecticut law professor and author of the 2005 book *The Medical Malpractice Myth,* argues that one of the best ways to reduce the number of misfire lawsuits in the malpractice system—the ones usually referred to as frivolous—is for doctors and hospitals to embrace a policy of full disclosure when they make mistakes. Giving patients better information about their injuries and whether those injuries were actual screw-ups would cut down significantly on the number of suits filed against the wrong parties, and even many suits over injuries that weren't actually the result of negligence. Of course, even though the American Medical Association's ethics rules require doctors to do this as a matter of course, it rarely happens.

Doctors argue that they don't disclose because they're afraid if they do, they'll get sued. But that argument, Baker notes, doesn't really hold water, because doctors who practice in places where they have little risk of personal liability—such as Veterans Administration hospitals, or in England, which has less liberal tort laws—still have dismal records at disclosing errors to patients.

In 1992 Bart A. Ross was diagnosed with mouth cancer, for which he eventually sought treatment and surgery at the University of Illinois Medical Center in Chicago. The cancer and the ensuing treatments left him disfigured. He lost most of his teeth and his lower jaw, making it difficult for him to talk and eat. Ross believed the hospital had botched the surgery on his jaw, creating most of the problems, and in 1995 he filed a medical malpractice lawsuit against the hospital. According to tort reform mythology, Ross should have had no trouble wringing money out of the hospital, but his case was quickly dismissed because he missed the filing deadline.

Nonetheless, Ross was obsessed, and by his own account, he consulted one hundred different lawyers, virtually none of whom would take his case. Ross would pursue his legal issue for twelve years, filing lawsuits without a lawyer until he finally made headline news in 2005 for murdering the mother and husband of federal judge Joan Lefkow, who was the latest in a long line of judges to reject his claim.

Ross's was an extreme case, but his travails in the legal system showed that frivolous lawsuits are harder to pursue than people think, largely because most lawyers aren't interested in taking them. That hasn't stopped tort reformers from pushing legislation supposedly designed to punish people for filing frivolous lawsuits. A perennial favorite is the loser-pays rule, a reform proposal touted by small-business lobbying groups and people like the Manhattan Institute's Walter Olson, who considers it one of the superior elements of the British legal system. The idea is that the number of frivolous lawsuits would be reduced if the losing party had to pay the winner's fees.

"The practical case for loser pays is equally compelling," Olson wrote in *Reason* magazine in June 1995, as a loser-pays provision was making its way through Congress as part of the Republicans' Contract with America. "Litigants naturally think too well of their cases; loser pays pushes them to size up their prospects more realistically. It also curbs the brand of extortion, so routine in American law as almost to have lost its ethical taint, by which lawyers use the costs of the process itself, or the risk of a fluke outcome found in any trial, to strong-arm their opponents into settlement."

In theory, it does seem like a good idea—so good it's often endorsed by liberals. Charles Peters, a lawyer himself and founding editor of the *Washington Monthly* magazine, has been a longtime proponent of the rule. Other liberal supporters in the media include the *Atlantic Monthly* writer James Fallows, former *Los Angeles Times* editorial-page editor Michael Kinsley, and former *American Lawyer* owner Steven Brill. All see loser pays as a reasonable legal reform that both conservatives and liberals can agree on.

The rule, though, has some problems. It raises the stakes substantially even for legitimate suits filed by a small business or individual against a deep-pocketed corporate defendant. Plaintiffs face steep odds of winning before juries, even when they have decent cases. Adding the risk of paying the other side's legal fees is just one more deterrent to filing a legitimate suit. Experience shows that loser pays also doesn't deliver any of the benefits that its promoters promise.

For instance, in Florida, the state medical association successfully lobbied for a loser-pays rule in medical malpractice lawsuits in the late 1970s. After ten years, the doctors begged the legislature to repeal it. As it turned out, the loser paying was frequently the defendant—the doctor or hospital—and the bills were significant. Even when plaintiffs lost, they rarely ended up paying the defense side's legal bills, for a pretty obvious reason: they were broke. The plaintiffs were generally injured people who suffered from severe disabilities that prevented them from working, and they often sued because they couldn't afford their medical bills. If they lost the lawsuit, they generally had few assets with which to pay the doctor's legal fees, and judges were reluctant to order them to try.

In 2003 the state of Texas passed a modified version of loser pays in its major overhaul of the civil justice system. The new Texas law requires that a losing party pay court costs if he or she refused a settlement offer from the defendant and then lost at trial or recovered less than 80 percent of the defendants proposed settlement. Not many lawyers have actually invoked the rule, but at least one has found out the hard way that it's not the magic bullet business groups think it is.

In 2004 a University of Texas Law School student sued a driver who'd run her down while she was crossing a street in Austin. The student demanded $14,500, and the driver and his lawyers offered $12,000. But instead of further negotiations, the driver and his lawyers invoked the loser-pays rule and took the case to trial. The jury found for the student and awarded her $29,819—more than 120 percent higher than the settlement offer—so the driver ended up having to pick up the tab for both the award and more than $16,000 in legal costs.

Loser pays also has the potential to backfire on its most adamant supporters, doctors in particular. "There are a huge number of clear-cut but small cases that don't get brought anymore because they don't make economic sense for the lawyers. If there was a loser-pays rule, it changes the economics," Kritzer explains. Whereas now a lawyer may be reluctant to bring a smaller but serious malpractice case because the cost of the experts needed to prove the case would eat up most of any award, under loser pays, the lawyer could recoup those costs at trial which they can't do now. "It would probably increase litigation," says Kritzer.

The legal system already has a mechanism in place to deal with genuinely frivolous lawsuits. It's called a judge. Judges in the civil courts have the authority to impose sanctions on litigants for filing frivolous suits, as they did in Kevin Muhammad's case. In the federal system, judges rely on what's known as Rule 11, which allows them to impose sanctions and also to force frivolous filers to pay the defendants' legal costs as well. Most states have their own version of Rule 11.

But business groups aren't happy with the current Rule 11 because they think judges don't use it often enough. They're now agitating for changes, including one that would force its application to all fifty state court systems, to create mandatory sanctions for frivolous filings, rather than leave their imposition to the judge's discretion. The change would return Rule 11 to the one that existed before 1993, when the U.S. Supreme Court modified it to make it less punitive. The business groups' yearning for the good ol' days of Rule 11, though, is based on a bit of wishful thinking.

In the debate over the changes to the federal rule, several researchers took a good look at the old Rule 11 to see how it actually worked. They discovered that the rule never really lived up to its billing, particularly in the tort cases that had business groups so up in arms. One 1992 study found that personal injury cases accounted for relatively few sanctions in federal court. Even though personal injury cases accounted for 19 percent of the federal caseload studied, only 15 percent of all Rule 11 sanctions were in those cases. The rule also had a disproportionate effect on civil rights cases, which made up only 11 percent of the filings but accounted for 23 percent of all the sanctions.

More importantly, "There was no evidence that it substantially reduced frivolous lawsuits," says Kritzer, who worked on the study. Historically, Rule 11 targeted lawyers, says Kritzer. But for it to work, as with loser pays, the frivolous filer has to have something to lose. "There's a fairly sizable group of litigants out there who are essentially judgment proof," says Kritzer, making the deterrent value of Rule 11 or loser pays pretty marginal.

The other problem, says Kritzer, is that "there's this image out there that there are all these frivolous lawsuits. But there's no evidence whatsoever that's the case. Are there frivolous lawsuits? Of course there are. Is there any evidence that it's a huge problem for the system? There's no systematic evidence that it is."

Kritzer has recently taken up a new research study on the practice of lawyers for insurance companies. He asked the defense lawyers how many of them had encountered a frivolous lawsuit in the previous year. The response, he says, was "almost none." Kritzer says that if the lawyers had seen a frivolous suit, it was generally filed by someone acting without a lawyer. His findings mirror a 2004 study by the consumer group Public Citizen that reviewed one hundred Rule 11 sanctions issued by federal judges. The vast majority— 35—came from pro se litigants who most likely were prison inmates. (Ninety-five percent of prison-inmate civil rights lawsuits in federal court are filed without the aid of a lawyer, vastly more than any other category of lawsuit.)

"There are definitely people out there who are nutty," says Kritzer, and those people account for many of what are clearly frivolous lawsuits, like those filed by Bart Ross. He says the British have a solution for "wackos" in the legal system. It's called the vexatious-litigant provision. In England, if a court deems you a vexatious litigant, you have to seek permission from the court to file a suit.

In the end, small-business owners may kvetch that they are constantly plagued with "nuisance" lawsuits of $5,000 from people who slip on the ice in front of their stores, but generally speaking, the reason their insurance companies pay is that while those cases may be small, under the law they aren't frivolous. The best defense against them isn't a radical overhaul of the tort system but aggressive snow shoveling.

★ ★ ★

Joan Guetschow and Trisha Stumpf are former Olympic athletes who live in Park City, Utah. During the 2002 Winter Games in Salt Lake City, the pair started up a little business called Utah Beer. The name was a joke: at various sporting events and in the ski resort town, the women sold bottled water with a label on it calling it "Utah Beer," as a spoof on the state's Mormon culture and reputation for state-mandated watered-down booze. When the pair sought to trademark their creation, though, they found themselves on the receiving end of a threatened legal challenge from none other than Anheuser-Busch, one of the world's largest beer companies.

The maker of Budweiser was challenging their trademark application. The women were shocked. "How do they even know about us?" asks Guetschow. They were forced to hire a lawyer to respond. When they finally talked to the beer company's attorneys, they learned that Anheuser-Busch made a practice of opposing any and all trademarks that included the word *beer*, even though in this case, the "beer" was actually water. In effect, Anheuser-Busch was attempting to squash smaller upstart competitors by forcing them to litigate expensive trademark challenges.

The women thought it was outrageous, but they couldn't afford to pay a lawyer to represent them. "Who's going to win against them?" Guetschow says. "We were going to be smothered in legal fees." When they could no longer afford the lawyer, Guetschow and Stumpf decided to handle the response on their own, with some guidance from the U.S. Patent and Trademark Office website, and eventually the beer company dropped the challenge. But she says it was clear that the whole goal of the threatened litigation was to keep small companies out of the market. "I think that their motive is to scare people," Guetschow says.

The Utah Beer story isn't just an outlier. While frivolous lawsuits don't offer individual plaintiffs much hope of making easy money, legal threats are useful for big companies looking to head off competition from smaller companies. For instance, pharmaceutical companies are notorious for using patent-infringement lawsuits against generic drug manufacturers as a way of keeping cheaper generics off the market, or at least delaying their entry.

In 2003 the Federal Trade Commission sanctioned Bristol-Myers Squibb for anticompetitive behavior that included using baseless lawsuits to delay the introduction of generic substitutes for an antianxiety medication, which may have cost consumers $100 million. In an order that required Bristol-Myers to cease and desist in filing any further "sham litigation," the FTC wrote that the company's conduct "constitutes a clear and systematic pattern of anticompetitive misuse of governmental processes, that is, abusive filings undertaken without regard to the merits, in order to use administrative and judicial processes—rather than the outcome of those processes—as a weapon to obstruct competition."

These types of lawsuits, though, never seem to mobilize tort-reform groups. Even in 2003, when Fox News sued comedian Al Franken and his publisher for allegedly violating the network's trademark slogan with his book *Lies and the Lying Liars Who Tell Them: A Fair and Balanced Look at the Right,* tort reform groups offered not a peep of criticism of the media giant. And, of course, most tort reform measures do nothing to restrict these types of lawsuits. (Victor Schwartz, ATRA's general counsel, insists that the proposed changes to Rule 11 to punish frivolous lawsuits would apply to these sorts of business cases as well and provide a deterrent to Fox News just as it would to the slip-and-fall plaintiffs who plague small businesses.)

Yet businesses account for a sizable number of Rule 11 sanctions for frivolous lawsuits. This makes sense given that the vast majority of civil litigation is initiated by businesses, not individuals. According to the National Center for State Courts, in the jurisdictions it studies, more than half of all incoming civil lawsuits involve a contract dispute—vastly more than tort lawsuits. Seven in ten of those are thought to be bill-collection lawsuits, a growth industry for businesses. Northwestern University law professor Lawrence Marshall and his colleagues conducted the analysis of Rule 11 sanctions before the rule was changed by Congress in 1993. They found that although noncontract commercial litigation, such as antitrust, securities, patent, and banking cases, then accounted for only about 10 percent of federal case filings, those lawsuits made up nearly 19 percent of all the Rule 11 sanctions imposed. Even so, the rule, if revived, isn't likely to provide much of a deterrent to frivolous filings by businesses that stand to make millions by harassing the competition with baseless lawsuits. Marshall found that the median financial penalty under the old Rule 11 was only $2,500.

There's no doubt that occasionally frivolous lawsuits do happen, and sometimes defendants do pay to get rid of them. Unfortunately, this is the price Americans pay for having a democratic legal system.

The American legal system is based on the notion of individualized justice. Every case is supposed to be decided on its merits, every person heard. So blanket tort reform measures that simply prevent lawsuits from being filed on the front end invariably will exclude legitimate cases along with any frivolous ones. Tort reformers understand that perfectly well. Unfortunately, most Americans who endorse their agenda really don't.

CHAPTER NINE

E Pluribus Screw 'Em:
Class Action Reform and the
Attack on Consumer Protection

aul Miller's life has been characterized by a string of bad luck. When he was in his twenties, a car accident left him with impaired hearing, rods in his back, and later he lost an eye. Then, in 1989, while covering the Khmer Rouge as a photojournalist in Thailand, he was beaten and left mentally disabled. Miller returned home to San Francisco, but his injuries eventually left him unable to work. He applied for federal disability benefits in 1992, and every month the government electronically deposited $670 into his checking account at Bank of America, where he had been a customer for more than twenty years. After paying the rent and utilities on his government-subsidized apartment and for some groceries, Miller usually had about $40 to $60 a month left over in disposable income.

In January 1998, the bank mistakenly deposited $1,799 into Miller's account and sent him a credit memo that made it appear that the money was a retroactive government-benefit payment. Miller used the windfall to pay some bills. Three months later, though, without warning, Bank of America took back the money, causing Miller's rent and other checks to bounce. Then the bank charged him a host of additional fees for the bounced checks. Penniless and on the verge of homelessness, a panicked Miller called the bank and pleaded with officials to let him work out a repayment schedule for the money. They refused and, instead, offered to sign him up for a high-interest credit card that he could use to pay back the money. When he noted that he had no assets, no job, and no income to make him eligible for a credit card, another bank official suggested he sell his car to repay the bank.

Fortunately, Miller connected with a volunteer lawyer at the Bar Association of San Francisco. The lawyer informed Bank of America that California law prohibited the bank from collecting debts from government-benefit accounts such as those holding Social Security and unemployment payments. A 1974 California Supreme Court decision also required banks to comply with the same laws that govern debts collected by J. C. Penney or any other consumer creditor. Just because it held Miller's money in an account, then, the bank couldn't just seize it to pay off a debt it claimed he owed.

When pressed by the lawyer, the bank agreed to put the money back into Miller's account and let him pay off his debt gradually. But not long afterward, the bank attempted to seize all the money from his account again, and the lawyer had to intervene. Finally, the bank gave Miller a new account where officials promised his disability benefits would be safe. But at some point the bank dipped into Miller's new account without his authorization. Miller's attorney was able to stave off the bank, and he finally paid off the debt in 2003.

Bank of America's practice of illegally raiding the accounts of elderly and disabled Social Security beneficiaries turned out to be widespread. As a result, in 1998, Miller became the lead plaintiff in a class action lawsuit against the bank that covered an estimated 1.3 million customers who'd had bank fees illegally withheld from their accounts. Miller's lawyers estimated that the practice netted Bank of America between $40 million and $50 million a year, just in overdraft fees. Evidence produced during the litigation showed that 85 percent of those fees came from accounts containing $1,000 or less. In effect, Bank of America was making a killing off little guys like Paul Miller.

For years, the bank attempted unsuccessfully to remove the Miller case to federal court, but after six years of legal wrangling, the case finally gave way to a trial in a state court in 2004. During the trial, Miller's team produced memos from the bank's own lawyers alerting management that withdrawing Social Security funds to pay overdraft fees was illegal, and yet the bank continued to do it. They also attempted to show how the bank's computer system processed checks in a way that intentionally encouraged people to overdraw their accounts. The impact of the system was most acute for customers like Miller, whose account balances were relatively small.

The jury found in favor of the Bank of America on a misrepresentation claim and a claim regarding the safety and security of direct deposit accounts. However, it found for Miller and the bank customers on other claims relating to false representations about using government benefits to pay overdrafts, hitting the bank with a $75-million verdict in compensatory damages. The judge believed that the bank should have to give back all the money it made through the illegal scheme and tacked on an additional $284 million for unfair competition and unfair business-practices violations. The jury also took advantage of a California consumer-protection law and ordered the bank to pay $1,000 in special damages per class member because the class members were all elderly or disabled. The full amount of the award could top $1 billion.

During the trial, according to Jim Sturdevant, Miller's lawyer, Bank of America didn't offer much of a defense. Much of the evidence presented at trial went undisputed. While Sturdevant and his team offered experts in gerontology to talk about the demographics of the plaintiffs—the increased occurrence of dementia, the declining ability to understand complex documents, their average income, and so on—the bank offered little in the way of expert testimony. But it did something else to protect itself. The bank did what any other trillion-dollar corporation would do when it can't win a court case on the merits: it used its financial might to make its case to Congress.

The same year the Miller case was filed, Bank of America joined with the rest of the finance industry and most of corporate America to change the rules governing class actions to make it harder for people like Miller to have their day in court. In 1998 Senator Chuck Grassley (R-Iowa), who in 1996 received more than $40,000 in campaign contributions from commercial banks, introduced one of the first versions of the Class Action Fairness Act. Grassley's bill would have forced consumer class actions into federal rather than state court, where procedural rules, judges hostile to consumers, and the lack of resources would essentially leave them dying on the vine. And where Bank of America had failed to get a judge to transfer the Miller case to federal court, Grassley's bill would have done it for them. Had the law passed, it would have applied to cases pending at the time it went into effect, thus forcing Miller to start his case all over again in federal court, at tremendous cost to his attorneys, who were footing the bill for the litigation.

Miller's wasn't the only class action against Bank of America that would have been affected by the law. The same year that Miller's case was filed, Bank of America merged with NationsBank, and within a month, seven class actions were filed in California state courts alleging fraudulent conduct in connection with the merger. In September 2001, the bank settled another case that alleged it had failed to credit car-loan payments when they were received so it could charge customers extra interest and late fees. Aggrieved customers recovered about $1 million. In 2002 BoA settled a $700,000 case with Washington State customers after it got caught disguising the ownership of its own ATMs and charging customers an out-of-network fee to use them. These types of fees have become lucrative business for huge banks and finance companies, which in 2004 generated $38 billion in service charges, according to the Center for Responsible Lending.

The potential profits available in nickel-and-diming its customers gave Bank of America a big incentive to pursue federal restrictions on class actions, one of the only ways consumers have to fight back when such charges are improper. The bank also had the deep pockets to sustain a protracted assault on the nation's elected class to get those restrictions passed. By the time the Miller case went to trial, Bank of America had undergone a series of megamergers to become the nation's third largest bank, with over $1 trillion in assets. It now controls almost 10 percent of the nation's bank deposits, the legal limit, and in June 2005 it announced it was purchasing MBNA, the world's largest independent credit-card lender and another frequent target of lawsuits. The move gave the bank twenty million more new customers and $143 billion in outstanding credit-card balances.

Bank executives were substantial contributors to and fund-raisers for the campaigns of President George W. Bush, who pledged to make class action reform a priority. In the 2004 election cycle alone, the bank donated $2.4 million to federal candidates, according to the Center for Responsive Politics. In Congress, Bank of America had four lobbyists working on class action legislation. It is also was a member of the Financial Services Roundtable, an industry group that employed twelve lobbyists working toward a bill, according to a study by the nonprofit consumer group Public Citizen. John Beisner, a lawyer credited with helping to write the class action legislation, works for O'Melveny & Myers, the same firm that represented Bank of America in the appeal of the Miller case. (Beisner did not return calls for comment.)

The business community's combined effort took six years and millions of dollars, including $23 million in lobbying fees spent by the U.S. Chamber of Commerce's Institute for Legal Reform just in 2004. But in February 2005 Congress passed and President Bush signed the Class Action Fairness Act, which would force most class actions into federal court, where consumer groups and plaintiff lawyers believe they will languish and die before ever coming to fruition. (The federal courts have vastly fewer resources and fewer judges than the state courts, especially in California.) The bill came a little too late, and without the retroactive provisions, to help Bank of America in the Miller case, but it would nevertheless ensure that the bank would be free to continue fleecing its own customers with abandon in the future, without much interference from customers, trial lawyers, or independent jurors.

Once upon a time, Congress actually worried about protecting consumers from fraud rather than from the lawsuits designed to punish it. During the heyday of the consumer movement in the late 1960s and early 1970s, Congress passed a package of consumer-protection laws designed to combat many of the problems in the unregulated marketplace. They included the Truth in Lending Act, the Unfair Trade Practices Act, and the Fair Credit Reporting Act.

Agencies like the Federal Trade Commission (FTC) were also empowered to prosecute fraud and other abusive behaviors by corporations under the new laws. But their tools were often limited to winning injunctive relief, that is, promises that a company will change its behavior, not money. Robert Pitofsky, the chair of the FTC during the Clinton administration, says that for many years, "The U.S. government's approach to consumer protection was to say to the person who had broken the law, 'go out and sin no more.' The wrongdoer kept the money, and the consumer didn't get anything." He says the agency has moved toward demanding that companies disgorge some of their ill-gotten profits, but even so, he says, "Violations of consumer rights are so ubiquitous that the government can't possibly bring all the cases that come to its attention."

Members of Congress recognized the government's limitations, so when they drafted the consumer-protection statutes, they provided measures that allowed private citizens to go to court on their own and seek relief, specifically through class actions. From the beginning, the class-action provisions were controversial, but the desire to protect consumers, and a lack of other viable—and cheaper—alternatives, prevailed. While it's hard to imagine a Republican administration embracing such a move today, President Richard Nixon supported the package, and his attorney general, John Mitchell, wrote, "The enactment of this legislation will constitute a significant step in protecting American consumers from fraud and deception."

The laws were a recognition that corporations were rapidly growing in size, thereby increasing the potential to engage in theft on a massive scale, a few pennies at a time. Senator Frank E. Moss chaired congressional hearings in 1971 on the legislation, and Rand Corporation researcher Deborah Hensler quotes him at length in her book *Class Action Dilemmas*, saying, "Even the most vigorous opponents to the class-action [bill] last year did not dispute the basic premise of the bill—that the deceived or defrauded consumer has no effective legal remedy. Despite his many rights in the law, the consumer is shut out of the courthouse by economic realities. . . . Neither was it disputed that consumers are cheated out of tremendous sums of money nor that they should have a remedy. Nonetheless, opponents of class action argue that the doors of the courthouse in the main should remain closed."

Since then, Congress and state legislators have continued to open up new legal channels for class actions to enforce laws governing everything from antitrust violations to securities fraud. Even as they were gearing up to pass a major tort reform package, legislators in Georgia in 2004 criminalized payday lending on the grounds that usurious lending was similar to racketeering. Along with the criminal penalties, the law also allowed consumers to file class actions against payday lenders with the potential to win triple damages, as an incentive for lawyers to take the small cases.

Politicians have written class action rights into so many laws because even though the laws give people defrauded out of relatively small sums the legal right to go to court to recoup their money, the cost of litigating their individual cases would far surpass the money being recovered. Class actions allow people to pool their cases, making them financially viable enough for a lawyer to take them on. The potentially large fees for lawyers in class actions serve as an incentive for lawyers to seek out fraud and other consumer abuses and represent the victims aggressively. By allowing class actions for consumer protection, members of Congress and other state legislators in effect created a market for doing good.

That market kicked into high gear in the 1990s, as years of Republican presidents, and then a Republican Congress, gutted the budgets and power of government agencies charged with enforcing the consumer-protection laws. The business world also changed, with consolidation of power among large corporations and new technology radically altering the way Americans manage their money. The government was slow to keep up, and business worked hard to ensure that it stayed that way.

For instance, the federal government, which regulates finance companies and banks through the Office of the Comptroller of the Currency (OCC) and the Federal Trade Commission, is ostensibly responsible for protecting consumers from banking and finance rip-offs like the one that snared Miller. But as banks and finance companies have gotten larger, they have plowed significant sums of money into the political system and succeeded in protecting themselves from government interference. In 2004 alone, banks, finance companies, and mortgage-lending companies donated almost $50 million to federal candidates, according to the Center for Responsive Politics, and the investment seems to have paid off.

Harvard law professor Elizabeth Warren, who has studied the financial-services industry, says that the consumer movement that took off in the 1970s stalled before laws could be promulgated to better regulate new financial instruments like ATM transactions and high-risk loans that are now sold on Wall Street and have led to widespread predatory lending abuses. "You saw the consumer movement lose steam when Reagan came into the White House," she says.

Since then, she says, the banks and credit card companies have consolidated their power so that they write the rules in Washington, leaving little hope that Congress will come to the aid of the little guy. The nation's biggest banks have more than a trillion dollars in assets each, meaning that the possible fines imposed by the government aren't even enough to slow them down, much less change their behavior. "The government doesn't have the will to reach out and regulate them," Warren says.

As a result, she says, while we now have health and safety regulations that prevent manufacturers from selling a toaster that has a one-in-ten chance of setting your house on fire, consumer financial instruments that burn people financially have no such regulation. "People can market mortgages that give you a one-in-ten chance of losing your house," she says. "And people who sell mortgages that give you a one-in-ten chance of foreclosure have a lot more incentive to do so than the toaster maker does in making a toaster that has a one-in-ten chance of setting your house on fire."

Consumers who have a beef with their bank, like Miller, can file a complaint with the OCC. But the agency, funded entirely by the banks, has only about forty people on staff to handle consumer complaints for the entire country. Its website actually instructs consumers with a dispute with a bank to consult a private attorney. Despite well-documented evidence of rampant

misconduct by the nation's credit card issuers and widespread lending discrimination among the nations' biggest banks, OCC's own data show that,
on average, it makes fewer than five referrals a year for fair-lending violations to the Department of Justice or the Department of Housing and Urban
Development (HUD) for further enforcement action. The OCC actually intervened in the Miller case on the bank's behalf, arguing the controversial
notion that the case should be thrown out because the state is barred from
enforcing its own laws against a federally regulated institution. In June 2005
the OCC sued New York attorney general Eliot Spitzer to prevent him from
investigating charges that some of the nation's biggest banks had engaged in
racial discrimination in their subprime lending operations.

Warren says, "The financial companies and banks are powerful against
the consumer, powerful against Washington." Without help from government regulators, she says, "The only thing to fight back with is the class action and punitive damages, both of which are being sharply curtailed."

Into that void, then, have stepped plaintiff lawyers representing consumers in class actions, where some judgments and settlements against the
nation's biggest finance companies and banks simply dwarf anything done
by the government. For instance, in 2003 Visa and MasterCard were
slammed in a lawsuit for hiding a 1 percent currency-conversion fee that
was tacked on to transactions cardholders made abroad. Evidence presented during a six-month trial showed that between 1996 and 2002, Visa
charged cardholders $630 million for currency conversions that cost the
company only $7 million. A disgusted California judge ordered the compa-
nies to refund the fees and disclose future fees on statements. This could require the companies to pay as much as $800 million to class members and
their lawyers. The case is on appeal.

The plaintiff lawyers' success in cases like these sparked a backlash in
the business community, which rallied behind a mammoth effort by the U.S.
Chamber of Commerce to put a stop to it.

All good tort reform campaigns need a couple of critical elements to work:
a "judicial hellhole," a trial lawyer villain, and concerted media coverage.
The corporate attacks on class actions had all three. Just as the U.S. Cham-

ber of Commerce made Jefferson County, Mississippi, emblematic of run-away juries and fraudulent mass-tort litigation, it turned Madison County, Illinois, into ground zero for the national battle over class actions.

A blue-collar area just over the Mississippi River from St. Louis, the county had a half-century-old reputation for liberal judges and juries, primarily due to the area's proximity to the railroads, which made it a hotbed of injured workers' litigation. Steel mills and other heavy industry gave the area a heavily unionized, and mostly Democratic, population. In 2003 Madison County Judge Nicholas Byron had awarded $10 billion to plaintiffs in a class action against Philip Morris in which they alleged the company had defrauded millions of smokers by hiding the risks of "light" cigarettes.

Not long after the verdict, U.S. Chamber of Commerce president Tom Donohue and the president of the American Tort Reform Association landed in front of the Madison County courthouse to unveil a ten-point "Madison County Manifesto," their plan to restore "fairness" to corporate defendants appearing in the court. Donohue said, "Madison County is the epicenter of class action filings in America. And how can it not be, considering the staggering 1,850 percent increase in class action filings here between 1998 and 2001?" (Filings in the county had jumped from two in 1998 to forty-three in 2001.) He announced plans to publish the manifesto not just in local Illinois papers but in *The Hill,* a DC paper widely read by members of Congress.

As in Mississippi, the staggering statistics about Madison County distributed to the media came courtesy of the Manhattan Institute, where Samuel B. Witt III, the former general counsel of tobacco giant RJR Nabisco, had overseen the data collection. John Beisner, a defense lawyer whose firm, O'Melveny & Myers, was defending a number of cases in Madison County, wrote the studies, which reflected the business community's complaints that class actions filed in state courts like the one in Madison were assuming a federal function by regulating national companies. A 2000 study noted that of the forty-three class actions filed in Madison County in 2001, twenty-five challenged the business practices of financial-service companies, insurance companies, and banks. "Should one state court assume responsibility for nationwide regulation of the insurance and financial industries?" asked the authors. The solution, of course, was to send all those cases to the judges who run the federal courts, through legislation pending in Congress, drafted with Beisner's input.

The drumbeat continued a year later, when Cardozo Law School's Lester Brickman published another Manhattan Institute report called,

"Anatomy of a Madison County (Illinois) Class Action: A Study of Pathology." In his usual style, Brickman declared that if class actions were filed nationally at the rate they were in Madison County, the nation would have seen forty-two thousand such cases in 2000. The media dutifully swooped in for a look at Madison County, returning with stories about thriving plaintiff lawyers and ridiculous lawsuits filed by people overcharged on special-edition Barbie dolls.

A 2002 New York Times profile of Madison County was a classic example. Within days of the Manhattan Institute's release of Brickman's monograph, the Times observed that the Madison County courts "never met a class action they didn't like." As evidence, reporter Adam Liptak, a former senior counsel for the Times, pointed to a recent settlement in a class action against a TV manufacturer filed by consumers who said the company's TVs had fuzzy pictures. The customers got $25 or $50 coupons to buy new TVs. The lawyers, noted Liptak, got $22 million. The rest of the story involved the case that was the primary subject of Brickman's report.

Naturally, ABC's John Stossel had to weigh in, too. His September 2003 20/20 broadcast featured a spokesman from the Illinois Lawsuit Abuse Watch, one of the state's CALA spin-offs, and Beisner. Beisner said on the air that plaintiff lawyers had come to Madison County because "the parasite circus moves from place to place. They pick out certain counties where they believe they will get traction with their lawsuits." With prompting from Stossel, Beisner equated class action lawsuits with "extortion" because he claimed that corporations frequently settle class actions for fear of losing a big case in the county.

Adding to the media assault on the county, in 2004 the U.S. Chamber of Commerce quietly started its own newspaper there, the Madison/St. Clair Record, to publish stories about the local legal system. Most readers weren't aware of the connection to the chamber, which was later disclosed nationally by the Washington Post. The chamber also spent $1 million that same year on a national advertising campaign calling for legal restrictions, particularly on class action suits.

President Bush boosted the chamber's work by making an appearance in Madison County to highlight the county's allegedly negative legal climate a few days before Congress was set to vote on the class action bill in 2005. Rather than try to explain the complexities of class action law, Bush used the time-honored technique of making a business issue all about the plight of doctors. When Bush traveled to Madison County, he focused on "lawsuit abuse," which he claimed was driving doctors out of the area. Yet in late

2003, the Madison County Circuit clerk had released figures showing the court had seen only eleven medical malpractice verdicts between 1996 and 2002. Plaintiffs won only four of them—hardly the stuff of a crisis.

Even with Bush's help, though, the publicity generated about Madison County didn't have quite the impact as similar efforts in Mississippi, perhaps because the juries and judges in Madison County were mostly white and middle class. But the chamber and other tort reform groups had an ample supply of ammunition for their attack on the class action, thanks to the third essential component in such campaigns: the trial lawyers.

In 1991 Chicago attorney Daniel Edelman sued the Bank of Boston in Alabama state court on behalf of more than seven hundred thousand customers who alleged that the bank had improperly held on to their mortgage escrow payments for taxes and insurance longer than it should have. In the settlement, the bank refunded some of the escrow money to customers, none of whom got more than about $9. The settlement netted Edelman and the other lawyers more than $8 million in fees. But the fees weren't paid by the bank, as they generally are in such cases. They were paid by its customers, many of whom didn't even know they were plaintiffs in the case but whose accounts were debited for the legal fees. One of those customers, Maine real-estate broker Dexter Kamilewicz, was so outraged he brought his own class action against Edelman for allegedly defrauding him and the other class members. The settlement negotiated by Edelman had netted Kamilewicz $2.19 in back escrow interest, while costing him $91.33 in attorneys' fees. Kamilewicz's case was tossed out for lack of jurisdiction. Edelman later countersued him and other class members for $25 million and that case was also thrown out on jurisdictional grounds.

The Bank of Boston case wasn't the only time Edelman's class action settlements have been criticized. In 1999 Edelman's firm settled a case with Bank of America in which homeowners ripped off by the bank on mortgages got discount coupons of $70 to $135 that they could use only if they refinanced with the same bank within five years. If they hurried, they could trade in the coupons for cash—up to $7.50 each. For their trouble, the lawyers got a half million dollars for costs and fees.

So-called "coupon cases" like these led a judge in one of Edelman's cases to observe, "I can think of no plague worse than to have a court impose the likes of Daniel Edelman . . . on absent and unsuspecting members of a class." Boston University School of Law professor Susan Koniak, a class action expert, told the *Washington Post*'s Joe Stephens in 2000 that Edelman "should be thrown out of the bar." Consumer advocates railed against Edelman in the *Post*, with one calling him the "Darth Vader of class action settlements." Edelman, however, noted that he and other class action lawyers are like bounty hunters searching for outlaw corporations and collecting fees for the service; they expose wrongdoing and force change.

For tort reformers, Edelman's work made their job easier, putting a human face on all the potential abuses of the class action system. Even though he worked in Chicago, Edelman had filed nationwide class actions in obscure Alabama state courts, another "magic jurisdiction" that critics said was too friendly to plaintiffs. Edelman showed how class action litigation could be driven by lawyers rather than clients victimized by serious fraud. (Edelman is now king of "junk fax" litigation.) And best of all, even lefty consumer advocates and lots of trial lawyers thought he was a problem.

Even though the Bank of Boston case was settled nearly a decade earlier, members of Congress continued to brandish it in their calls for class action reform. Representative Bob Goodlatte (R-VA), who sponsored the class action reform bills in the House, invoked the case nearly every time he took the House floor on the subject.

As with much of the tort reform rhetoric, the anecdotal evidence offered up by the tort reformers about the evils of class actions was rarely representative of the whole system. For instance, while Madison County may have seen some class actions that should have been in federal court, the cases filed there were but a tiny portion of the class actions filed nationally. Every year, thousands of class actions are filed across the country, but the Madison County courthouse had 107 the year before Congress passed class action reform. The Illinois courts themselves had the ability to weed out the ones that really didn't belong there, which they eventually did, without any intervention from Congress. Yet the federal legislation was written as if the whole country looked like Madison County, even when some solid government research showed that, for the most part, the class action system was working as it should, allowing people with relatively small losses to band together and bring cases to court.

For instance, while the "coupon cases" made for good copy, they were not representative of the vast majority of class actions. A 2004 study done by the Federal Judicial Center, the research arm of the federal judiciary, found that in class actions terminated between July 1, 1999, and December 31, 2002, only 9 percent resulted in a coupon settlement, and of those cases, the majority also included some cash for the class and other relief along with the coupons.

The same study found that the typical class action resulted in a win of about $800,000 for class members, working out to $350 per class member in state court and $517 per member in cases in federal court. Earlier numbers from an FJC study in 1996 that looked at a broader range of cases found that 75 percent of the awards in class actions in federal court, after attorneys' fees, ranged from $645 to $3,341 per person—a decent amount of money, given that class action cases are brought specifically because the amounts of money involved in individual cases are too small to warrant an individual lawsuit.

A 2004 study published in the *Journal of Empirical Legal Studies* by Cornell University law professor Theodore Eisenberg and New York University law professor Geoffrey P. Miller found that the median recovery in a class action was $11.6 million, and the mean was $100 million, a level that had remained relatively stable over the past decade. And despite claims by critics that class action lawyers frequently gobbled up as much as 70 percent of settlements in fees, the study found that legal fees ranged from a modest 10 to 30 percent of the class award, and the percentage actually went down the bigger the award.

Nonetheless, during the years of debate over potential class action reform, reporters continued to crank out stories about consumers who got settlement checks for 34 cents while their lawyers reaped millions. Such news coverage rarely provided an in-depth look at the fraud and deceptive practices that lead to many class actions in the first place, and it showed just how little reporters really understood about the function of the class action in keeping business honest. "It is completely meaningless that the consumer got fifty dollars and the plaintiffs' lawyers got one million dollars," says Brian Wolfman, the director of Public Citizen's litigation group. "It's totally irrelevant. Is it critically important to put fifty dollars into the hands of consumer A? The real question is do you want the defendant to escape a $50 million or $100 million rip-off."

That's not to say that there haven't been some problems with class actions. Many of the coupon cases were bad news, but one reason they got used as much as they did is because corporate defendants like them so much. When companies like Blockbuster Video or Bank of America are caught fleecing customers, a friendly coupon settlement can help limit their liability on the cheap. By issuing coupons instead of cash, Blockbuster ensures that the class members have to plow their recoveries back into the same business that scammed them in the first place. Most settlement coupons also never get redeemed at all, so the additional settlement funds often revert back to the company.

More importantly, a national coupon settlement can wipe out other pending litigation. Generally, class action settlements apply to everyone similarly situated unless they make a conscious effort to "opt out," meaning that, for instance, anybody Blockbuster overcharged on late fees during the class period is covered by the agreement whether he knows it or not, even if it turns out that he has a particularly egregious case that could be worth a significant amount of money if tried on its own. Cheap coupon settlements allow companies to tell stockholders that their legal liability is under control. "Defendants generally favor class actions if it will help them settle cases they want to settle," says Yale Law School professor Peter Schuck.

A friendly class action settlement is so useful for companies with a big legal exposure for some sort of misdeed that corporations have an incentive to encourage plaintiff lawyers to file a class action that they can then settle for peanuts. Matthew Lee, director of the New York–based nonprofit Fair Finance Watch, says that when Citigroup was in negotiations with the FTC to settle longstanding charges of predatory lending, the company did not settle with the government without a private class action to settle as well; a settlement with the government wouldn't wipe out all the civil litigation against Citigroup elsewhere.

Lawyers in California ended up filing suit against Citigroup in February 2002 and settled it six months later when the FTC case settled for $215 million, one of the largest settlements in the agency's history. But, in fact, the settlement netted consumers only $120 each, and because of the private-lawsuit component, class members lost any right to defend themselves against foreclosure on their homes, a big problem in the predatory-lending cases, says Lee. The class action was settled for $25 million for the class and a whopping $25 million for the lawyers who seemed to do little more work than filing it.

In spite of the occasional abuses, though, the class action system had long had checks and balances in place to protect consumers from abusive settlements before Congress got involved. Judges have a tremendous amount of power over such settlements; they only need to be asked to exercise it. And more and more often, they are. Nonprofit advocacy groups like Public Citizen and Trial Lawyers for Public Justice represent consumers objecting to bad class action settlements, with a great deal of success, as do trial lawyers who've created a new subspecialty: representing objectors in class action settlements. They've received a fair amount of derision from parties on both sides of the table as "claim jumpers" who come in at the last minute and threaten to scuttle a settlement as a form of extorting a fee to go away, but many of them represent legitimate consumers and add another element of oversight to the process.

None of this, apparently, factored into Congress's decision to reform the class action system in 2005. And for all their harping on the coupon cases, members of Congress didn't even address them in the bill until pressed at the last minute by consumer groups.

In 1999 David McIntyre of Bessemer, Alabama, got a credit card offer in the mail from Household Bank stating that he was preapproved for a credit card with a $1,500 credit line. McIntyre worked sixteen hours a day assembling jewelry and as a clerk in a convenience store to support his family. In his off-hours, he worked as a preacher for the Bessemer Independent Church of God. Despite all his labors, McIntyre struggled to make ends meet. So when he got the credit card offer, he jumped at the chance to have a little float between paychecks.

He filled out the form and returned it to Household with the $19 application fee. But when his card came in the mail, the credit line was only $300, not the $1,500 he'd been promised. On top of that, the first $79 had to pay for the annual fee on the card, and the interest rate was very high. So McIntyre and his wife of thirty-two years decided not to use it. He put it in a desk drawer and forgot about it.

About a year later, McIntyre got a letter from a collection agency informing him that he owed $263 to Household Bank for a MasterCard bill. He thought the letter was a mistake because he'd never had a MasterCard. After he got another bill a few months later, he called the agency to inform it of its error. The agency, however, said that it wasn't an error. Household Bank had automatically activated the card and charged McIntyre the $79 annual fee, then tacked on late fees and interest, which the collection agency was trying to get him to cough up.

A call to Household confirmed that McIntyre had never bought anything with the card, but the collection agency continued to hound him. After a nightmarish back and forth, McIntyre told the collection agent that the bill was illegal. The agent dared him to go to court over the bill, saying, "Go ahead and find yourself a good $1,000-an-hour lawyer to sue over $263!"

McIntyre knew only one lawyer, a guy who defended insurance companies who had deposed him after he witnessed a car accident. The lawyer had given him his card, so McIntyre called him and told him his story. The attorney thought he had a good case and referred him to his friend Brian Warwick, an attorney in Florida who specializes in consumer class actions. Warwick filed the class action in Illinois federal court, where Household was headquartered, using the Illinois state consumer-protection laws. He would have preferred to file it in Alabama, where McIntyre lived, but Alabama's consumer-protection statute not only bans class actions but exempts financial institutions from suits over deceptive trade practices, so the case wasn't viable there.

Warwick learned that Household actually made a policy of charging people for the credit cards they never used, and as many as fifty thousand other low-income consumers were in similar straits as McIntyre. But U.S. District Judge Ruben Castillo, a Clinton appointee and former counsel for the Mexican American Legal Defense and Educational Fund, said that he was sympathetic to McIntyre's situation, but that the law required him to send the case to arbitration. The credit card agreement had an arbitration clause that barred users from suing the company in court. Castillo felt it was for the arbitrator to determine whether the agreement was enforceable against McIntyre. But the arbitration clause in the credit card contract only went in to effect once the card was used, and McIntyre had never used the card—a point the arbitrator recognized when he sent the case back to the judge. When McIntyre went back before the judge, Warwick says Castillo kept asking why this "old" case was still on his docket. In any event, Castillo ultimately did not certify a class action in the case, noting that the particular facts surrounding McIntyre's case were not typical to a class. McIntyre was able to settle his case separately with Household after Warwick threatened to refile the case in California, but fifty thousand other people were left without a cost-efficient legal procedure for correcting their credit records or getting their money back. (McIntyre's settlement is confidential.)

McIntyre's story may be the future of consumer class actions. The new federal law passed in 2005 forces most consumers to bring class actions into federal court, where consumer groups and plaintiff lawyers believe many judges are disinclined to certify classes. They point to the conservative judges who now make up most of the federal judiciary. (Eleven of the thirteen circuit courts have a Republican majority, and 55 percent of sitting federal judges were appointed by Republican presidents.) There's not much empirical evidence that federal judges are more ideologically hostile to plaintiffs or less inclined to certify a class action than state court judges are. A 2005 study by the Federal Judicial Center found that state and federal judges certify such cases at about the same rate and that both are equally likely to approve a settlement. The real issue with sending more class actions to federal court is one of resources and caseloads.

Federal judges have made it clear that they don't want cases like McIntyre's showing up on their dockets. Led by the late U.S. Supreme Court Chief Justice William Rehnquist, the Judicial Conference of the United States—the formal organization of federal judges—officially opposed the class action bill in letters to Congress, arguing that cases based on state law ought to stay in state court.

Ten years ago, in its long-range plan, the Judicial Conference stated emphatically: "If federal courts were to begin exercising, in the normal course, the broad range of subject-matter jurisdiction traditionally allocated to the states, they would lose both their distinctive nature and, due to burgeoning dockets, their ability to resolve fairly and efficiently those cases of clear national import and interest that properly fall within the scope of federal concern."

The federal judges' opposition to the class action bill is also partly based on money. In 2004 the federal courts saw a nearly 10 percent increase in new filings over the previous year. At the same time, the courts laid off nearly one thousand employees due to restricted budgets, and the judges have insisted that court backlogs will only grow with the new responsibilities for state class actions. At a House Budget hearing in 2004, Chief Judge John G. Heyburn II, chair of the Judicial Conference's budget committee, testified, "The courts' workload and the resources provided to handle that workload are headed in opposite directions."

Indeed, the Congressional Budget Office estimated that the new class action law would cost the federal courts about $7 million a year, not including the cost of the additional judges it suggested would be needed. Congress has not allocated any more money or created new judgeships to handle the new class action workload. State courts have far more judicial resources. There are only 877 federal judgeships, 44 of which were vacant as of the summer of 2006. By comparison, the state of California alone has nearly 1,500 state court judges, and that doesn't even include appellate court judges.

The federal courts' ability to manage the new class actions is one reason why critics of the bill suspect that it was designed simply to keep such cases out of court altogether. "This is a major effort by big corporations to transfer jurisdiction from state courts, where there is relatively quick resolution of people's claims, to the dark hole of the federal judiciary, which doesn't want them," says West Virginia State Supreme Court of Appeals Judge Larry Starcher, whose court lost authority for many class actions under the new law. Starcher notes that the West Virginia state courts aren't exactly flush, but he believes they are much better equipped to handle the state class actions than the federal court. "As a trial court judge, I tried about twenty thousand individual asbestos cases. I know a little about mass litigation," he says.

Warwick has filed cases in both federal and state courts and says the difference for consumers is like night and day. "A federal court judge's time is already in such high demand. A state court judge's day is full of crap," he says. "He's got a divorce case, a meth lab sentencing, car accidents. So you give him a $5-million case against a big corporation, and he's like hey, this is interesting. He'll take the time to listen to what you have to say."

CHAPTER TEN

Slip and Call: Merchants' (Irrational)
Fear of Getting Sued

When President George Bush stood in the Rose Garden and signed the Class Action Fairness Act in February 2005, at his side was a woman named Hilda Bankston, who had come all the way from Fayette, Mississippi, to witness the event. Bankston had been a prominent figure in the debate over class actions, testifying before Congress twice and appearing at the president's economic summit in December 2004 for a session about "the high cost of lawsuit abuse."

Bankston made for good copy. She had immigrated from Guatemala in 1958 and joined the Marines, where she met Mitch Bankston, a navy seaman. They married in 1964, and Mitch went to pharmacy school at Ole Miss, while Bankston worked as a seamstress. As she told it, the Bankstons moved to Fayette in 1971 and bought a local drugstore. They lived the American dream until one day in 1999, when a band of greedy trial lawyers named the Bankston drugstore in a mass action against American Home Products, the manufacturer of the diet drugs Pondimin and Redux, better known as the "fen" in fen-phen.

In her congressional testimony, Bankston said that the lawsuit caused her husband a great deal of distress and anxiety over how his customers would think of them. Three weeks after being named in the suit, Mitch, whom Bankston said had been perfectly healthy, died of a massive heart attack. She said she was forced to sell the pharmacy soon afterward, but "even though I no longer own the drugstore, I still get named as a defendant time and again."

Bankston thus secured her spot as a star player in the tort reform movement. Hers became a popular anecdote for reporters chronicling the alleged excesses of the litigation system, especially in Mississippi. Bankston appeared on *60 Minutes,* MSNBC, and Fox News. She was interviewed by the *New York Times,* the *National Law Journal,* the *Washington Times,* and by her own state press corps. The news stories on Bankston generally began like the one in the Jackson *Clarion-Ledger's* June 2001 series, "Hitting the Jackpot in Mississippi Courtrooms": "Former Fayette pharmacy owner Hilda Bankston lost track of how many times she has been sued since 1999."

As she would do repeatedly in the years to come, Bankston detailed the indignities of being sued: the book work, the records searches, the expense of hiring staff to fill in for her while she was "dragged into court on numerous occasions to testify." In her July 2002 congressional testimony, Bankston said, "I have spent many sleepless nights wondering if my business would survive the tidal wave of lawsuits cresting over it."

She then explained that her predicament arose because of a quirk in Mississippi law that allowed plaintiffs to bring suit against any large corporation in any jurisdiction in the state, rather than federal, court so long as they had a legitimate local defendant and a local plaintiff. In drug cases, the defendant was usually a pharmacy, and Bankston's store was the only pharmacy in the county. So lawyers would name Bankston Drugstore as a defendant to keep lawsuits in state court rather than federal court, which was thought to be more hostile to plaintiffs.

Signing up Bankston as a tort reform lobbyist was a coup by the big corporate interests backing the class action bill in Congress. The companies already had on the payroll roughly five lobbyists for every U.S. senator in their pursuit of limits on class actions, according to a study done by the nonprofit group Public Citizen. Big companies organized through the U.S. Chamber of Commerce's Institute for Legal Reform spent $24 million on lobbying just in 2004 to pass the Class Action Fairness Act.

Their pleas for lawsuit relief though were not especially sympathetic. Take, for instance, Wal-Mart, which was defending dozens of class actions from its own employees who claimed the company had locked them in stores, denied them lunch breaks, and forced them to work overtime off the clock. Or there were the pharmaceutical giants like Bristol-Myers Squibb, facing legal charges that it engaged in price fixing for baby formula (the case ultimately settled).

These companies needed a sympathetic victim, particularly one who could represent small business and espouse the tort reform activists' longstanding claim that small-business owners are at risk of bankruptcy because of frivolous lawsuits. The problem with that strategy is that very few small-business owners ever go bankrupt because of a frivolous class action, much less a meritorious one. So tort reform groups have had a hard time finding sympathetic spokespeople. (Another "small-business owner" who appeared with Bankston at the White House economic summit was Robert Nardelli, the CEO of Home Depot.)

Bankston, though, had it all: she was an immigrant, a small-business owner, and, best of all, she could argue compellingly that trial lawyers had killed her husband. Not surprisingly, tort reform proponents seized on her as the quintessential victim of lawsuit abuse. She was recruited by the Civil Justice Reform Group, an industry tort reform group, and flown to Washington by Marsha Rabiteau, the general counsel and vice president of the Hartford Financial Services Group in Connecticut. Before coming to Hartford, Rabiteau had been the in-house counsel for the Dow Chemical Company, where she dealt with the company's silicone breast implant litigation. The group paid the DC PR firm Porter Novelli to train Bankston in the fine art of media courtship and to prep her with talking points for her congressional testimony. The effect was powerful.

Over and over again, members of Congress held up Bankston's story as proof positive of the evils of litigation. Representative James Sensenbrenner (R-WI) wrote op-eds claiming that "hard-working Americans like Mrs. Bankston are being victimized—many even bankrupted—each day by plaintiff attorneys shopping for the county court system most likely to pay out big money."

Bankston's testimony was quoted by everyone from members of Congress to conservative think-tank researchers to U.S. District Court Judge Harvey Bartle III, the federal judge overseeing all the federal fen-phen litigation. Her story even appeared in Spanish on the White House website. And her populist fame helped furnish a political victory on the class action bill. The bill had been opposed by many Democrats, but at least one critical vote on the bill came as a result of Bankston's testimony. Senator Dianne Feinstein (D-CA), one of the nonlawyers on the Senate Judiciary Committee, said on the Senate floor in July 2004 that Bankston's testimony had persuaded her to support the legislation. "I use this case because, of all the hearings that have been held in the Judiciary Committee in twelve years, this woman made a profound impression on me as I sat there hour after hour and listened to the testimony," she said.

With her grandmotherly demeanor and spunky one-liners, Bankston deftly avoided any critical questioning. Even the trial lawyers left her alone. And yet Bankston's story withers under cross-examination.

Start with her repeated claims that she continued to get named as a defendant in lawsuits even after she sold the drugstore in Fayette. At least one part of that story is true. According to the Mississippi secretary of state's office, Bankston did sell the pharmacy in November 1999, about a month before the end of the big fen-phen trial in the case that allegedly killed her husband. Bankston filed her last quarterly report for Bankston-Rexall Drugs—the corporate owner for the Bankston drugstore—in March 2000, and the state dissolved the corporation for lack of activity in October 2001.

Strangely, though, in all of Bankston's public appearances and media spots, not a single reporter or member of Congress has ever asked her why all those lawyers would waste their time and money suing a widow who no longer owned the county drugstore. Everyone, it seemed, including the trial lawyers themselves, were willing to believe the worst about lawyers.

In the spring of 2005, I made a trip to the Jefferson County courthouse and attempted to count up the number of lawsuits filed against Bankston before she sold the pharmacy. The court records are difficult to cull. The courthouse has no computerized docketing system. Instead, legal records are entered in longhand into big leather docket books by court clerks, and the files are stored next door in "the dungeon," the decaying old jail. No doubt some of the names have been left out when there are multiple parties in a case. But in my search of the court records, I came up with only a single suit against Bankston-Rexall Drugs: the fen-phen case. That case contained more than eight hundred plaintiffs, but only a handful of them were from Jefferson County and had filled their prescriptions at Bankston's store, meaning that Bankston's role in document production would likely have been limited to turning over a small handful of prescriptions to plaintiff attorneys.

My research did not reveal anything indicating that Bankston was even deposed in that case, much less called to testify in court. In fact, despite putting in calls to numerous plaintiff lawyers in Mississippi and Texas who handled mass drug cases in Jefferson County, I have yet to find a single one who deposed Bankston in a lawsuit or put her on the witness stand in court. That's not to say there might not be one I've missed, but neither Bankston nor her lawyer offered any specific examples to prove me wrong when I spoke with them.

Bankston-Rexall may have been named in a mass-tort suit involving the drug Propulsid, at about the time when the store was being transferred to the new owner, but after that, lawsuits against Jefferson County's drugstore were filed against Bankston Drugs LLC, a different corporate entity created in October 1999 and owned by someone else. To check my research, I asked Bankston's lawyer, Luke Dove, for supporting evidence that Bankston had been sued repeatedly even after she no longer owned the store. He offered no examples of specific lawsuits and declined to comment further.

My numbers square with research done for the pro–tort reform Manhattan Institute's Center for Legal Reform, which commissioned a study of Jefferson County's docket for a report on magnet courts published in April 2003. In 1999 the small rural county had only 178 civil complaints filed in its courthouse, which would have included everything from credit-card collections to car-crash cases to big multiparty drug litigation. According to the MI study, of those cases, only three were mass actions filed against out-of-state pharmaceutical companies that would have also needed to name Bankston's drugstore to keep the cases out of federal court.

To be sure, Jefferson County has played host to a huge amount of litigation relative to its size, but the high-water mark came the year *after* Bankston sold her pharmacy, in 2000, when the FDA removed three different widely prescribed drugs from the market. While only 166 civil complaints were filed that year (as well as 480 identical asbestos suits filed to enforce a settlement in an earlier case), the Manhattan Institute found 17 mass-tort drug cases with more than 3,000 plaintiffs in Jefferson County in 2000. All of those cases were likely to have named the local pharmacy, but the vast majority, if not all of them, were filed against Bankston's successor.

Tort reformers have actively marketed Bankston as the exemplar of the compelling victim. They have sought to apply each and every example of "lawsuit abuse" to Bankston's case, leading to some serious distortions and outright falsehoods in the media. One common piece of misinformation is the notion that Bankston faced financial ruin at the hands of greedy plaintiff lawyers. In August 2001 the *New York Times* reported that although Bankston and her late husband had not been found liable in any drug lawsuit, "they have incurred sizable legal expenses." In 2004, after the White House economic summit, the *Sacramento Bee* went so far as to report that Bankston had said that the drugstore she and her husband owned went bankrupt after it was sued as part of a class action against manufacturers of fen-phen.

It's not too hard to see where these ideas come from. In September

2004 the Federal Trade Commission hosted a workshop on protecting con-sumer interests in class actions. James Wootton, the former director of the U.S. Chamber of Commerce's Institute for Legal Reform, invoked Bankston's story in his pitch for the class action bill pending in Congress. He claimed that Bankston was "driven out of business after being named in numerous lawsuits" over defective drugs, and that she had been forced "to spend thousands of dollars in legal fees."

Reporters have repeated such allegations as fact starting almost imme-diately after Bankston arrived on the national scene, but few explained that her drugstore did not go bankrupt, nor was it ever found liable in any law-suit. And what reporters and members of Congress never seemed to realize is that Bankston and her store were *never* at risk of bankruptcy from any of the lawsuits. Mississippi state law generally required that a manufacturer pay the legal expenses for a retailer sued for selling its allegedly defective product. That meant that the drug companies were obligated to pick up the tab for both Bankston's defense and any jury verdicts or settlements against the pharmacy.

In a brief conversation I had with Bankston on the phone in March 2005, she actually volunteered, "I never knew how much my attorney got paid, because he never told me." She said her lawyer was paid by the drug companies. "My insurance company never had to do anything," she said. "It was just a hassle." Dove, the attorney for Bankston-Rexall, confirmed that the pharmacy had been indemnified by the drug manufacturers. Despite all the hype, Bankston and Bankston-Rexall never paid a dime as a result of lawsuits, not even in legal fees.

Bankston's story did highlight a problem that had arisen in Mississippi, but what wasn't included in the tale of woe before Congress and the media is that the state of Mississippi pretty easily addressed the excesses at work in the court system, without any help from Congress and without making serious compromises to its residents' constitutional rights.

Mississippi is one of the few places in the country that does not have a class action rule in its civil procedure rules. Instead, it has a joinder rule, which allows judges to aggregate similar cases for expediency and economy. The less restrictive joinder rule was attractive to plaintiff lawyers looking to bring large mass actions on drugs like fen-phen and Propulsid. All they had to do was find a few local plaintiffs and name the local drugstore that dis-pensed the prescriptions, and they could bring large-scale lawsuits in small rural counties rather than federal court.

Initially, when the first wave of these suits landed in Jefferson County,

Circuit Judge Lamar Pickard was receptive to linking them together, in the face of the difficulties of trying all the cases individually. But later, as the lawsuits poured in, and he came under intense criticism for his decision to let several large drug cases proceed, Pickard changed his tune. In July 2001, more than six months before Bankston's first congressional testimony on the class action bill, Pickard stated from the bench that he would be giving much greater scrutiny to mass torts with large numbers of out-of-state plaintiffs. His ruling, and subsequent refusal to allow new mass actions in his court unless all the plaintiffs were from the county, helped put a damper on the flood of litigation.

Then, in April 2002, the Mississippi Supreme Court extended further protections to pharmacies by covering them under what's known as the "learned intermediary" rule, meaning that people injured by a defective prescription drug can't sue their pharmacy if the prescription was properly and legally filled. These two steps essentially closed the door on any more big drug lawsuits against drugstores like the one Bankston had owned. Yet Bankston continued to lobby in favor of the congressional bill to limit class actions for everyone.

As late as December 2004, Bankston claimed publicly that she was still spending countless hours searching for pharmacy records in response to subpoenas from greedy plaintiff lawyers, as she had been complaining for the past three years. A year earlier, though, the FBI had subpoenaed copies of those same records from Bankston in an investigation into fraudulent fen-phen claims. As it turned out, Bankston didn't have them. The records had been conveyed with the store when Bankston sold it in 1999.

As perfect as Bankston may have seemed as a sympathetic victim of so-called lawsuit abuse, no one focused on a few omissions that would have undermined her effectiveness had they come out during the debate over the class action bill.

At the time Bankston appeared in the Rose Garden with Bush decrying the high cost of lawsuit abuse, she was the plaintiff in a lawsuit against United Mississippi Bank and a state senator who worked at the bank.

Bankston alleged in the lawsuit (originally filed in Jefferson County in 1999) that the bank had wrongfully canceled the credit life insurance on a loan her husband procured from the bank. When she tried to make a claim on the insurance after her husband died, Bankston learned that the bank had canceled the policy and that she was on the hook for $12,686, the balance of the loan. In her lawsuit, Bankston not only demanded recovery of the loan balance but another $500,000 in actual damages and $25 million in punitive damages for wrongfully denying her credit life claim. The case, which was refiled in the court in Jackson, was still pending in 2006. It's just the kind of punitive damages claim case that tort reformers love to hold up as outrageous and which the tort reform agenda, if ever fully materialized, might stamp out altogether (and has in some states).

When I first called Bankston in March 2005 to arrange a meeting in Fayette, she seemed perfectly happy to meet with me. But by the time I arrived in Jefferson County a few weeks later to ask her about all of this, Bankston had clammed up. In a brief phone conversation canceling our meeting, she alluded to the fact that a lot of people in this debate have been used for political purposes, that the president signed a good bill, and that if I wanted to know the answers to questions like who paid for her travel expenses on all her trips to Washington that I would have to work for my money. Then she hung up.

The plight of the small-business owner, at the mercy of greedy lawyers and irresponsible plaintiffs, has been a staple of tort reform rhetoric for many years. The National Federation of Independent Business (NFIB), the premiere small-business lobby, has been a reliable and vociferous ally in the fight to restrict lawsuits. Its members routinely traipse up to Capitol Hill to testify about the evils of lawsuit abuse and its threat to their livelihoods. As with Hilda Bankston, they put a mom-and-pop face on an issue that otherwise would be dominated by big chemical companies like Monsanto or oil giants like Exxon Mobil Corporation, whose financial interests are much more threatened in big tort lawsuits. Like a mantra, NFIB insists repeatedly that small businesses are only one lawsuit away from bankruptcy.

One of the talking points that NFIB distributes to its members on lawsuit abuse says, "With the average small-business owner's salary being less than $50,000 per year, it's easy to see how one frivolous lawsuit can wipe out an entire small business." Ohio NFIB director Roger Geiger told the House Judiciary Committee in 1999, "Our members tell us that being sued is one of the most terrifying experiences a small-business owner can have. It is even more frightening for the smallest of the small businesses, who fear being put out of business for good with one lawsuit."

But much of the rhetoric from the small businesses is a long way from reality.

In 2004, Karen Harned, executive director of the NFIB Legal Foundation, testified in support of a bill "limiting lawsuit abuse" before the House Judiciary Committee. Her main evidence in support of the bill wasn't a mountain of empirical data documenting all those wiped-out small companies. It wasn't even actual lawsuits that plagued her members, but the "'fear' of getting sued, even if a suit is not filed." She noted that a recent NFIB poll found that about half of small-business owners surveyed either were "very concerned" or "somewhat concerned" about the possibility of being sued. This, she claimed, created a climate of fear that was having a negative impact on small businesses.

Harned's testimony may well mark the first time that a trade association has complained to Congress about the effectiveness of its very own PR. Fear of lawsuits, after all, is one of the emotions that NFIB has spent millions of dollars promoting over the past 10 or 15 years. The group has sponsored national TV advertising warning about the threats of products liability lawsuits and continually updates its own members on alleged victims like Bankston to support a legislative agenda that includes caps on punitive damages, limits on obesity lawsuits against fast-food companies, and a host of restrictions on medical malpractice lawsuits.

Harned testified that for the really small-business owner, with five employees or less, "the problem is the $5,000 and $10,000 settlements, not the million-dollar verdicts." Harned said that the settlements themselves are costly, but mostly because they drive up the cost of liability insurance premiums, and that occasionally the companies pay them out of their own pockets so as to avoid increases in their premiums.

Despite all of the NFIB's ominous warnings that its members are but one lawsuit away from going out of business, the group has rarely been able to find a compelling witness to testify before Congress that his or her business had actually been shut down by a lawsuit. The truth is, few companies are ever put out of business because of a lawsuit. Harvard Law professor Elizabeth Warren and Jay Westbrook, a bankruptcy expert at the University of Texas School of Law, created a database of nearly 3,300 business bankruptcy cases filed across the country. The database covered a broad cross section of companies, but they are mostly small firms. Westbrook and Warren then attempted to break out the reasons the companies filed bankruptcy.

After combing through a subset of 386 bankruptcy cases, they could come up with only three that included a tort claim. Warren and Westbrook acknowledge that the number could be higher, given the difficulties of iden-tifying tort claims in the data. But their research led them to the conclusion that very few small firms went bankrupt because of a tort lawsuit. "It's quite rare," says Westbrook. "We find that tort claims are a pretty darn small portion of the claims." He is suspicious of the small-business lobby's complaints that it is plagued by hundreds of extortionlike settlements de-manding $5,000 or $10,000, because if it were true, he says, the data would also show a whole bunch of big judgments out there that did put people under.

Nor are big companies running from the courthouse's civil chambers to the bankruptcy division of litigation. UCLA School of Law professor Lynn LoPucki has created a database of corporate bankruptcies going back twenty-five years that includes all the reasons the companies filed and how they fared once they were reorganized. A quick search of the database turns up thirteen bankruptcies related to tort claims (eleven of which stem from asbestos claims), barely 2 percent of all the filings in the database.

Companies that go into bankruptcy over tort claims also aren't gasping their last breath. To the contrary, LoPucki's data show that companies that file bankruptcy because of a tort judgment generally survive, largely because they use bankruptcy to get out of the judgment. Most companies in bank-ruptcy for other reasons are back in bankruptcy five years later, he says. LoPucki observes that virtually all of the asbestos companies that filed Chapter 11 survived. "Bankruptcy discharges the tort judgment, and man-agers never miss a paycheck," he says.

In 2003 University of Texas law professor Charles Silver, who, like many academics has done work for plaintiff attorneys, published a study on class actions and attempted to catalog the number of firms put out of busi-ness or into bankruptcy from a class action. After extensive research, he couldn't find a single one. Many companies, Silver discovered, used class ac-tions as a way of avoiding liability, because they could put a lid on future lawsuits. But the main explanation for so few belly flops, he concluded, was simple: insurance. Most businesses today have some sort of liability insur-ance to pay both the legal costs of defending a suit and any settlement or judgment. Most of the time, even when successful plaintiffs get a big verdict against a company, they would prefer to settle for what's available from the insurance policy than to put the company into bankruptcy and get nothing. Other researchers have made similar findings. A 1991 study by Stanford University law professor Janet Cooper Alexander noted that insurance money paid about 50 percent to 80 percent of settlements in shareholder lawsuits against public companies.

That's not to say that small companies never lose at trial or that companies on the losing end of lawsuits never file bankruptcy. They do, but often times they do it to escape pending litigation or adverse judgments they don't want to pay. Asbestos companies are the classic example. More than twenty million people were exposed to serious levels of asbestos between 1946 and 1980, causing between eight and ten thousands deaths a year from asbestos-related cancer well into the twenty-first century. The related lawsuits created a flood of liability for the companies that manufactured and used the dangerous fire retardant.

In 1982 Johns Manville started a trend when it filed bankruptcy as a way of halting thousands of legitimate lawsuits from sick workers who contracted asbestos-related diseases, many from working in World War II shipyards. The company was getting hit over and over again with large punitive-damage awards in court because of conduct that one judge deemed "reckless disregard for human life." Johns Manville had hidden the dangers of asbestos for decades, while making little effort to protect workers and their families who were exposed to it, and juries were scandalized. Bankruptcy court offered a friendlier venue for settling the outstanding claims.

With $2 billion in assets and twenty-five thousand employees, the company was the largest American industrial company to ever file Chapter 11 at the time—and one of the first financially healthy firms to do so. The move sent scores of other asbestos firms to bankruptcy court for similar reasons. Seventy-eight asbestos companies filed bankruptcy between 1982 and 2002. What's more, in 1994 Congress actually *encouraged* asbestos companies to file bankruptcy by creating special protections for them in the bankruptcy code that would allow them to escape future liability for asbestos claims that hadn't even been filed yet. The legislation helped accelerate the bankruptcy filings.

But asbestos litigation is in a category of its own because of the huge number of actual victims, the severity of the injuries, and the conduct of the companies. As LoPucki notes, "That's not one lawsuit. That's lots of lawsuits." Indeed, at the time it filed Chapter 11, Johns Manville alone estimated that it would face some fifty-two thousand asbestos-related lawsuits over the coming years.

When lawsuits do put companies out of business, they are often performing a public service. A recent example is the California-based Bryco Arms, one of the nation's makers of "Saturday Night Specials." The company has long specialized in making junk guns that sell cheaply, starting at $50. In 1994 seven-year-old Brandon Maxwell was shot in the face with a Bryco Arms pistol when his babysitter attempted to unload it. The gun was defectively designed so that a user had to take the safety off to take out the bullets. When the twenty-year-old babysitter tried to unload the gun, he accidentally shot Maxwell, who was sitting across the room. Maxwell ended up with massive brain injuries and is now confined to a wheelchair. Maxwell's family sued Bryco Arms for making a defective product and won a landmark judgment against the company for $50 million, which was reduced by the judge to $24 million. The jury award came down on May 13, 2003. On May 14 Bryco filed for bankruptcy.

Richard Jennings, the owner of the company, foreshadowed the move in 1999 when he told *Business Week* that his company and others like it would deal with any lawsuits through bankruptcy. "They can file for bankruptcy, dissolve, go away until the litigation passes by, then reform and build guns to the new standard—if there is a new standard."

He's living up to his prediction: in 2005 a former plant manager for Bryco, with no discernable assets, bought Bryco out of bankruptcy using funds from a company owned by Bryco's former president, who is also Jennings ex-wife.

For all the complaints about the threat of litigation to small businesses, there's plenty of evidence that small businesses actually need some of the very measures in the legal system they have actively sought to restrict, particularly class actions. That's what some of the nation's car dealers discovered in the mid-1990s, when they discovered that they weren't getting their fair allocation of Hondas because some of their larger competitors were bribing company executives to get the choice cars. The small dealers banded together in a class action lawsuit against Honda, and the case was settled in 1998 for $330 million, with Honda dramatically changing the way it handed out inventory.

Small retailers have been duking it out with credit card giants Master-Card and Visa, alleging that they've been bilked out of millions of dollars in excessive fees. In 2005 Michael Schumann, the co-owner of a Minnesota furniture store, initiated a class action against Visa and MasterCard alleging that the companies are a monopoly that rip off merchants on credit card processing fees, which total nearly $30 billion a year. The only way Schumann was able to take on the credit card giants was through the class action mechanism, which allowed him to sue on behalf of all small businesses nationally, making the case potentially profitable enough to convince one of the nation's wealthiest law firms to front the many millions needed to bring the case. (The case was still pending at press time.)

All this is not to say that small businesses aren't plagued by the occasional frivolous lawsuit. For example, in California in 2003, three lawyers resigned from the bar after being accused of shaking down thousands of small car repair shops and restaurants, many owned by immigrants, with frivolous lawsuits. Relying on a quirk in California's consumer-protection law, the lawyers allegedly created their own consumer group to serve as a plaintiff in the cases, and would file suits against small firms that had been issued citations by the state for health violations or other minor legal infractions, and then demand a few thousand dollars to go away. The state attorney general and the state bar association eventually investigated and cracked down on the lawyers, shattering their operation.

The California cases were extreme because of the scale, in part due to the uniqueness of the law there, but such cases are not unheard of elsewhere in the country. For a small-business owner, they are a problem. So it would make sense for NFIB to push countermeasures, like better policing by state bar authorities and attorneys general. Instead, these groups are proposing a different set of remedies, primarily caps on punitive damages and loser-pays statutes. Far from assisting the little guys, such proposals only threaten their ability to compete against corporate conglomerates.

Take caps on punitive damages. Why this cap is such a priority for tiny businesses is something of a mystery, because small businesses rarely face punitive-damage awards. And punitive damages are, of course, never part of the $5,000 settlement that Harned says is her members' biggest concern.

The real beneficiaries of a cap on punitive damages are not the local minimarts, but huge corporations like Exxon that frequently see punitive damages tacked on to jury awards for especially egregious conduct, such as the *Exxon Valdez* oil spill in 1989. Small businesses are essentially using their political cache as the romanticized foundation of American enterprise to do the dirty work of less sympathetic corporate polluters and other global corporations. What the small-business owners don't seem to realize is that what's good for corporate America isn't necessarily good for mom and pop. The legal system offers small businesses the possibility of a level playing field when they encounter anticompetitive behavior from larger companies (think Microsoft). Lawsuits are often the only way for small companies to fight back against antitrade violations, contract fraud, deceptive trade practices, and other tactics large companies use to crush their up-start competitors.

Furniture store owner and class action plaintiff Michael Schumann il-lustrates the paradox at work in the thinking of small businesses when it comes to "lawsuit abuse." He loves his own lawyer and is deeply impressed with the law firm's strategizing on his behalf, and he fully understands that without the ability to bring a class action, he would have absolutely no re-course against the rip-offs by Visa and MasterCard. Nonetheless, he still believes in the need for restrictions on lawsuits. In an interview, he rattles off several examples of class actions he thinks are frivolous and points to the recently documented fraud in mass silicosis litigation. The difference, he says, is that "our case is a very valid case. It's not a sham case."

But taken to their logical extension, the measures pushed by small-business lobbying groups show that restrictions on alleged "sham cases" have a deleterious effect on the very legitimate cases that small businesses often need to bring. Houston businessman Walt Shofner found out about that the hard way.

A few years ago, if you had asked Shofner whether he supported limits on lawsuits, he would have said yes. But in 2000 Shofner discovered the re-ality behind the PR campaign. His company designed software for insurance companies and had recently beaten out a larger competitor on a bid to up-grade software at the Prudential Insurance Company of America, in New Jersey. Afterward, the competitor, Computer Sciences Corporation (CSC), accused his firm of violating a nondisclosure contract and asked American Express and Prudential to cancel their contracts with Shofner, which they did. Shofner sued, arguing that CSC, a corporate giant with nearly $10 bil-lion in revenues in 2000, was simply trying to squelch the competition. The jury agreed and awarded Shofner $8 million in punitive damages.

But after the jury announced its verdict, the judge declared that he had to reduce the award to $200,000. In 1995, Governor George W. Bush had signed into law a cap on punitive damages similar to the one groups like NFIB have pushed nationally. It left the judge no other choice. Shofner—as well as the jury—was shocked. Fred Kronz, one of the jurors in the case, says he couldn't believe the news. Kronz says the jurors took their job seri-ously and spent a lot of time trying to come up with an adequate punish-ment for CSC, which they believed was clearly in the wrong. During the trial, everyone in the courtroom knew about the damage cap except the ju-rors, who learned of it only after they announced their verdict, making their deliberations seem like a charade, says Kronz.

The decision essentially killed that part of Shofner's software business. He says, "CSC had no trouble paying me off. They got two or three million dollars of revenue after I left [the other firms]. I got zapped for chump change by my competition. They have almost a monopoly on the software now." Shofner's now a vocal critic of lawsuit restrictions. "Tort reform assumes that all plaintiffs are crooks. But if a case gets far enough to get an award, that's not frivolous. I was a Republican. I guess I still am. But I've seen the light." Thanks to the tort reforms passed in Texas, Shofner says, "Any small business person in Texas is at risk."

CHAPTER ELEVEN

The Hypocritical Oath: When Doctors Double as Tort-Reform Lobbyists

When he went on strike in January 2003, Dr. Robert Zaleski earned his fifteen minutes of fame. The Wheeling, West Virginia, orthopedic surgeon was one of two dozen surgeons to walk off the job to protest his state's high costs of malpractice insurance. Arguing that "frivolous lawsuits" were driving up insurance premiums and forcing physicians to leave the state, Zaleski and his colleagues threatened to stay out for thirty days unless the legislature passed a bill that would cap pain-and-suffering awards in such suits at $250,000. As the walkout turned into a national story, Zaleski became one of its most visible faces, making the rounds of TV news shows and telling CNN, "I would certainly jump in front of a bus if I could to continue to serve my patients as I have for twenty-three years." Just a few weeks later, Zaleski's mug shot appeared with those of five other doctors in the *New York Times Magazine,* where he claimed to be "on the brink" of moving out of state because of high insurance rates and lawsuits.

Zaleski and his colleagues are the leading edge of a much broader movement. Since 2001, across the country, doctors like him have been telling reporters, legislators, and even their patients that frivolous lawsuits are driving up insurance costs and forcing doctors out of practice and out of state, threatening access to care. They've mobilized around state legislation to limit malpractice lawsuits and linked arms with President Bush and Republicans in Congress who have been pushing similar bills in Washington. Indeed, Zaleski himself was even personally invited to attend a speech President Bush delivered in Scranton, Pennsylvania, where

Bush railed against the threat to patient care posed by out-of-control law-suits.

Between 1987 and 2002, according to the West Virginia Board of Medicine, patients filed fourteen lawsuits against Zaleski, eight of which re-sulted in payouts that together came to $1.7 million. By contrast, according to a Public Citizen study, only 1 percent of the state's doctors made five or more malpractice payouts over the decade 1993–2003. And while Zaleski says the settlement figures are misleading because they also include defense costs, his record is hardly squeaky clean. In a 1983 lawsuit (one *not* among the fourteen reported to the Board of Medicine), he admitted in a deposi-tion to being addicted to prescription painkillers for a substantial part of the time that he was operating on people in the early 1980s. Not only was he a drug addict, but to maintain his Percodan habit, Zaleski allegedly wrote pre-scriptions for other local addicts, who filled them and kicked back some pills to the doctor, according to court documents that include copies of the prescriptions and depositions from some of the addicts.

Even though a suspicious police officer reported him to the state med-ical board, Zaleski was never disciplined by his fellow physicians. (In a 2003 interview, he told me that he does not remember the specifics of the case, and while he acknowledges a past substance-abuse problem, he insists that he has been clean and sober for more than twenty years.) Given this his-tory, the real scandal may not be how high Zaleski's insurance premiums are, but the fact that he can get insurance at all.

Zaleski's malpractice record may have been extreme, but it was not un-usual among the doctors who walked out of West Virginia hospitals that January. According to a *Charleston Gazette* report, nine of the eighteen doc-tors striking at Wheeling Hospital, including Zaleski, had cost their insurers more than $6 million in malpractice settlements and judgments. At least some of the suits don't seem to merit the adjective *frivolous,* including one in which a surgeon cut into his patient's stomach wall during surgery, causing a massive, fatal infection. Indeed, a number of those doctors involved in the protest movement include former drug addicts, felons, doctors whose li-censes have been revoked, and many, many others who get sued a lot—and far more than most of their colleagues.

Few physicians angry about malpractice lawsuits and high insurance have checkered histories. Many ethical and responsible doctors say the sys-tem invites frivolous litigation, subjecting them to considerable hassle and anxiety. But even Congress's nonpartisan investigative arm, the Govern-ment Accountability Office (GAO), has concluded that there's little evidence to back the striking doctors' main claim that lawsuits are forcing many of them to abandon the practice of medicine or to avoid high-risk procedures. While there's no doubt that malpractice insurance premiums increased significantly in the early part of the new millennium—about 30 percent to 40 percent annually between 2000 and 2003—the increase is largely due to the ailing stock market and poor business practices in a virtually unregulated industry. As a result, there's no reason to think that capping jury awards would bring down premiums, a fact the insurance industry itself acknowledges.

Robert E. White Jr., president of First Professional Insurance Company, the leading medical malpractice insurer in Florida, told the *Palm Beach Post* in January 2003, "No responsible insurer can cut its rates after a [medical malpractice] bill passes."

That's one reason why the doctors' protests aren't about good policy. They're about good politics. Although the malpractice strikes over the past few years look like a natural outgrowth of physician frustration, they are, in fact, the product of a sophisticated lobbying campaign coordinated by Republican operatives and underwritten by business groups with little interest in the practice of medicine.

Limits on malpractice suits have proved to be a powerful inducement to the medical community at a time when frustration with managed care has been alienating this once reliably Republican constituency. (Lawsuit-prone doctors have proven especially eager to lead the crusade against trial lawyers.) To that end, GOP leaders made malpractice lawsuits a pivotal issue for the 2004 presidential campaign. With health-care costs exploding on its watch, the GOP was eager to shift blame onto the Democrats and John Edwards, their trial lawyer vice-presidential candidate. Doctors, who enjoy great credibility among voters, were key to linking rising health-care costs to frivolous medical lawsuits and rallying their senior citizen patients to the cause.

Beyond the electoral politics, though, doctors have served as enormously effective front men for the broader corporate campaign to restrict lawsuits. White-coated physicians have provided reassuring cover for any number of legislative measures that have nothing to do with health care and would never fly on their own. Here's how it works: with their protests and complaints about insurance premiums, doctors get bills to restrict malpractice lawsuits on the table in Congress and state legislatures. Then Republicans slip in legal protections for errant drug companies, the insurance industry, and other corporations.

For instance, a malpractice bill passed by the House in March 2003—and again in July 2005—with backing from the American Medical Association would completely exempt not just doctors but also drug companies, medical-device manufacturers, nursing-home operators, and HMOs from punitive-damage awards for reckless conduct in private lawsuits. Using doctors to advance broader tort reform has been a brilliant strategy for both corporations and the GOP. The only losers are injured people who don't realize what's been lost until it's too late.

The doctors who walked off the job in West Virginia were primarily from the Wheeling and Weirton areas of West Virginia, right in the heart of steel country and on the borders of Ohio and Pennsylvania—the only solidly Republican section of historically Democratic West Virginia. Nestled in the Ohio Valley, Wheeling is a relic of the Industrial Revolution. Once home to bustling steel, glass, and tobacco industries, the area today offers a rusting landscape of smokestacks and dying steel mills. Downtown Wheeling is nearly deserted, its once grand Victorian architecture blackened from years of neglect. The "Coffee Shop" on the main drag is actually a video poker hall with a single coffee pot to provide an occasional "pick-me-up" to the pasty, overweight gamblers glued to video poker machines and smoking cigarettes in dark rooms.

Like much of West Virginia, Wheeling and surrounding Ohio County rank among the poorest places in the country. Thanks to the closing of the steel mills, Ohio County has lost 30 percent of its population since 1968, leaving it with one of the oldest populations of any county in the country. Today's residents are thus heavily dependent on the local hospitals, which also happen to be the area's largest employers. Wheeling Hospital, where most of the doctors went on strike, employs some three thousand local residents.

Thanks to the health-care-based economy, doctors make up the area's upper crust, and their patients are mostly poor and elderly folks reliant upon government health-care programs like Medicaid and Medicare. As trial lawyers are quick to point out, with its high rates of poverty and uninsured residents—as many as one in five—Wheeling is not exactly a magnet for medical talent, especially because it must compete with the highly acclaimed University of Pittsburgh Medical Center only sixty miles away.

As a result, many of West Virginia's striking doctors were foreign born and trained, and even some of the native doctors were trained in places like Guadalajara, Mexico. At the same time, Ohio County has an unusually active and talented trial bar, lawyers who honed their skills through decades representing injured union workers. The tension between the two groups had been brewing for years, and by 2001, when malpractice insurance companies imposed stiff premium increases on doctors, conditions were ripe for conflict.

While the jury verdicts aren't nearly as outrageous as the doctors make them out to be, there have been a few whoppers in Ohio County—albeit usually in cases involving egregious malpractice. The case that most upsets the doctors is that of Dr. Fred Payne. Payne had been sued sixteen times between 1986 and 2002, resulting in nearly $9 million in payouts, according to the state board of medicine.

In 1998 Payne operated to repair a minor spine injury on a spry seventy-six-year-old World War II veteran who had fallen out of a tree. On his way to the operating room, Payne ran into a medical-equipment salesman who encouraged him to try out a new type of clamp. The patient hadn't consented to the procedure, nor had Payne ever even seen the tool used or studied its use; he tried it out anyway. After Payne left the hospital, a nurse paged him to let him know that the patient wasn't doing well in recovery. An examination found that the clamp had slipped into the spinal canal and paralyzed the man from the neck down—a hideously worse injury than he had initially sustained. He died a year later. A lawsuit over the case, which charged that the man didn't even need surgery in the first place, was settled for $4.6 million.

The Ohio Valley Medical Center agreed to pay $3.5 million of the settlement but left Payne responsible for the rest. Payne's minimal insurance didn't cover the balance, so the judge on the case, Fred Risovich II, insisted that he use his personal assets to pay his share of the settlement, a rare move in a malpractice case. "The negligence was so gross, and the injury so bad, that justice required that he pay something," says Risovich. Payne has not practiced medicine since.

Doctors in Wheeling had not been particularly politically active before this, but they were outraged by the case—not by Payne's behavior, but by Risovich's. The doctors organized to oust him in a nasty campaign that would foreshadow the tenor of the battle over malpractice suit caps two years later. According to Risovich and people in the local medical community, during the 2000 judicial race, anonymous flyers appeared on the windshields of cars at the local supermarket accusing Risovich of beating his wife and being a racist. Risovich says one night someone set fire to his campaign materials in his front yard and urinated on his stoop. "Someone sent investigators to call my children at college, asked my stepchildren if they'd ever been molested. It was horrible," says Risovich. Dozens of Republican physicians changed their party affiliation so they could vote against Risovich in the Democratic primary, and many today take credit for his crushing defeat.

It's not a coincidence that the nation's doctors were becoming politically energized just as the malpractice-insurance industry went into a financial tailspin. Historically, physicians' loudest demands for caps on jury verdicts have always coincided with problems in the insurance market. The first wave came in the 1970s, when doctors succeeded in passing medical malpractice—reform measures in California and elsewhere, then again in the mid-1980s. The pattern is always the same: doctors' insurance premiums start to skyrocket, the insurance companies pull out of various states, and the doctors complain that lawsuits are driving them out of state, out of high-risk practices, and out of the business of delivering babies. And their proposed cures are always the same: not insurance reform, but restrictions on malpractice lawsuits. The latest wave is no exception.

As doctors put the blame for their insurance woes on trial lawyers, malpractice suits, and juries during the protests in West Virginia, they had some help in staying focused: between 1995 and 2001, Medical Assurance of West Virginia, a large company that provided medical malpractice insurance to doctors to cover their legal costs and damages in lawsuits, paid the state medical association at least $115,000 to lobby on the company's behalf, according to a story in the *Charleston Gazette* by Lawrence Messina. Medical Assurance offered members breaks on their insurance premiums for attending "White Coat Day" at the legislature and provided the glossy brochures and information on "meritless lawsuits" and "outrageous" damage awards that doctors used in their talking points with reporters and elected officials.

Similarly, the PR materials on "lawsuit abuse" and patient petitions that began to fill doctors' offices in 2002 came from the West Virginia Care Coalition. The coalition was actually a project of Maple Creative, a Charleston-based PR firm with close ties to the Bush administration. Those groups footing the bill for Maple's services included several with a direct stake in medical issues. The state HMO association and the local hospital association, according to Wheeling Hospital CEO Donald Hofreuter, gave the Care Coalition more than $200,000. But other business groups also pitched in, including the West Virginia Oil and Gas Coalition, the state chambers of commerce, the West Virginia Building and Industry Coalition, and the Business Roundtable.

Once corralled behind malpractice caps, doctors came up with their own innovations. At one point, physicians in Wheeling began adding a "tax" to their bills, $5 or $10 above and beyond what insurance would pay for, telling patients it was intended to cover their outrageous malpractice insurance premiums. Predictably, older people on fixed incomes flooded their elected officials with calls for lawsuit restrictions.

All in all, claims about a lawsuit-abuse crisis proved remarkably effective in West Virginia—and resistant to contradictory evidence. In February 2001, responding to the doctors' allegations, the *Charleston Gazette* undertook a computer-assisted analysis of more than two thousand medical malpractice claims reported to the West Virginia Board of Medicine. The paper determined that far from being in a state of crisis, West Virginia ranked thirty-fifth in the country for median malpractice payouts. The paper also found that both the number of malpractice claims and the dollar amounts of the settlements and verdicts had actually declined between 1993 and 2001. Nor was West Virginia suffering under an epidemic of "disappearing doctors."

In August 2002 the *Gazette*'s Messina attended a rally at which the West Virginia Medical Society set out thirty-seven empty chairs labeled with the names of local doctors who supposedly had been forced out of practice because of insurance costs. He discovered that at least two of the doctors named were indeed not practicing—because they were dead. Another two were still actually treating Wheeling patients. A Public Citizen study of the state medical board records later found that the number of doctors in West Virginia increased by more than 350 between 1997 and 2002.

In the fall of 2003, the GAO reached a similar conclusion: of five states identified by the American Medical Association as malpractice "crisis" states, including West Virginia, it found that "many of the reported provider actions taken in response to malpractice pressures were not substantiated or did not widely affect access to health care . . . some reports of physicians relocating to other states, retiring, or closing practices were not accurate or involved relatively few physicians." Nor, in those same states, could the GAO "identify any major reductions in the utilization of certain services some physicians reported reducing because they consider the services to be high risk."

As doctors and insurance companies in West Virginia mobilized to impose caps, Republicans in Washington began to ramp up their own campaign for lawsuit restrictions. In July 2002 the Bush administration kicked off the effort with the release of a report called, "Confronting the New Health Care Crisis: Improving Health Care Quality and Lowering Costs by Fixing Our Medical Liability System," which claimed that the "critical element" for expanding health insurance to uninsured Americans was "curbing excessive litigation." Soon after, in July, congressional Republicans launched a hearing titled "Harming Patient Access to Care: The Impact of Excessive Litigation."

The supposed travails of West Virginia doctors made a perfect case study. Representative Shelley Moore Capito (R-WV), a close confidant of White House adviser Karl Rove, personally escorted a West Virginia doctor named Dr. Samuel Roberts to the House floor to testify. Roberts, one of only three doctors who testified, told the committee that he could not afford the insurance to continue delivering babies and claimed that soon "I will have to stop, leaving seven counties around me with no family physician delivering prenatal or maternity care."

As with so much of the malpractice campaign, Roberts's testimony omitted some critical facts that might have explained some of his insurance woes: in 1987 he pleaded guilty to five counts of cocaine possession and was sentenced to five years' probation, according to the *Charleston Gazette.* In response, the state suspended his medical license for a year, though it later reduced the penalty to five years of supervised probation. (Incidentally, a year after his dire warnings to Congress, Roberts was still delivering babies, according to his office.)

Nonetheless, the campaign gained steam, and in July 2002 Bush gave a major speech on medical malpractice in North Carolina, home state of trial lawyer and Democratic presidential hopeful John Edwards. "Health care costs are up because docs are worried about getting sued," the president declared. Before the speech, Bush met privately with AMA president-elect Donald Palmisano, who told the *Wall Street Journal* that Bush had counseled him to "get out the grassroots" if he wanted caps on malpractice damages. The West Virginia doctors took his advice. When they staged their strike in January 2003, it coincided perfectly with Bush's State of the Union address, in which he raised the malpractice issue before a national TV audience.

The West Virginia strike did inconvenience a few patients, but its real sting was felt—as intended—at the statehouse. Joe DeLong, a delegate from Weirton, where some of the surgeons walked out, views the doctors' strike as a form of extortion. "When I grew up, a strike was a sacrifice," he says. "The doctors' livelihoods were never at stake. This was a movement to inflict pain on the sick and the elderly." He recalls being flooded with calls, including one from a ninety-six-year-old woman in tears because she was dependent on a state transportation program to get to her doctors. The shuttle wouldn't cross state lines to take her to Pennsylvania or Ohio if doctors in West Virginia quit practicing; she calmed down only when DeLong offered to drive her should it prove necessary.

Such calls sent the legislature into a frenzy. "It's an emotional issue for them," DeLong says, noting that the doctors have done a good job of turning their insurance problems into an antilawyer issue. Aside from the trial lawyers, there has been very little organized opposition on the other side. In March 2003 state legislators, most of them Democratic, voted overwhelmingly in favor of a sweeping malpractice bill. (DeLong was among them.) Governor Bob Wise practically begged to sign it.

Thanks in part to the ripple effect of the West Virginia strike, the national campaign by protesting doctors was a smashing success. In state after state, doctors had only to threaten walkouts to win promises of damage caps from local legislators. Shortly after the West Virginia doctors went on strike, for instance, doctors in Scranton sat down to talk strategy with Frank Galitski, a former Bush campaign worker and insurance industry lobbyist. He admits that there was "some coordination" between the doctors' protests and the White House, which saw the doctors' protests as a useful tool for bashing Democrats in key swing states like Pennsylvania.

After the West Virginia success, the AMA pledged to spend a whopping $22 million in 2003 campaigning for the malpractice issue alone, establishing a nationwide, state-level grassroots operation that came in handy during the 2004 election. That figure was nearly eight times larger than the entire budget of the Association of Trial Lawyers of America. And Bush's reelection campaign netted more than $8.2 million from doctors, hospitals, nursing homes, and other health care professionals, according to the Center for Responsive Politics.

It's worth noting that the walkouts would never have been so effective had the media taken a closer look at the doctors involved—and the interests backing them. Aside from a few skeptical reporters in West Virginia, most of the press has taken the doctors' claims at face value, rarely challenging their evidence and anecdotes. In June 2003, for instance, *Time* magazine devoted an entire cover story to "disappearing doctors," complete with data supplied by the AMA—the same data that previously had been challenged by consumer groups around the country and later was authoritatively debunked by the GAO. Reporters have also abetted the campaign by portraying wealthy doctors as the impoverished victims of "lawsuit abuse" and the often poor and injured plaintiffs as the greedy pawns of billionaire trial lawyers. Yet as with the AMA's data, that image doesn't hold up under inspection.

Take Dr. Rajai Khoury, a striking Wheeling cardiovascular surgeon who told a local TV news interviewer during the doctors' 2003 strike, "We're hurting, our patients are hurting, the community is suffering." It's no secret in Wheeling that Khoury recently built a 12,000-square-foot mansion with a five-car garage, a pool, and a lovely view of the countryside from "Pill Hill," the ritzy neighborhood that's home to many doctors. (According to county building records, the house is valued at close to $3 million, in a town where houses go for as little as $19,000.) This, too, despite the fact that Khoury has been sued six times between 1992 and 2002, resulting in nearly $1 million in settlements and judgments paid out to his patients by insurance companies and the hospitals he worked for, according to the state board of medicine. Even Zaleski seems to be doing pretty well, despite his claims on television. He says his malpractice insurance of $150,000 a year is about 30 percent of his income, which would net him $300,000 annually. "I'm not starving," he admits.

Dr. Greg Saracco, the telegenic surgeon who became the unofficial spokesman for the Wheeling walkout, defends his profession, saying, "I don't think it's really an issue how much a doctor makes. Who says we have to do this for free?" When I interviewed him in February 2003, Saracco railed against the "outrageous jury awards" given in Wheeling, offering the story of a local man who violated company rules and safety guidelines on the job and used a broomstick to unstick some kind of machine, which then cut his arm off. Saracco said the man then sued the company for safety violations, and a jury awarded him $4 million for his stupidity.

"Is somebody's arm worth $4 million?" he said with amazement. Alas, the story may be apocryphal, as many frivolous-lawsuit stories often are. Verdicts over $1 million are rare in West Virginia (there was none the year before the doctors went on strike), and none of the trial lawyers I spoke with in Wheeling could recall such a case. They suggest Saracco may be confusing it with a similar case—lost leg, not arm—but the suit was against an insurance company, a very different issue.

When asked whether he'd ever been sued, Saracco said he had just settled a "crappola" suit for $25,000. In that "crappola" suit, James Westfall, a man in his mid-fifties, came into the hospital for a hernia repair surgery, performed by Saracco and his partner, Dr. Robert Cross. According to allegations in the suit, during surgery Saracco pierced Westfall's bowel while stitching him up and sewed it into his abdomen. The wound closure later tore and created a hole in Westfall's bowel, causing it to leak. Cross allegedly failed to respond to nurses' reports of complications until Westfall was in critical condition—too late, as it turned out. Westfall died a miserable death two days later. The lawsuit was ultimately settled by Saracco for $25,000, and by Cross and the hospital for well over $1 million.

Sitting in his Wheeling office, Saracco suggests that most of the people who suffer from "malpractice" usually have themselves to blame, like obese people and the smokers he says are getting money from asbestos lawsuits. The solution, he insists, is a cap on jury awards like the one passed in California in 1976, known as MICRA, the Medical Injury Compensation Reform Act. That law capped pain-and-suffering awards in malpractice suits at $250,000 and is the model for legislation pushed by doctors today—without adjusting for inflation—because they believe it kept a lid on insurance premiums. But Saracco and his fellow physicians have a short memory.

California passed its law after malpractice insurers, blaming out-of-control lawsuits, suddenly hiked doctors' premiums by more than 300 percent in a single year. Some years after the law took effect, insurance premiums had shown no sign of going down. California doctors ended up suing Traveler's Insurance Company, alleging that it grossly overcharged in the name of a nonexistent malpractice crisis. (Here, too, the plaintiffs' bar came in handy: a trial lawyer won the doctors a $50 million refund.) The state ultimately passed strict insurance reform that kept a lid on future premium increases.

History has repeated itself. Six months after West Virginia passed strict caps of $250,000 on noneconomic damages in malpractice cases, insurance companies were already requesting big increases in doctors' premiums. The Commonwealth Medical Liability Insurance Company asked for a 54 percent rate hike and was granted a 22 percent increase by West Virginia insurance regulators. The Doctors Company, a California firm that has been heavily involved in lobbying for caps, requested a 45 percent increase and got a 17 percent hike.

A year later most of the firms were back asking for equally large rate increases and received approval for a portion of them, even though the number of malpractice verdicts and settlements filed in the state dropped precipitously, from 411 in 2001 to 177 in 2004. During the same time, the amount of money paid out in verdicts and settlements in the state reported to the board of medicine dropped from $62 million to about $25 million. The insurance companies were making out like bandits, even as doctors were still waiting for relief.

A year after Texas passed draconian restrictions on malpractice lawsuits, including the $250,000 cap on noneconomic damages, one malpractice insurer requested a 39 percent increase in malpractice insurance rates. In an October 2003 memo, General Electric's Medical Protective company (MedPro), which sells malpractice insurance to many Texas doctors, explained why it wouldn't be reducing its rates in light of the new legal changes: "capping noneconomic damages will show loss savings of 1.0%," it said. The same memo observed that all the savings promised from Governor George Bush's sweeping 1995 tort reform "did not materialize completely."

Eventually, malpractice insurance rates started to level off in some states that had passed damage caps. But they also leveled in states that didn't pass any new lawsuit restrictions. For instance, in late 2005, in Connecticut, where doctors' premiums had increased as much as 90 percent annually in previous years, several big insurers declined to raise rates, and others asked for much smaller increases than they'd sought in recent years.

(Connecticut Medical Insurance Company admitted, too, that despite claims of dire straits during the tort reform debate, it netted $7.6 million in profits in 2004 from all those hefty charges to doctors.) In Washington State, one malpractice firm dropped its rates nearly 8 percent, also without any changes in the legal system.

In the end, the doctors' insurance problems had very little to do with a supposed lawsuit crisis. Even before the doctors started protesting, the number of medical malpractice suits filed nationally had fallen by 1 percent between 1998 and 2002, according to the National Center for State Courts. In many of the AMA's so-called crisis states, medical malpractice lawsuits had been falling even more dramatically. In Minnesota, for instance, they fell a whopping 44 percent between 1997 and 2001, according to the NCSC.

Doctors' groups, chastened by the new data, decided that the real problem with malpractice lawsuits isn't the volume but the dollar amount of jury verdicts, which are indeed getting larger. The Bureau of Justice Statistics found that in 2001, the median malpractice award was $431,000, up from $287,000 just five years earlier. The percentage of verdicts over $1 million also rose from 25 percent to 32 percent during that same time period.

From a purely statistical viewpoint, though, the verdicts are misleading because today there are simply fewer trials, with far fewer plaintiff winners than there were in the early 1990s—a factor that can drive up a statistical average. In 1992, according to the BJS, there were 1,370 medical-malpractice trials in the nation's seventy-five most populous counties. By 2001 there were 1,038 even though the American population had grown by 12 percent. Plaintiffs were also winning fewer of these. In 1992 nearly one-third of medical malpractice plaintiffs won before juries, but by 2001 they were winning just one-quarter of the time. The cases that did go to trial were significantly more serious, involving more instances of wrongful death and permanent, total disability, which also drives up the dollar value of verdicts.

As much as insurance companies like to blame juries for the rising awards, the increase is largely a factor of rising health care costs, which make up the bulk of the damages in most malpractice lawsuits. In 2005 the Kaiser Family Foundation published a study of the government-sponsored National Practitioner Data Bank, which consists of paid malpractice claims against the nation's doctors. The study also included research from an insurance industry database of paid claims. Kaiser researchers found that the number of paid claims against doctors between 1991 and 2003 had remained relatively stable, increasing about 1 percent a year. The dollar amount for the average claim did increase, but when adjusted for medical inflation, the average increase in malpractice payments was a modest 2 percent a year.

Jury verdicts themselves seem to have no real relationship to the increase in doctors' malpractice insurance premiums. In March 2005 several researchers published a study of the Texas Department of Insurance database that contained all malpractice claims resolved between 1988 and 2002. They found that medical-malpractice filings, verdicts, and settlements, once adjusted for population growth and inflation, were surprisingly stable.

The Texas study did reveal unsavory details about the insurance industry's practices. While malpractice insurance premiums in Texas had jumped 135 percent between 1999 and 2003, the number of paid claims per one hundred practicing physicians in Texas fell to fewer than five in 2002, and the percentage of big claims, with payments of more than $1 million, was consistently about 6 percent of all the large claims over a fourteen-year period. The total payouts in the state, when adjusted for economic growth, actually fell by $6 million. And malpractice lawsuits accounted for less than 1 percent of the state's health care expenditures.

Elsewhere, a few insurers actually jacked up doctors' premiums when both their current claims and future payouts were falling. For instance, Medical Assurance, the biggest insurer in West Virginia, increased doctors' premiums by nearly 90 percent at the same time that its claims fell by one third. The resulting price increases left the insurers with record amounts of surplus cash. Several state attorneys general sniffed signs of price gouging. Wall Street, though, saw signs of lucrative business. The stock prices of the few malpractice insurance companies that are publicly traded doubled between 2002 and 2005, even in a sluggish market.

Consumer groups and trial lawyers have accused insurance companies of gouging doctors to make up for poor investment strategies and mismanagement. To be sure, some of that was at play. For instance, the St. Paul Companies, once the nation's largest malpractice insurance firm, pulled out of West Virginia in 2001 not long after losing more than $100 million when Enron went belly up—leaving one thousand state doctors without insurance. The company blamed skyrocketing jury verdicts for its decision to leave the state.

In Illinois, the state's largest malpractice insurer, ISMIE Mutual, gave a $4.9-million severance package to its former CEO, Donald Udstuen, after he pled guilty to tax fraud conspiracy after being charged with taking part in a scheme to steer government contractors to business paying kickbacks. This was part of the scandal surrounding the state's former governor

George Ryan. The following year, ISMIE raised doctors' premiums 35 per-cent, turning a $19-million profit. Rather than reduce doctors' insurance rates, the company gave pay raises to seven top executives. The company also admitted to state regulators that it lost a significant amount of money in the stock market from the sales of WorldCom, Tyco, and Qwest securities.

Some of the doctors' insurance woes stem from a structural problem with the insurance market, which is subject to regular boom and bust cy-cles. This insurance cycle rarely makes big news when it happens, because historically, when insurers have hiked doctors' premiums, they've initiated massive media and legislative campaigns calling for yet more restrictions on lawsuits, which make the business more profitable but rarely benefit doc-tors. One thing lawsuit restrictions do successfully, though, is make it much, much harder for people to get into the courthouse to file malpractice suits, and they also shortchange those who do sue successfully and most need the money.

In the spring of 1988, forty-one-year-old Maryland resident Bonnie Harri-son took her mother and aunt on vacation to Florida. On the drive down, she was feeling unusually sleepy, so when she got back, she went to see her internist. At the time, she was also having some blood spotting and irregu-lar periods. The internist gave her some antibiotics and told her that if the bleeding didn't stop in a week, he'd send her for a sonogram. "I wish he had," Harrison laments.

Instead, her doctor referred her to ob/gyn Mark Seigel, who, Harrison says, did one of the quickest internal exams she'd ever had. After the exam, Seigel told her she needed a D&C—a dilation and curettage procedure, which scrapes out the uterus. It's the same technique often used to perform abortions. When she came out of surgery, Seigel told Harrison that he'd found an "unusually large polyp" and that he'd had some difficulty getting it out. According to Harrison, he also told her that he'd had a difficult time stopping the bleeding but that she was OK by the time she came out of sur-gery.

Six weeks later, Harrison still didn't feel right. She returned to see Seigel, who, she says, dismissed her complaints and told her to go back to the plastic surgeon who'd done some work on her abdomen a year earlier. So she did. The plastic surgeon compared some of the post-op photos to her current state, and, puzzled, performed an internal exam. Afterward, he asked, "Bon, is there a chance you could be pregnant?" She said, "If I am, Harv, I'm six and a half months pregnant."

Harrison didn't think it was possible. An administrative officer at the FDA, she had been previously married for a decade and had tried unsuccessfully for seven of those ten years to get pregnant. Although Seigel says he had asked Harrison if she was pregnant and she said no, he did not do a pregnancy test before the D&C. The concerned plastic surgeon sent Harrison back to see Seigel, who denied that she could be pregnant according to Harrison. Checking would have been easy enough. "All that time, the [heart monitor] was right there on the counter," says Harrison. "He could have put it on my stomach right there and heard the heartbeat. But he was so firmly convinced that I wasn't pregnant." Seigel finally referred her for a sonogram, which not only showed she was pregnant but that the baby weighed two pounds already.

Harrison was shocked. She transferred to another doctor, who, she says, told her that she should come to the hospital immediately if she suffered from any pain or complications, as he suspected that Seigel may have nicked the amniotic sac during the D&C. "I was deprived emotionally, financially, and physically the opportunity to prepare for his birth, which occurred five weeks later," says Harrison. Tommy Harrison arrived eight weeks premature, and nine days after his birth, he suffered two brain hemorrhages, resulting in cerebral palsy. He would need extensive spine surgery and has multiple physical problems that will require him to walk with crutches for the rest of his life.

Harrison sued Seigel, alleging that the D&C he performed had ruptured her membrane and caused the premature birth that led to her son's injuries. In his defense, Seigel said in an interview that he had asked Harrison before the procedure whether she could be pregnant, and that she said no. "I just believed her and didn't see any reason to do a pregnancy test." Seigel also says that because the injuries to the baby didn't occur for several weeks after he performed the D&C, he did not believe he was responsible. Any side-effects from the D&C, he says, would have been apparent immediately. Ultimately, Seigel says, it was the doctors at the hospital who handled the rest of Harrison's care who were to blame for some of Harrison's son's problems.

Harrison faced an uphill battle in court. She had a hard time finding expert witnesses after even a good doctor friend refused to testify on her behalf. She says he told her that "he would be blackballed up and down the East Coast" if he dared testify against another doctor. Meanwhile, Seigel brought in big shots from Harvard and Johns Hopkins.

Most of the original lawsuit was a claim for damages for Thomas, who had extensive medical expenses. As an afterthought, John Gill, Harrison's lawyer, also asked the jury to award Harrison money for the mental anguish she suffered during those weeks when she was pregnant and knew that the D&C Seigel had performed might have severely injured her unborn child. After twelve hours of deliberation, the jury found in Seigel's favor on the claims relating to Thomas's injuries. But they gave Harrison $602,960, of which all but about $3,000 was for her pain and suffering. Gill believes the jurors really didn't want to punish the doctor, who showed contrition on the stand, but felt that the Harrisons deserved something.

What the jurors didn't know, however, was that Maryland law re-quires judges to automatically reduce pain-and-suffering awards to a statu-tory cap, which was then $350,000. After lawyers' fees and expenses, Harrison says she ended up with about $218,000. Gill says he would have liked to appeal the case, but Harrison needed the money. She was a single parent of a disabled child, and she says that by the time of the verdict, she was deeply in debt because of the costs of Tommy's physical therapy. The verdict allowed her to pay off the medical debts and to move from her town house to a rambler that could be outfitted to accommodate her son's disabil-ities. Since then, she's had to refinance the house several times to pull out money to keep herself and her son afloat. Today she's scrimping to save money so that Tommy can go to college to study computer design.

Seigel, meanwhile, went on to become the president of the Maryland Medical Society and a prominent figure in the doctors' attack on lawsuits during the malpractice "crisis" that started in the state in 2003. One of their primary demands was a 50 percent reduction in the cap on noneconomic damages.

Lucinda Finley, a professor at the State University of New York at Buf-falo Law School, has spent years chronicling the effects these types of caps have, and she's come to the conclusion that it's women like Harrison who are disproportionately affected by them, along with the elderly and children. She has found that jury awards, like the average workplace, tend to under-compensate women, largely because women tend to make less money than men who've suffered similar injuries. Because women don't have large eco-nomic damages to recover, juries tend to make up the difference by giving them bigger pain-and-suffering awards than they give to men.

Women also suffer unusual injuries that are unique to their gender, such as impaired fertility, miscarriage, and trauma to intimate parts of their bodies that don't translate easily into pure economic terms, as was the case with now-famous Wisconsin resident Linda McDougal. In 2002 the mother of three underwent a double mastectomy after her doctor told her she had aggressive breast cancer. As it turned out, she didn't have cancer at all. The lab had mixed up her test results with someone else. Because this type of injury doesn't cause significant economic damage—for instance, by preventing someone from working—juries tend to compensate people like McDougal with awards for her pain and suffering.

The doctors' favored legal reform these days is a strict cap on these types of awards, and to Finley, it's highly discriminatory. She took a look at the effects of the vaunted California MICRA law that caps noneconomic damages at $250,000. Studying 131 cases between 1992 and 2002, Finley found that noneconomic damages made up 76 percent of jury verdicts for women, while they only made up 48 percent of the awards for men. As a result, when the caps kicked in, women saw their total compensation in malpractice cases reduced dramatically, by about 57 percent. Men, on the other hand, lost only about 31 percent of their awards to the caps.

Thanks to the MICRA cap, babies and small children in California aren't worth much in the courts these days either. Finley found that the cap reduces the amount of money recovered in a wrongful death lawsuit for a child by fully 80 percent. Juries, though, continue to believe that these families deserve to be compensated for such a devastating loss. Juries aren't told about the cap during a trial, and as a result, the median award in a malpractice case that resulted in a child's death is $1.2 million. But the jurors' feelings don't really count for much. The statute cuts those jury awards to about $254,000, so little that most California lawyers simply won't take these cases, as the cost of trying them can be more than the family can recover.

Indeed, caps on damages and other tort reforms make many medical malpractice cases so hard to bring that lawyers just don't bother. West Virginia plaintiff attorney Bob Fitzsimmons is one of the state's most prominent malpractice attorneys. He says he used to get about twenty calls a week from people who thought they had medical malpractice claims or from other lawyers referring him cases. Before the state passed a $250,000 cap on pain-and-suffering awards in 2003, he would take about one new case every two weeks. Now, he says, he still gets the same number of calls, but

"I take about one out of every five hundred calls." Patients who have suffered at the hands of their doctors are simply out of luck.

★　★　★

In a speech in Little Rock, Arkansas, in early 2004, President Bush declared that "one of the major cost drivers in the delivery of health care are these junk and frivolous lawsuits." As part of Bush's attempt to make malpractice lawsuits a campaign issue, his Department of Health and Human Services has claimed that a federal cap on pain-and-suffering awards would reduce health care costs by an astonishing $108 billion a year. No reliable researcher has ever proved that caps on damages save money in overall health care costs. Indeed, the costs associated with medical malpractice don't just disappear into the ether because the lawsuits do.

The Institute of Medicine, part of the federally created National Academy of Sciences, estimated in 1999 that avoidable medical errors cost the country somewhere along the lines of $17 billion annually. In 2004 Health Grades, a private health care ratings company, released a study on patient safety in American hospitals. The study of the Medicare population found that the economic consequences of medical errors was "staggering": about $3 billion annually. When Healthy Grades extrapolated the numbers for the population as a whole, it calculated that between 2000 and 2002, 575,000 people (not including obstetric patients) died from preventable errors in hospitals, at a cost of a whopping $19 billion.

Respected medical groups have documented repeatedly that medical malpractice is epidemic in this country and that it costs the public dearly both in lives lost and in cold cash. Bush's plan to get rid of the lawsuits that arise from substandard health care simply shifts the cost of those errors onto the people who are least able to afford it: the injured patients and their families, and ultimately, the taxpayers.

Consider the case of the Gourley family. In November 1993 Nebraskan Lisa Gourley was thirty-six weeks pregnant with twins. The day before her regular prenatal visit, she noticed that the babies had stopped moving around as much as they had been. She told the doctor the next day. After checking the heartbeats, the doctor told her not to worry and that it was normal at that point, since she expected Lisa to go into labor that week.

Over the following two days, Lisa grew concerned as the babies' move-ment grew even less frequent, and she called her doctor. After several hours of delay, another partner in the practice finally saw Lisa and deter-mined that the babies were in distress. A series of further delays kept her from getting to the hospital for several hours. Finally, after another ultra-sound, the doctor decided the babies needed to come out immediately. Even then, though, Lisa says, nothing happened very quickly.

When they were finally delivered, neither boy was breathing, and both were put on ventilators. After five days, Connor started to improve, but his identical twin, Colin, took a turn for the worse. The day before Thanksgiv-ing, the doctors asked Lisa and her husband about removing the ventilator, but the couple waited until their whole family had arrived in Omaha for the holiday before agreeing to remove it. When they did, Colin started to breathe on his own. But he had suffered a severe brain injury that left him profoundly physically and mentally disabled.

The Gourleys filed suit against their obstetrician, alleging that she was largely responsible for the injury because she failed to adequately monitor the high-risk pregnancy. A jury agreed and found that both the doctor and the hospital were responsible for Colin's injuries. They awarded the family $5.625 million to pay for Colin's past and future medical expenses. But thanks to a nearly thirty-year-old state law, a relic of one of the nation's first malpractice insurance "crises," the award was automatically reduced to $1.25 million. Nebraska is one of only three states that cap both economic dam-ages as well as pain-and-suffering awards.

The Gourleys appealed the reduction on constitutional grounds, and an appellate court ruled in their favor. (The Gourleys' case was only the sec-ond verdict in Nebraska to actually exceed the cap, a sign that the Midwest-ern juries weren't exactly loose with insurance companies' money, and perhaps the best argument that the cap was both unfair and unnecessary.) The case dragged on for another three and a half years, until the Nebraska Supreme Court, with some misgivings, ruled against them in 2003.

During the course of the litigation, Lisa had to quit her job to stay home to care for Colin because the insurance company wouldn't provide for in-home nursing care that he needed. Plus, Colin was a fussy child, and Lisa says she worried that someone else might get frustrated with him, so she learned nursing on the job. Overwhelmed by the responsibilities of Colin plus three other children, she got depressed. Sleep deprivation only made things worse, as Colin didn't sleep at night.

When the twins were four, the Gourleys were forced to sell their house and move in with Lisa's in-laws to pay for Colin's care. "We sur-vived for four years on credit cards," Lisa says. "If the house didn't sell, we would have had to file bankruptcy." The family's credit was ruined. While the family of six shared cramped quarters with her in-laws, Lisa says Colin underwent seven major surgeries, including one after his hips dislocated that left him in a body cast for eight weeks. Another round of surgery in-cluded fifteen different procedures to rebuild Colin's legs, cutting his thigh bones and replacing bone in the collapsed arches of his feet. He required ex-tensive physical, speech, and occupational therapies, for which his parents drove eighty miles round-trip for each appointment. The gas alone for the Chevy Suburban needed to carry his wheelchair cost $700 a month.

Lisa says that while they litigated their case, their attorney got into huge fights with the lawyers on the other side, who told them, "This family just needs to move on." To which Lisa responded, "We can't move on. This is our life. We can't move on."

Colin couldn't speak until he was five and is confined to a wheelchair. His lifetime medical expenses have been estimated at about $12.5 million. Even the original jury award wouldn't have completely covered the associ-ated expenses. But with the reduction in the jury verdict, says Lisa, "After ten years of the attorney, ten years of past medical bills, there was hardly anything left."

She says the family's insurance is fairly good, but it caps the annual number of physical therapy visits at thirty. "By March or April, we've gone through that," she says. Colin needs braces for his legs, which cost "three thousand dollars every time his feet grow. Insurance won't pay for it," says Lisa. The family can't afford the cost either, "so the taxpayers get to pay for this instead of the [doctor's and hospital's] insurance company," she says, ex-plaining that the government health care program Medicaid now picks up the tab for the rest of Colin's care. The cap on damages that is supposed to be saving the public so much money is likely to cost the state more than $10 million in Medicaid costs for a single child.

At one time, the Gourleys were stalwart Nebraska Republicans. But in 2005, Lisa was home sick and happened to catch President Bush's Illinois speech on medical malpractice lawsuits. She says she heard him going on and on about frivolous lawsuits and "jackpot justice," and "I just about went out of my head." Obviously she didn't vote for him.

Caps on damages aren't the only one of doctors' favored reforms that will end up costing the public money. A little-understood measure that is often part of tort reform proposals is a repeal of something known as the collateral-source rule. Once a staple of tort law in most states, the rule allowed injured people to collect the full cost of their injuries, regardless of whether a third party, such as workers' comp or private health insurance, picked up the tab for some of it. Then the insurance companies, or Medicaid or Medicare, could put a lien on the award and recoup the money they paid out for the malpractice.

The rule is supposed to ensure that the cost of injury is born by those most responsible and most able to prevent such injuries in the first place. It's an incentive for doctors and hospitals to be more careful. Doctors and other business groups have slowly chipped away at the collateral-source rule. Since 1986, according to ATRA, twenty-four states have modified or repealed it so that plaintiffs essentially can't recover damages that were paid by a third party such as Medicare. As a result, taxpayers and anyone with private health insurance are now picking up the tab for a lot of malpractice that used to be paid for by the doctors and hospitals that caused it.

These kinds of hidden costs of tort reform have not been well studied or publicized. But in Nevada, lawyers mounted a challenge to a 2004 ballot measure that repealed the state's collateral-source rule. In an affidavit filed in the court case, they concluded that in just a single recent lawsuit, the state would have lost $4.7 million in Medicaid funds had the new law been in place at the time of the verdict.

Howard Fletcher was a fourth-generation Texas Republican who came from a long line of small-business owners. As part of their political activism, the Fletcher family gave thousands of dollars to groups like Citizens Against Lawsuit Abuse. Fletcher prominently displayed the famous CALA Stop Lawsuit Abuse stop-sign stickers in his office windows. He supported then governor Bush's legal reforms, which Bush signed in 1995 after declaring a war on "junk lawsuits."

All that changed, though, in 1997, when Fletcher's pregnant wife went into labor. The delivery was done with forceps and fundal pressure, and their son's skull was crushed. The baby hemorrhaged out of his eyes, nose, ears, and mouth, losing most of the blood in his body. He went without oxygen for thirteen minutes before doctors revived him. As Fletcher sat at the hospital waiting to see whether his child would live or die, he says he was overwhelmed with the potential looming costs of caring for his now badly brain-damaged baby. After a couple of weeks of watching the bills mount, he recalled the CALA representatives who frequented his office and regaled him with tales about irresponsible plaintiffs who'd hit the "legal lottery."

"I figured that if someone can slip and fall on a banana peel and get millions of dollars, surely in a just society someone will look at my son's case, and we'll get compensated," he says.

So the Fletchers sued the delivery doctor and others involved in the birth. The malpractice involved seemed obvious. Nonetheless, the defense dragged out the litigation for more than three years. And then, the Fletchers were shocked to learn that, despite all the headlines about million-dollar jury verdicts, in Texas, doctors aren't required to carry more than $500,000 in insurance. As a result, even if they won a big verdict at trial, the most they could recover was exactly what the doctor had in insurance: a half million dollars, an amount eaten up by their son's medical bills in the first three weeks of his life. But the money had to cover more than just medical bills. It also had to cover their lawyer's out-of-pocket costs, which topped $100,000 without even taking the case to trial. The case resulted in a confidential settlement.

The longer the case dragged on, the more Fletcher realized that the portrait of the legal system painted by Bush and his supporters was simply false. "These people seem to think that people like myself are just a bunch of gold diggers," he says. Fletcher, whose family business went bankrupt because of the cost of caring for his child, has become a vocal opponent of the tort reform movement. "These people are liars," he says.

Slanted media coverage and propaganda from doctors' groups and politicians like Bush have had a pernicious side effect on the public. While they've convinced people that the legal system is out of control, they've also persuaded them that if they are injured, they can get compensation through the courts. Unfortunately, most malpractice lawyers say they spend most of their time telling people they don't have a case or that it's not economically feasible. In fact, as the Fletchers and the Gourleys learned the hard way, even those people lucky enough to get a jury award rarely see most of it— and not because their lawyers charged too much.

Most plaintiffs in medical malpractice cases receive but a fraction of their jury awards, either because the verdicts are reduced by statutory caps or on appeal; because the defendants can't pay, thanks to too little insurance coverage; or because of pretrial settlement agreements that limit any pay-outs. And the bigger the award, the more it's likely to fall after a trial. Over the years, Duke University professor Neil Vidmar has conducted several empirical studies of postverdict reductions, with pretty surprising results. In New York, between 1985 and 1997, he found that some of the largest mal-practice verdicts resulted in settlements that were between 5 and 10 per-cent of the original award.

In a more recent study of closed claims reported by insurance compa-nies to the Florida State Insurance Commissioner, Vidmar took a look at verdicts over $1 million to see how plaintiffs actually fared after the trial. Out of the fifty cases for which the data was available, Vidmar and his col-leagues discovered that the defendants paid the full verdict in only ten of those cases. On average, the final settlement was just 63 percent of the orig-inal jury verdict. For the verdicts that exceeded $4 million, the reductions were even more dramatic. Plaintiffs received only about 37 percent of the jury award, on average.

And those are just the award figures. They don't factor in the events that occur later, when the lawyers, insurance companies, and Medicaid or Medicare take their share of the awards. In a 1991 study of Indiana's Med-ical Malpractice Act, which caps all damages in malpractice cases at $750,000, researchers Elanor Kinney, William Gronfein, and Thomas Gan-non described the case of a forty-three-year-old woman who had a botched surgery that left her without mobility in her left arm and both legs. She also lost bladder and bowel control, and ended up confined to a nursing home for the rest of her life. In 1987 she won a $400,000 annuity in a lawsuit. After all the lawyers' fees and after repaying Medicaid for the costs of her past care, the balance of the award wasn't even enough to cover her nurs-ing home bills for a single year.

CHAPTER TWELVE

In Big Government We Trust: How the GOP Learned to Love Bureaucrats

One day in early 2005, more than one hundred attorneys from the Association of Trial Lawyers of America came out early to a windowless conference room at the La Quinta Resort & Club outside of Palm Springs, California. Rather than hit the links for early-morning golf, they ventured to watch Colorado attorney Stuart Ollanik lead a seminar on expert-witness testimony. The arcane subject deals with trial admissibility issues that could easily glaze the eyes. But Ollanik's presentation is anything but dull, and it shows why the gregarious, bespectacled lawyer has won tens of millions in jury verdicts and settlements on behalf of his injured clients over the past fifteen years.

Ollanik has made a career out of persuading juries that some American car manufacturers have callously disregarded passenger safety in designing many of their vehicles. Successes like his have led the auto industry and other big corporations to invest millions in trying to convince elected officials and influential voices in the media that Ollanik and American juries are wrecking the economy by second-guessing federal regulators over the safety and design of products, from Ford Explorers to pacemakers to Vioxx. Ollanik's presentation, though, shows why that argument rings hollow in practice.

Ollanik begins with photos of Stephanie Jackson, a pretty, blond twenty-four-year-old special-ed teacher and tennis coach at a high school near Atlanta. The wholesome-looking woman radiates from the big screen, first dressed as a bridesmaid, next smiling with her happy father, the owner of the local Lincoln Mercury dealership. And then the photos get grisly.

In June 2001 Jackson was en route to give a tennis lesson when she and another driver both attempted to move into the center lane at the same time. The other driver swerved back into her lane and continued on. But Jackson wasn't so lucky. She was driving a Mercury Mountaineer, a swankier version of the Ford Explorer. Ollanik explains that when Jackson swerved to avoid hitting the other driver, the Mountaineer fishtailed and then flipped over three times. Jackson was wearing a seat belt, but the belt was attached to the pillar holding up the roof, which collapsed when the car rolled over. The seat belt went slack, and Jackson was partially thrown from the vehicle, killing her almost immediately. The next photos show the skid marks on the road, and then Jackson's car, upside down; and as Ollanik points out, there is beautiful Stephanie, with "only her elbow left in that seat belt."

In the old days, an accident like this might have been chalked up to driver error or simply bad luck. But Ollanik represents the family in a law-suit that alleges that the automaker knowingly sold a car with high risks of rollover. "There are two problems with this car," Ollanik explains: "stability and crashworthiness." Ollanik flashes to video of an Explorer dangerously tottering on its side while driven at 41 miles an hour on the race track by Bobby Unser, the legendary three-time Indy 500 winner hired by the firm as a test driver.

The footage comes compliments of the firm's in-house engineering staff, which does nothing but test cars, re-create accidents in sophisticated com-puter modeling, and gin up trial exhibits by sawing apart real car parts. The firm's engineers also do what the manufacturers generally didn't in these cases: redesign the cars to make them safer, showing how simple and often inexpensive modifications could have saved lives. In the next shot, Unser is performing a "fishhook" test at over 70 miles an hour in an Explorer re-designed by Ollanik's engineers, who had instructed Unser to do everything he could to make the car roll. All four wheels are still safely on the ground. "It's not going anywhere," Ollanik observes, noting that the test used by his firm was later adopted as a safety-testing standard by federal regulators.

Ollanik moves on to another similar case, this time of a Halliburton em-ployee who was driving a company Explorer after getting her wedding dress fitted. The heavy car rolled over, the flimsy roof buckled, and the woman was paralyzed as a result. In defending against such roof-crush law-suits, Ford has argued that there was nothing the company could have done to make the Explorer safer. "To show that we can fix these things, we have to do the test," says Ollanik.

Next video: footage of two Ford Explorers being dropped on their roofs to simulate a rollover accident, including inside-the-cab footage of crash-test dummies. The dummies get squashed by the collapsing roof in the stock Explorer, but the dummies survive the drop in an Explorer redesigned by Ollanik's engineers. Even though the roof-drop test had been around since the mid-1960s and was common among other carmakers, including Volvo (now owned by Ford), Ford never did the test when it developed the Explorer, Ollanik says.

Lawsuits over roof-crush injuries have become increasingly common, largely because for three decades the auto industry had successfully fought off new safety regulations that would have required them to make stronger roofs, particularly in SUVs. Federal regulators have proved mostly tooth-less in policing the safety of American cars. In 2004 the National Highway Traffic Safety Administration (NHTSA) issued only $10 million in civil penalties against auto companies, mostly for violating gas mileage rules. A 2003 verdict in one roof-crush lawsuit resulted in a jury verdict twice that large, against a single automaker.

When roof-strength regulations were first proposed in the early 1970s, they were never seen as a priority because few people used seat belts, so most victims of rollover accidents were thrown from the vehicle before they had a chance to get crushed by the roof. Once people started wearing seat belts, though, roof crush became the leading cause of injury in rollover accidents. An NHTSA study released in 2001 noted that 14 percent of people killed or seriously injured in rollover accidents were wearing seat belts and had been hit by the roof failing, a problem identified by federal regulators at least a decade earlier. Yet the federal government had still not updated the design standards.

As a result, lawyers stepped in to fill the regulatory void. Some one thousand lawsuits a year are filed over collapsing roofs during rollover accidents, which are estimated to cause about twenty-seven thousand injuries or deaths annually. Some of the verdicts have been substantial. It's fair to say that the auto industry hates these cases. It hates that lawyers like Ollanik have not only the gall but the financial resources to perform engineering tests that second-guess the nation's biggest automakers in a way that government regulators never do. Not surprisingly, then, American automakers have been lobbying for restrictions on lawsuits for years, with some measured success. But their prayers were answered with the election of George Bush.

Lobbying for restrictions on lawsuits in all fifty states is expensive and difficult business. But Bush, through his control of the federal regulatory agencies, has found a convenient way of getting around those pesky state legislators—and Congress, too—to aid automakers and other big corporations seeking immunity from lawsuits. Bush has made an art out of stealth tort reform, using executive power to quietly chip away at citizens' right to sue. The basis of all these new rules is something known as "preemption." The idea is that federal rule-making agencies should take precedence over state laws, even when those state laws go further in protecting the health and well-being of citizens.

It's a controversial notion, especially when it's advanced by Republicans whose party platform champions states' rights over those of the federal government. But Bush and his administration have all but thrown that party doctrine out the window when it comes to protecting corporations from lawsuits.

In the case of the auto industry, for instance, Bush has used regulations issued by NHTSA, the nation's leading safety agency for cars, to try to put Ollanik and his car lab out of business. In 2005, after thirty-four years of dodging the issue, and in the wake of numerous deaths in SUV rollovers, NHTSA finally came out with new regulations governing roof strength. But the rule offered up a weak new standard for the roofs. NHTSA didn't require the drop test used by Ollanik (*and* by other carmakers). Instead it just required automakers to put a little more pressure on the roofs and hope they would hold. As a result, the wimpy new standards would cost the industry only about $11 per car—and save almost no lives. Even NHTSA estimated that eight of ten vehicles would pass the new standard without any changes under the rule, which NHTSA estimated would save only thirteen to forty-four lives annually.

What the new federal rule would do, though, is to strip consumers of the ability to file products-liability lawsuits when roofs built to those new weak standards failed by preempting any state action against automakers on this front. In defending its proposal, NHTSA put forth the incredible argument that the fear of lawsuits might lead automakers to make poorly engineered cars by making roofs too strong, causing them to roll over more often. Volvo laid waste to this argument by designing the safest SUV on the market, with a roof many times stronger than that required by the new regs.

The roof-strength rule wasn't the only place where NHTSA slipped in protections for industry while purportedly protecting the public from dangerous vehicles. A few months before issuing the roof standard, NHTSA actually made a similar proposal for new regs governing seat-belt placement, and consumer advocates expect the preemption language to become standard fare in all new federal safety regulations. Those advocates argue that immunizing manufacturers from lawsuits removes a critical incentive for them to make safer products. Allison Zieve, an attorney with the Public Citizen Litigation Group, says, "Now they have one less incentive to do another test without the threat of lawsuits. It just seems so shortsighted, and it potentially affects everyone's safety."

The new rules are a radical departure from the way the tort law historically has dealt with federal regulations. Since the 1960s, the courts have said that federal safety standards are the minimum, not the maximum, standards for safety, leaving tort law to provide an additional incentive—without burdensome bureaucratic interference—for companies to make safer products. The new rules turn that notion on its head, and safety experts fear dire consequences—for good reason. Federal agencies are notoriously slow to respond to emerging problems, and they are vulnerable to political winds that can seriously impede their effectiveness. In addition, lawsuits provide a treasure trove of data and information about accident trends and dangerous products that federal regulatory agencies rely on to do their jobs.

For instance, as Keith Bradsher writes in his book on the evolution of the SUV, *High and Mighty,* much of the data that NHTSA collects on car accidents and complaints about safety problems with specific models of cars come from personal injury lawyers, who submit detailed information on the cases they file, giving the agency's safety engineers a critical source of information. Without the lawyers digging up new safety and design problems with new cars, NHTSA would be even less effective at regulating auto safety than it is now.

The agency has also established a dismal track record in investigating the sorts of problems with cars and trucks that plaintiff lawyers have been regularly rooting out and punishing. The classic example is the agency's handling of the Ford Bronco II rollovers. In 1990, plaintiff lawyers lobbied NHTSA to open an investigation into the rollover problem based on evidence they'd turned up in lawsuits. In the end, NHTSA opened an investigation but then abandoned it without taking any action. Several key agency officials then left to go to work for Ford as expert witnesses in Bronco II litigation.

NHTSA, like many federal agencies, particularly during the Bush administration, employs people with priorities of the industry. In 2002, for instance, the agency got a new chief counsel: Jacqueline Glassman, formerly a senior lawyer for DaimlerChrysler, a longtime member of the nation's tort reform movement. In 2005 she was promoted to deputy administrator.

Eliminating lawsuits over things like roof crush or other safety design flaws in American cars, then, leaves American drivers at the mercy of the political winds blowing at NHTSA. But the Bush administration has been aggressive in pursuing the preemption doctrine in new regulations all over the federal safety apparatus. It's also gone a step further and directly intervened in private lawsuits on the side of industry to assert that the federal government has the last word on safety, even if that word isn't much of one.

The current debate over preemption is just the latest iteration of the corporate world's attempt to roll back the revolution in products-liability law that took place in the 1960s. The old tort laws dating back to the Industrial Revolution insisted on clear relationships between wronged and wrongdoer, as well as assignment of fault, which meant, for instance, that usually drivers were legally to blame for auto accidents, not the makers of the car. But starting in the late 1950s, the courts began to rule that manufacturers of products should shoulder the cost of the injuries caused by their products, regardless of what drivers or other users did with them. The idea was that society at large was picking up the tab for all the injuries that manufacturers could have prevented with better design, more information, and improved premarket testing, but the law could provide a mechanism for forcing companies to shoulder more of those costs. William L. Prosser explained in his 1941 *Handbook of the Law of Torts* that this new law often forced defendants to pay despite "well-intentioned and entirely moral and reasonable conduct" because it is "good social policy . . . enterprises should pay their way by bearing the loss they inflict."

The newer, softer tort law was helped along by one exploding Coke bottle, a progressive California Supreme Court justice, a handful of creative trial lawyers, and one cranky consumer advocate. First, the Coke bottle: In the early 1940s, Gladys Escola was working as a waitress in a California restaurant when a Coke bottle she was putting in a refrigerator exploded in her hand. The broken glass sliced five inches of her hand and thumb, severing blood vessels, nerves, and muscles in her palm. Represented by the original "King of Torts," attorney Melvin Belli, Escola sued Coca-Cola, with help from a delivery driver who testified that he had seen other bottles blow up in the past. She won a jury verdict, and the case was appealed all the way to the California Supreme Court, which upheld the verdict in 1944.

The court found that Coca-Cola had been negligent enough in causing Escola's injury. The decision became famous because of the concurrence written by Justice Roger Traynor, long seen as the anti-Christ by the tort reform movement. In upholding the verdict, he argued that negligence shouldn't affect whether Escola could recover damages or not. He wrote, "Even if there is no negligence, however, public policy demands that responsibility be fixed wherever it will most effectively reduce the hazards to life and health inherent in defective products that reach the market."

Traynor's vision was a radical one, as it meant that even if manufacturers hadn't intentionally done anything wrong in making a product, they should nonetheless pay for any injuries it caused. The decision lies at the heart of Ollanik's car crash law practice. But the leap from Traynor to Ollanik didn't fully materialize until the 1960s, thanks to a big boost from consumer advocate Ralph Nader. After Nader's ill-conceived foray into presidential politics, it's hard now to fully fathom the profound impact he has had on American life. But Nader probably had more to do with changing the way modern courts look at products liability than any other individual in the second half of the twentieth century.

In 1965 the American Law Institute published the *Restatement (Second) of Torts,* codifying the strict liability doctrine that had been evolving for a half century. The move might not have been so revolutionary, except that it happened the same year that Nader published *Unsafe at Any Speed,* the exposé of the designed-in dangers of the American automobile. The book began by tracing the design history of the Chevrolet Corvair, which Nader declared "one of the greatest acts of industrial irresponsibility in the present century."

Nader showed how General Motors's poor design made the Corvair prone to swing out of control and flip over for no obvious reason. For years, Detroit had been insisting that all auto accidents were solely the fault of bad driving—the famous "nut behind the wheel" defense—and poor road conditions. Nader's research on "crashworthiness" obliterated that argument by showing that accidents involving Corvairs and other American cars were not always random, freak accidents caused by bad drivers but often calculated casualties that automakers could have easily prevented. By publicizing General Motors's callous disregard for life in the design of its cars,

Nader changed the way people looked at accidents. He made clear that many of the fifty thousand annual highway deaths and two million disabling injuries were part of a very large systemic failure.

Nader called upon the nation to attack the designed-in dangers of the automobile with the same vigor it was applying to civil rights. His vision went further than cars, however. As he saw it, "A great problem of contemporary life is how to control the power of economic interests which ignore the harmful effects of their applied science and technology." With his clarion call, Nader launched the nation's consumer movement, which would take its battle for safer cars and other mass-marketed products to Congress, but particularly to the courts. Three years later, Nader's analysis found its way into a landmark federal court decision that automakers would be ruing for decades.

In February 1964, Michigan resident Erling David Larsen was driving a friend's Chevy Corvair when he had a head-on collision with another car. Larsen was impaled on the steering mechanism, suffering significant injuries. Larsen sued General Motors, alleging that the design of the car exposed him to unreasonable risk of injury because, as Eighth Circuit Judge Floyd Gibson wrote, the steering column acted "as a spear aimed at a vital part of the driver's anatomy" during head-on accidents.

Larsen didn't argue that the faulty design had caused the accident, only that it enhanced his injuries from the crash. GM argued, with a great deal of precedent, that it had "no duty whatsoever" to design a car that would be safer during a collision, and that the car was safe for its intended use, which was driving, not crashing. The trial court had agreed, and granted GM a summary judgment.

To the contrary, ruled the Eighth Circuit. Crashing was as much a part of the car's use as driving. In his decision, Gibson noted that as many as two-thirds of all cars were involved in an accident that kills or seriously injures someone. The court also noted that in 1965, 49,000 people had been killed and 1.8 million disabled by injuries in car accidents, numbers that a year later had ticked up to 52,000 and 1.9 million, respectively. Given how frequently cars crash, Gibson wrote, "Where the manufacturer's negligence in design causes an unreasonable risk to be imposed upon the user of its products, the manufacturer should be liable for the injury caused by its failure to exercise reasonable care in the design."

Joan Claybrook, the longtime president of Public Citizen who served as the NHTSA administrator in the 1970s, says that with Larsen, the court finally accepted that "the way motor vehicles were designed had a lot to do with if you lived or died." The ruling meant that not only could manufacturers be sued for making a faulty wheel, but they could be punished for failing to make cars safe enough for occupants to survive a crash, even where the driver was drunk or falling asleep at the wheel without a seat belt. It was a tremendous departure from the old tort rules, where the fault of the victim played the leading role in whether damages could be sought.

Suddenly, individual Americans were taking on the world's biggest conglomerates, arguing that they too often put profit over safety, and the courts were sympathetic. Lawsuits were forcing companies to consider consumer safety in making products, from children's pajamas to prescription drugs. And each lawsuit seemed to expose corporate decision making at its greed-driven worst. Even more troubling for business, the ultimate arbiters in these disputes were not legislators, who could be plied with campaign cash, or government regulators who could be enticed toward favorable rulings with lucrative private-sector job offers, but with twelve average Joes.

The constitution guaranteed that juries would decide whether or not Chevy did enough tests on the Corvair or whether a fabric company knowingly sold children's pajamas that were prone to catching fire. And in the minds of the nation's business leaders, juries were far too unpredictable to trust with such matters involving large sums of money. Faced with this new threat to corporate profits, business almost immediately set about unraveling it.

The early tort reform movement, in fact, focused almost exclusively on restricting product-liability lawsuits. President Jimmy Carter convened the first Interagency Task Force on Product Liability in 1977, with Victor Schwartz, now the general counsel to the American Tort Reform Association, as its chairman. The task force didn't result in any legislation. It wasn't until the mid-1980s that Congress took up the issue. It haggled over a bill for a decade before finally passing one in 1996. That would have capped punitive-damage awards in products-liability lawsuits at $250,000 or twice compensatory damages, whichever was greater. The bill also would have limited liability for pain and suffering and done away with joint and several liability, a measure that makes each defendant in a lawsuit liable for 100 percent of the damages, even if it was only partially responsible for the injuries. It's a way of ensuring that an injured party is made whole, even if one of the defendants can't pay or goes bankrupt, and it's highly controversial.

Business groups created a special organization to lobby for the bill, the Civil Justice Reform Group, which was chaired by John Martin Jr., the general counsel for Ford Motor Company. Among the lobbyists working for the group was Theodore Olson, who would later become George W. Bush's solicitor general. General Motors alone spent nearly $7 million on lobbying just in the first half of 1996, when the bill was under consideration. All told, business groups are thought to have invested more than $10 million in the effort. But in 1996 President Bill Clinton vetoed the bill, arguing, oddly enough, that it trampled states' rights, a traditionally Republican position. Clinton said at the time of the veto, "This bill overrides the laws of all fifty states, in spite of the fact that forty of the fifty states in the last ten years have acted on their own to reform the tort laws, and more than thirty of them have acted in the area of product liability."

Congress couldn't come up with the votes to override the veto, and it went down in flames. In regrouping, business groups ultimately revised their strategy and began to take a more subtle approach to winning restrictions on products-liability lawsuits. Among those tactics was a renewed focus on federal preemption of state law, an idea heartily embraced by the Bush administration. Business groups have spun the idea in the media with some frequency over the past few years, in a spiel that goes something like this: Why should a company be punished in court for making a product that was produced in accordance with government safety standards? And why should a jury or state court be able to second-guess scientific agencies like NHTSA or the Food and Drug Administration in deciding that a company didn't go far enough in protecting consumers from flaws in its product? It's a seductive argument, and one that's been taken up with sympathetic commentators in the media, particularly in recent years over the flurry of prescription-drug litigation.

Michael Kinsley, then the editorial-page editor of the *Los Angeles Times,* complained in August 2005 that a recent verdict against Merck over its dangerous painkiller Vioxx was an absurd event given that the drug was on the market legally and that it had been approved by the FDA. He argued that only the government, not individual juries, can make consistent and uniform regulatory rules that drugmakers need to do business. "But in our current system, the government plays two conflicting roles. The FDA approves or disapproves a new pharmaceutical, weighing the trade-off between risk and benefit. And then the court system comes along and sees that trade-off differently. The fact that Vioxx was approved by the FDA carries little authority in Tort World, where thousands of juries in hundreds of courts of the fifty states will draw the line in other places."

While Kinsley and others have been making this argument in the press, the Bush administration has been actively making the argument in new regulations, like those from NHTSA. The administration has also come to the aid of industry defendants in private lawsuits to assert federal authority. The most well known of these efforts has come from the FDA, the agency charged with protecting Americans from dangerous drugs and medical devices.

After Bush took office in 2001, he appointed a new general counsel to the FDA, one Daniel Troy, a brilliant conservative lawyer who had once clerked for Robert Bork, the conservative former judge nominated to the Supreme Court by Ronald Reagan and rejected by the Senate. Troy was one of the nation's leading proponents of the preemption doctrine. Bush made the FDA job a political appointment, and Troy avoided the scrutiny of a Senate confirmation.

Before going to the FDA, Troy had worked at the DC powerhouse firm of Wiley Rein & Fielding, where he had spent most of his career suing the FDA on behalf of tobacco and drug companies over regulations they didn't like. In the year before Troy went to FDA, the drug company Pfizer had paid Wiley Rein more than $350,000 for services provided by Troy. Pfizer, which had a great deal of interest in seeing an ally in the FDA's counsel office, was not disappointed with Bush's selection. A year after the ban on working on behalf of a former client had passed, Troy began to work on a Pfizer matter, much to the surprise of some victims of prescription-drug injuries, who had believed that the FDA was there to protect them.

One of those people was a California woman named Flora Motus. In 1998 her husband, Victor Motus, had been suffering from insomnia. He went to see his doctor, who prescribed Zoloft, an antidepressant made by Pfizer. Almost immediately after taking the drug, Motus realized it was making him crazy. He told his wife. He consulted with two relatives, a pharmacist, and a psychologist, asking if his symptoms could be caused by the drug. Both said that the drug probably wasn't the cause, since there was no indication on the label of such problems being related to the drug. Six days after Motus first took Zoloft, his brother arrived at his house to take him to the airport, where he was scheduled to fly to Washington to accept an award from President Clinton for his work at a local school district. Instead, his brother discovered that Motus had killed himself with a shotgun.

Flora Motus filed suit against Pfizer, alleging that the company should have warned doctors that the drug causes suicidal tendencies in some people. A judge threw out the case in December 2001 on the grounds that even such a warning would not have changed Motus's doctor's prescribing habits. But Pfizer was worried about the appeal after a similar case against GlaxoSmithKline over its drug Paxil had been successful. Pfizer attorney Malcolm Wheeler called Troy to enlist his help.

In September 2002 Troy and the FDA legal staff filed a brief in support of Pfizer's position that the FDA didn't believe antidepressants increased some people's risk of suicide, and therefore any warning label to that effect would have been "false or misleading and would have misbranded the drug in violation of federal law." Troy and the FDA suggested that such mislabeling might in fact harm the public health by leading to the "underutilization of beneficial treatments."

Of course, later it became clear that Zoloft did indeed increase the risk of suicide in some people, particularly healthy people like Motus with no history of depression. Lawyers in private lawsuits were discovering that drug companies for years had been underreporting the number of suicidal acts that took place during clinical trials of many antidepressants. As a result, in October 2004 the FDA decided to require all antidepressants to carry a black-box warning on the risk of suicide associated with these drugs.

While at FDA, Troy continued the crusade for preemption. As soon as he took office, the FDA began aggressively seeking out cases in which to intervene. In December 2003 Troy gave a talk to a conference of defense lawyers and in-house counsel to drug companies on "The Case for Preemption," where, after making some jokes about plaintiff lawyers and runaway juries, he coached industry lawyers on how best to use the preemption doctrine in defending their cases. He also invited lawyers to refer cases to his office and said the FDA would consider helping them out. "We can't afford to get involved in every case," he said. "We have to pick our shots," so "make it sound like a Hollywood pitch."

To many observers, Troy was reversing years of precedent by intervening in at least five different private lawsuits to argue that state courts and juries have no authority to impose safety standards on drugs or medical devices approved by the FDA. Yet such lawsuits were consumers' only re-course for compensation when they were injured by drugs and medical de-vices the agency regulated. The U.S. Supreme Court, too, has ruled that FDA regulation does not preempt state law in all cases.

One of the cases Troy took up involved a Mississippi man named Gary Murphree, who filed a suit in 2000 in Tennessee against the pacemaker manufacturer Pacesetter, Inc. Murphree had received three different Pace-setter devices, and all were recalled, leaving him with serious heart-rhythm problems and at high risk for cardiac arrest. Pacesetter lost a motion in the case for summary judgment, but it soon got help from the FDA. Troy's of-fice, through the U.S. Department of Justice, filed a brief in the case argu-ing that Murphree's claim was barred because it conflicted with federal authority over medical devices. The brief argued that "the prospect of hun-dreds of individual juries determining the propriety of particular device ap-provals, or the appropriate standards to apply to those approvals, is the antithesis of the orderly scheme Congress put in place and charged FDA with implementing." Allowing private lawsuits over flaws in these devices, the FDA argued, would create chaos "for both the regulated industry and FDA."

The trial judge was not persuaded, and the case is headed toward a jury trial sometime in early 2007. For his part, though, Murphree was stunned to find himself battling not just the pacemaker manufacturer but also the U.S. Justice Department and the FDA. At the time he filed suit, he was the hon-orary chairman of the Mississippi Republican Party and a heavy donor to GOP political causes. He says the FDA sent three lawyers to a hearing, where they essentially said, "'We're not arguing that [Pacesetter] didn't hurt him. We're not arguing that he didn't have damages. We're just saying 'tough titty,'" explains Murphree, who has now spent eight years trying to get the case before a jury.

Murphree says he's not in the lawsuit for the money. He's more wor-ried about the other cases that are waiting behind his. Because he has such good facts—three faulty pacemakers, eight surgeries, and evidence that Pace-setter was using unapproved materials to make the faulty pacemakers—if he loses, no one else who has been injured or killed by one of the thousands of recalled devices will have much success in winning compensation. "This is a bellwether case," he says.

As vice president of Dutch Lubricants, an oil-shipping firm, Murphree is also worried about the effects on big business if the preemption argument prevails. He says the threat of lawsuits makes him more careful about the way he runs his own operation. Remove that threat, he says, and business will just focus on the bottom line. "If you can't sue big business—if you can't sue me—all we're going to do is reap billions of profits and screw everybody else," Murphree says.

The experience with the FDA has left Murphree deeply unhappy with the GOP as well, largely because he sees the Bush administration abandoning one of the party's basic tenants: respect for states' rights. He didn't vote for Bush in 2004, and he says that whereas he donated $100,000 to the party the year before his face-off with the FDA, he's not donating a cent until Bush leaves office. "I'm for tort reform, but not for taking people's rights away," says Murphree. "I don't know how we got this far off the platform."

Meanwhile, Dan Troy resigned from the FDA in November 2004, but his legacy lives on in the briefs filed by his office under his leadership. They're still being used in court to fend off private lawsuits, with mixed success.

Pharmaceutical companies have also stepped up their attempts to put preemption arguments into legislation as another backdoor method of barring lawsuits against drug companies and medical product manufacturers. In early 2006, after extensive consultation behind the scenes with drug companies, the FDA promulgated a new regulation stating that if the FDA approves a drug warning label but the product nonetheless goes on to kill or injure people, those people no longer have the right to sue for compensation under state laws. The measure was not included in the publicly circulated draft of the regulations, and it was inserted over the objections of career drug-safety officials at FDA. The courts will have to decide how to interpret the new regulations, but it clearly comes in handy for drug companies fending off lawsuits like those in the Vioxx cases, where plaintiffs allege that the manufacturers withheld information about the dangers of their products on the labels.

In most states, the debate over preemption is still a lofty and, frankly, dull technical legal question. But there is one state that's seen firsthand what the world would look like if Dan Troy's vision were implemented and the federal government had the last word on safety standards for consumer products.

★ ★ ★

One day in April 2003, Dr. David Cox was working in his Michigan office teaching residents the ins and outs of family practice medicine. As he was talking to one of the residents, he was suddenly overcome by excruciating pain in his head. "It was like getting shot in the head," he says. Cox told the resident he had to leave and stumbled outside to his car, where he collapsed. A woman in the parking lot eventually came over and asked him if he was OK, and he regained consciousness. Somehow Cox managed to start driving, but halfway to his house, he had to pull over, afraid of passing out again. He doesn't remember the ride, but somehow he got himself home, where his wife realized that there was something seriously wrong with him.

She raced him to the emergency room. Some of Cox's colleagues in the neurology department did an MRI of his brain and informed him that they believed he had an aneurism, a weak spot in an artery, in a part of the brain that doesn't respond well to surgery. The neurosurgeons told Cox that they were going to perform an arteriogram to confirm the diagnosis, and if it looked bad, they'd take him right into surgery, which was extremely risky. Cox says the doctors, his friends, looked like they were attending a funeral when they asked him, "Are your affairs in order? Do you have a will?" He says they gave him twenty minutes to make all the critical decisions about what might happen if he was left in a persistent vegetative state, and to make any last phone calls.

As it turned out, he wasn't suffering from an aneurism but a blood clot in his brain. Essentially, he'd had a stroke, which left him unable to walk; he had difficulty talking. Before that day in April, Cox had worked twelve- to fourteen-hour days, he had a busy medical practice, coached all his kids' sports teams. Afterward, the stroke left Cox with disabling migranes, slurred speech, and serious fatigue. He's no longer able to drive and hasn't been able to work. "Overnight, boom, it was all gone," he says.

Because blood clots are usually caused when pieces of plaque in the arteries break off and block the blood flow, they usually occur in people with high cholesterol, whose arteries are lined with plaque from years of high-fat diets. But Cox didn't have high cholesterol, didn't smoke (another risk factor), and an arteriogram of his brain showed that he had no plaque in his arteries. At forty-two, the father of five was a healthy man, and he was perplexed about what had happened. Cox consulted many of his colleagues trying to find an answer. None of them could come up with one, and most said he was lucky to be alive and not a quadriplegic.

It wasn't until one day, when Cox put on the lab coat he'd been wearing the day of his stroke that the light bulb went off: in the pocket was a drug-company sample of the painkiller Vioxx. Cox had been taking Vioxx for a herniated disc in his neck, the result of a sledding injury. The drug was taken off the market in late 2004 after evidence that it radically increased the chance of patients' suffering a heart attack, stroke, or blood-clotting problem, and Cox suspected that the drug was the source of his problems. He decided to find a lawyer.

Cox is a trial lawyer's dream client. A sympathetic victim, he had no contributing factors like obesity or high blood pressure that the drugmaker could blame for his condition. He had clear documentary evidence that Vioxx likely caused his stroke. As a young, healthy white-collar profes- sional, his injury caused him to lose twenty years or more of future income from a high-paying job, not to mention the possibility of pain-and-suffering damages he could potentially claim. In short, Cox's case was worth a lot of money. Finding a lawyer to take it on should have been a breeze.

Cox had done some legal reviews for plaintiff lawyers in the past and contacted one of the firms he'd done work for in Florida, headed up by leg- endary trial lawyer Willie Gary. When he told people at the firm what hap- pened to him, they said, "Oh, you're from Michigan? Don't you know? You can't sue."

That's when Cox discovered that under the leadership of former gover- nor John Engler, in 1996 Michigan passed a law that prevents its residents from filing suit against a drug company if they were harmed by a prescrip- tion drug that had been approved by the FDA. Cox was dumbfounded. "I have no rights in my own state," he says. Indeed, Cox is one of hundreds of Michigan residents who believe they or a loved one were seriously injured or killed by a dangerous prescription drug and who now have no recourse to recoup damages against the drugmakers.

"Our former governor is now the CEO of the National Association of Manufacturers (NAM), which is one of the largest lobbying groups for pharmaceutical companies in Washington, and he made this happen," says Cox. "The representatives from his association say they want to reduce frivolous lawsuits. I'd be all for a law like that. I think that's what people think they're getting with tort reform." But Cox says that after working with other people like him who've been injured by prescription drugs, he believes that the preemption law is limiting legitimate cases. "The people I've seen, they're not frivolous cases," he says.

The number of people now shut out of Michigan courts as a result of the immunity law is growing. In 2003 the ultraconservative Michigan Supreme Court threw out the cases of several people who alleged injuries from the deadly diet drug fen-phen, ruling that the state's drug-company im-munity law was constitutional. The ruling effectively put an end to any fen-phen litigation by Michigan residents. Then, in February 2005, a New York federal judge overseeing national litigation over the recalled diabetes drug Rezulin threw out the cases of 187 Michigan residents injured by the drug. The judge cited the Michigan statute, even though the cases were in a dif-ferent federal court. The courts have ruled that the drug industry's immu-nity in Michigan is absolute.

Back in the mid-1990s, Engler and his business backers in the drug in-dustry sold the preemption law as a way of reducing the cost of prescrip-tion drugs for state residents and of saving state jobs in the drug industry. Now, as head of NAM, the former governor has touted the law as a model for the rest of the country. Engler declined several requests for an inter-view, but in November 2004 he told *Crain's Detroit Business,* "I believe that for something like drugs, national standards make a lot of sense. Federal reg-ulators such as the FDA must do their job well, and we should be able to rely on them. I think the Michigan law reflects a rational approach, and a federal law modeled after it would be a rational way to protect bringing new products to market."

Yet the Michigan law hasn't quite lived up to Engler's billing. State res-idents still pay some of the highest prices in the nation for prescription drugs, and the state has lost jobs in the drug industry. Because of the law, too, taxpayers are now picking up the tab for the medical care and lost in-come of many of the people who in the past might have been able to get compensation from the drug companies that injured them.

Two of the women whose fen-phen cases were dismissed by the state supreme court in 2003, lead plaintiffs Tamara Taylor and Lee Anne Rintz, both suffer from primary pulmonary hypertension, a rare and deadly lung and heart disorder that is a side effect of the diet drug. But even though the makers of fen-phen badly deceived the public and the FDA about the safety of the diet pill in seeking its approval, the company will not be picking up the tab for Taylor's and Rintz's medical care. That cost will be shouldered by the taxpayers, who are subsidizing the drug company's wrongdoing through Medicaid, which now pays their medical bills, according to their lawyer, J. Douglas Peters.

The drug industry shield law has been such a disaster for consumers that even the state's Republican attorney general has said publicly that the law needs another look, while several Republicans in the state legislature are seeking to repeal it. Among them is State Senator Alan Cropsey, a graduate of Bob Jones University, and an evangelical Christian lawyer who is progun, antiabortion, and the former field director of one of former House Majority Leader Tom DeLay's political action committees. In the 1980s, Cropsey had been a leading proponent of tort reform in Michigan and had sponsored several bills in the legislature to restrict lawsuits. But in the 1990s, during the next wave of tort reform, Cropsey says he greeted business requests for more tort reform with skepticism, after realizing that the attacks on the civil-justice system ebbed and flowed along with swings in the insurance business.

In those years, Cropsey was also deeply suspicious of the FDA under Bill Clinton, who was an abortion-rights supporter. Cropsey feared that Clinton would push the FDA to fast-track abortion drugs without proper testing, leaving women at risk of serious injury. If the Michigan drug-company shield law passed, women injured by abortion drugs would have no recourse in the courts, so Cropsey voted against it. "I was worried about taking power from juries and giving it to a bureaucracy," Cropsey says. "Why would conservative Republicans be putting so much faith in a bureaucracy?" For him, he says, "It's not a question of tort reform but of what's right and what's just. Most of the time, the jury will do the right thing."

He says today, after watching the way the FDA handled the approval of fen-phen and then seeing Michigan residents shut out of court after they were harmed by dangerous drugs, he's more convinced than ever that the law was a bad idea. "I'm so glad I didn't vote for it," he says.

Another Republican legislator, Representative Ed Gaffney, who represents the wealthy Detroit suburbs around Grosse Pointe, was persuaded to introduce legislation that would modify the statute to allow victims of dangerous drugs to rebut the law's assumption that just because the FDA approved a drug, it was safe. He got on board after hearing Cox's story.

Gaffney says of the law, "It's unfair, and I don't think it's right. We all know the FDA's made mistakes." He says Michigan has plenty of other measures in place to protect industry, including caps on punitive damages. He believes the FDA immunity law goes too far. "I call this tort reform gone wild. Why would you exempt an entire industry that put a dangerous product into the commerce stream and then say people can't sue when they're hurt?" Gaffney suggests that the law leads to all sorts of crazy contradictions about which industries ought to be protected. "In Michigan, why wouldn't we do it for the auto industry?" He doesn't mind that opposing the law puts him at odds with the GOP. "I don't care about the party line. If

somebody's damaged, they should be compensated." And if there's a dispute, he says, "I think people should be able to fight it out in court."

The legislature is considering several different proposals for changing
the preemption law. Getting those bills passed will be a big job, and the ob-
stacles show how difficult it is to reclaim a legal right once it's been lost. As
Gaffney notes, the victims' rights group that has sprung up to lobby for it is
not exactly a powerhouse. Its members are too sick or financially strapped
because of their devastating injuries to make them much of a force to be
reckoned with.

"They're total amateurs. They have no idea what they're doing," he
says. "They don't have the resources to fight the drug companies, PhRMA
[the national lobbying organization for drug companies] and the best lobbying firms in town hired by the drug companies. It's very difficult for them."

Cropsey, too, at the moment isn't sanguine about repealing the law. He
says that even though several Republicans support changes to the law, for
the most part it's bogged down in partisan politics. Until more victims really
start to demand change and talk to their legislators, he says, not much will
happen. "If it's just trial lawyers, that's not enough."

CHAPTER THIRTEEN

In the Tanker: Exxon's Stealth Campaign against Punitive Damages

One day in 1976, seventy-two-year-old Elmer Norman went to see his doctor for some hearing tests. The doctor wrote him a prescription for antibiotics to treat an ear infection. Afterward, he submitted the bills to Colonial Penn Franklin, through which he had a group health insurance policy for seniors. Much to Norman's surprise, the company denied his $48 claim, arguing that, among other things, the prescription drug he'd received wasn't a *prescription* drug and therefore wasn't covered. Incensed, Norman went to see William Shernoff, a famous California trial attorney who'd won a landmark lawsuit against an insurance company a few years earlier.

Blind in one eye and mostly deaf—he wore a homemade hearing aid made from big stereo headphones connected to a box on his belt—Norman eventually persuaded Shernoff to take his $48 case against the insurance company. During the litigation, Shernoff discovered that Colonial had replaced the policies of about one hundred thousand seniors like Norman with a "new and improved plan." The new plan was intentionally designed to dupe seniors into believing they were getting something better for the same premiums, when, in fact, it actually cut coverage to save the company $4.5 million annually. Colonial Penn's treatment of the seniors so outraged the jury that it awarded Norman the $48 Colonial Penn had stiffed him, plus $4.5 million in punitive damages, the same amount the company had saved in one year by cheating all the seniors.

The Norman case became famous among consumer advocates fighting unscrupulous insurance companies. J. Robert Hunter, a former Texas insurance commissioner and current director of insurance for the nonprofit Consumer Federation of America, says Norman's case "did more in one year to reform claims practices than years of regulation." He says that for years afterward, lawyers would turn up claim documents from national insurance companies with notes to the adjusters saying, "Handle this one right. It's from California."

Punitive damages are the capital punishment of the civil justice system, the ultimate sanction society can levy against especially egregious conduct. To do the job right, they're supposed to be big enough to get a defendant's attention, punish wrongdoing, and deter such wrongdoing in the future. Unlike a schedule of government fines, punitive damages are frequently awarded based on the assets of the defendant, to ensure that they cause pain commensurate with the heinousness of the wrongdoing. As law professors Marc Galanter and David Luban put it, punitive damages "constitute the best available means for social control and moral sanction of economically formidable wrongdoers. . . . High punitive-damage awards hit homo economicus where it hurts: an eye for an eye, a tooth for a tooth, and a bottom line for a bottom line." High awards, too, are supposed to provide an incentive for lawyers and citizens to pursue and punish wrongdoing and to reward people like Norman, whose relentless pursuit of justice over a $48 rip-off helped thousands of other consumers.

Generally speaking, businesses that make an occasional mistake doing honest work don't get tagged with punitive damages. As West Virginia Supreme Court Justice Richard Neely once wrote in a famous decision, people and companies who tend to draw punitive-damage awards fall into three categories: "really stupid defendants, really mean defendants, and really stupid defendants who could have caused a great deal of harm by their actions but who actually caused minimal harm."

Even though the law specifically reserves punitive damages only for especially egregious conduct—something that's willful, malicious, reckless, or fraudulent—tort reformers have long insisted that huge awards, like those in the Texas Vioxx case, or the $145-billion verdict against the tobacco industry in 2000, are commonplace events that are threatening the very fabric of the nation's economy. Yet in reality, punitive awards are rare, they're generally not very big, and most people who win them in a jury trial never actually get the money. In 2001 the federal Bureau of Justice Statistics found that out of the nearly 12,000 civil jury trials in the nation's seventy-five largest counties, only 260 resulted in a punitive-damage award—about 3 per county. The median punitive award was only $50,000, down from $63,000 in 1992. Large awards do happen, but if they aren't already capped by state law, judges frequently reduce them on appeal. The bigger the award, the more likely it is to get cut. One study by Harvard law professor W. Kip Viscusi found that in products-liability cases, plaintiffs received only 29 percent of the original punitive award.

Such figures haven't deterred the nation's really mean and really stupid defendants from trying to stamp out punitive damages. Usually they argue that the awards are bad for business because they add an untenable level of uncertainty to the marketplace. Of course, one reason why punitive-damage awards are thought to have a deterrent effect on misconduct is precisely because they aren't fixed by a schedule. The potential for variability means that companies can't, say, factor in how much it would cost to kill a person into the bottom line and adjust their procedures accordingly, in what's often called "Pinto math." The name dates to the 1970s exploding gas tank scandal involving the Ford Pinto, where the giant automaker calculated that a human life was worth approximately $200,000, and that based on the number, it was cheaper to let 180 people die each year in fiery car crashes than to spend $5.80 per car to make the life-saving safety improvement in the Pinto. The prospect of high punitive-damage awards raises the dollar value of human life and then, in theory, helps tilt the corporate balance sheet in favor of public safety.

But there are other good reasons why insurance and other big companies don't like punitive damages—and money is only one of them. Big punitive awards generate a fair amount of media coverage, drawing attention to a company's illicit or immoral behavior. Shame is a powerful motivator, as are stock prices, which can be affected by news of such awards, too, at least temporarily.

Punitive-damage awards have also helped to get dangerous but lucrative products off the market long before any government agency stepped in to protect the public. Take the case of the dietary supplement ephedra, which led to the deaths of more than 150 people and seriously injured hundreds more before it was finally banned in 2004. The federal government had been receiving reports about the dangers of the supplement for a decade, but thanks to the political influence of the supplement industry, ephedra remained legally on the market.

By the time U.S. Health and Human Services Director Tommy Thompson announced the ban in 2004, the decision was largely meaningless; by then, ephedra had already become scarce, and the campaign contributions of many of the supplement companies that sold it were drying up in bankruptcy court, thanks to hundreds of lawsuits—including one in 2001 that resulted in a $12 million punitive-damage award against a Utah company. The lawsuits revealed that many of the supplement makers had engaged in massive cover-ups of the dangers of their products and that they'd occasionally dosed their products with synthetic compounds to boost the addictiveness. The onslaught of lawsuits by injured customers and big punitive-damage awards was enough to cause insurance companies to stop insuring many of the supplement makers, who then pulled the product from the market a couple of years before Thompson announced the FDA ban.

In addition, after twenty years of deregulation and a shrinking government, punitive damages in lawsuits brought by private citizens are often the only meaningful punishment a company will receive for actions that have killed lots of people or lead thousands of others to financial ruin. For instance, on June 23, 1999, twenty-four-year-old Juan Martinez, a contract worker at a Phillips Chemical plant in Pasadena, Texas, and his uncle Jose Inez Rangel were on a scaffold hydrotesting a pipe. The pipe was about ten feet from a reactor used to manufacture a plastic used to make drinking cups, food containers, and medical equipment. After a series of mishaps, the reactor exploded, coating Martinez and Rangel with 500-degree molten plastic and burning them alive.

Martinez and Rangel were not the first workers killed at the Phillips plant. In the ensuing lawsuit filed by Martinez's widow, attorney John Eddie Williams wrote, "No other serial killer in this state has been allowed to go unpunished and virtually unbridled for so long." Thirty workers had been killed and hundreds severely wounded at the plant over an eleven-year period. A jury found that Phillips had been negligent in Martinez's death, and awarded his family $7.8 million in actual damages and $110 million in punitive damages—the equivalent of one month's profits. Even with Texas's punitive-damage cap, which reduced the punitive award to $3.2 million, the jury award still dwarfed the federal penalty for Phillips's well-documented safety violations, which came to a grand total of $140,000.

Antilawsuit crusaders love to deride this kind of activity as "regulation through litigation," which it is. Tort law in this country was designed that way on purpose. Private lawsuits, with their opportunity for punitive damages, allow lawyers to work like bounty hunters rooting out malfeasance as a way of making money. The law makes them and their clients "private attorneys general," allowing them the spoils of punitive damages as a reward for performing a public service. The lawsuits are not supposed to replace the government but to complement it. Legislators, both at the state and federal levels, have recognized that Americans neither support nor want to pay for a bureaucracy large enough and intrusive enough to catch every wrongdoer or every flawed product before it hits the market, but they still want to see the public health and safety protected.

In a perfect world, Americans wouldn't need punitive-damage awards, because the FDA would force supplement companies to sell safe products from the beginning, and regulators would enforce workplace safety before the refinery blows up. But they don't. As a result, lawsuits and punitive damages have taken on a bigger role in policing corporate conduct. That's why, since about the mid-1980s, big corporations—with insurance companies leading the charge—have been waging an aggressive war to not only limit punitive damages but to eliminate them entirely.

Punitive damages are financial judgments, but they're also moral ones, with deep religious roots. Provisions for punishing wrongdoing with damage awards many times larger than the injury involved date back to biblical times and are even mentioned in the Old Testament. The British courts, though, refined the concept as a way of punishing abuses of power by bullies, by the rich, and by the government, allowing the courts to assess the fines based on the offender's wealth or "other circumstances that the rigid rules of ancient law had ignored." (The British also allowed these sorts of damages in civil suits based on insults as a way of avoiding the more lethal tradition of settling such disputes: dueling.) In the British common law, punitive (or exemplary) damages allowed the little guy a mechanism for winning justice against stronger, richer, and more powerful entities who had wronged him. The concept was imported to America.

With their religious roots and history as a power equalizer in a society stratified by class, punitive damages have always been controversial, and attempts to abolish them are nearly as old as the provisions themselves. A Harvard Law School professor launched a movement to abolish them in 1834, arguing that punitive damages were too nebulous, a weird merger of public and private, civil and criminal law, that had no place in American society. Forty years later, the railroads would take up the cause, and Justice William Foster of the New Hampshire Supreme Court would pronounce in 1873 that the idea of punitive damages "is a monstrous heresy. It is an unsightly and unhealthy excrescence, deforming the symmetry of the body of the law." One hundred years later, his state would abolish punitive damages all together, in a renewed national campaign that started up in earnest in the mid-1980s.

The political attacks started in the media, with prominent business leaders raising the specter of a "crisis" in escalating punitive-damage awards that were threatening the health and vitality of the nation's economy. In the 1980s, one of the leading business voices attacking punitive damages was Richard Mahoney, chairman and CEO of Monsanto, the agricultural chemical company, which, during the Vietnam War, was a major supplier of the defoliant Agent Orange but now makes herbicides like Roundup and specializes in genetically modified seeds.

Monsanto became a leading funder of academic research bashing the tort system while Mahoney worked the media, penning several high-profile news articles calling for restrictions on punitive damages. In 1988 he argued in the *New York Times* that punitive damages needed to be strictly limited because "conduct liable for punitive damages is whatever a single jury says it is." He cited a survey of CEOs that claimed a fear of lawsuits had led almost 50 percent to cancel products and 40 percent to withhold new products, including new pharmaceuticals. Mahoney added that his own company had decided to forgo marketing an asbestos substitute out of fear of getting sued. "The punitive-damages system makes it too easy for lawyers to persuade a jury—possessing little scientific background but believing in the possibility of a risk-free society—to enrich plaintiffs and contingent-fee lawyers with multimillion-dollar windfalls," he complained bitterly.

At the time of Mahoney's public campaign, his company was appealing a $16 million punitive-damage award in the Illinois state courts. In 1987, after a three-year trial, a jury had found the company liable for polluting the air and soil of a small Missouri town after a train carrying a shipment of Monsanto chemicals derailed and spilled toxins for a half mile along the track. (The courts eventually threw out the punitive damages award.) In 1986 another jury had hit the company with more than a $100 million punitive-damage award in a case filed by one of its employees who died of leukemia after working with the chemical benzene in a Texas plant. (The judge overruled the verdict as excessive and the family eventually settled with Monsanto.) In 1988 one of Monsanto's subsidiaries, G. D. Searle & Company, incurred a $7 million punitive-damage award over problems with the copper-7 intrauterine birth-control device.

Needless to say, Monsanto's self-interest in securing limits on punitive damages was crystal clear. Thirty-four states would eventually "reform" punitive damages by 2005, either by passing strict caps on awards, raising the evidentiary standard for awarding them, forcing parts to be paid to a state fund rather than to the plaintiffs, or banning them all together, as was the case in New Hampshire. Despite all the new restrictions, though, juries had the nerve to keep awarding punitive damages when they saw especially outrageous misconduct. So, many of the nation's biggest corporations decided to pursue a parallel campaign to severely restrict punitive awards through the courts themselves.

Today, when Birmingham, Alabama, Dr. Ira Gore gets his name in the newspapers, it's usually in the obituaries, where families of his cancer patients frequently thank him for caring for their loved ones. But for a long time, Gore's name was synonymous with the alleged excesses of the American court system.

In 1990 Gore purchased a black BMW 535i for $40,750 from a German car dealer in Birmingham. About nine months later, he took the car to Slick Finish to have it detailed and snazzed up. Leonard Slick, the owner of the detailing shop, took a look at the car and gave Gore some bad news: His new Beemer had likely suffered paint damage from acid rain during the shipping from Europe, and BMW had repainted the car once it arrived in the U.S. without disclosing the damage to either its dealers or its customers. Slick encouraged Gore to file a lawsuit based on the car's diminished resale value.

Despite objections from his family and colleagues, Gore went ahead and sued BMW. "He did this because what BMW did was wrong," says A. W. Bolt, Gore's lawyer, who notes that BMW went to great lengths to disguise its practice of repainting the cars. The day the case went to trial, says Bolt, BMW offered Gore "a lot of money to settle." But Gore wanted to know if he took the money would the company change its policy of failing to disclose the paint damage. It wouldn't, so Gore decided to go to trial. His gamble paid off. Finding BMW's conduct reprehensible, the jury awarded Gore $4,000 in compensatory damages for the reduced value of his car, and $4 million in punitive damages, the amount BMW profited from its repaint-ing scheme on the other one thousand repainted cars it sold to American consumers over the previous decade. Almost immediately, BMW changed its nationwide policy to disclose even minor repairs made to cars before they were sold new.

At the time of the 1993 verdict, Alabama was in the thick of a nasty political fight over lawsuits, and the state's business community, with the help of Karl Rove, was waging a full-blown assault on the state supreme court to install Republican, pro-tort reform justices. The BMW case be-came a rallying cry during the campaign. Under siege from the business community, the state supreme court sat on the case for more than a year before finally handing down a decision upholding the awarding of punitive damages but reducing the verdict to $2 million. The case was such a polit-ical hot potato, says Bolt, no justice wanted to put his name on the opin-ion, and it was issued unsigned in 1994.

BMW appealed the decision all the way to the U.S. Supreme Court, at-tracting the attention of the nation's tort reform infrastructure. Bolt says business groups filed nearly forty amici briefs on BMW's behalf. Even the *Washington Post* and a host of large national media corporations filed a brief arguing that punitive damages were a threat to free speech (not to mention their bottom lines). On Gore's side, there were three. The high court was receptive to the appeal. By 1994 it had already heard four major constitu-tional challenges to punitive damages since 1988, including another one out of Alabama, and Justice Sandra Day O'Connor had been a consistent critic of punitive damages.

The earlier cases had rejected business groups' arguments that punitive awards were so excessive that they violated the Eighth Amendment's pro-hibition of "excessive fines," largely because none of the money at issue went to the government. But in a 1989 case, *Browning-Ferris Industries v. Kelco Disposal*, a majority of the justices suggested they would be open to a punitive-damages challenge under a different argument, namely that a large punitive-damage award may be a violation of a defendant's Fourteenth Amendment right to due process if it's substantially larger than the compen-satory award.

So for the next several years, business groups would search for the per-fect case to challenge. Their first couple of efforts, involving unsympathetic defendants and complex legal issues, floundered. But then along came Dr. Gore and his BMW.

When his story was pared down for the media, Gore came off like the classic greedy plaintiff, a rich guy looking to get richer off a frivolous lawsuit because his luxury car had a tape line in the paint job. BMW, which hired big Washington PR firms to sell its side of the story, painted itself as the innocent victim of rapacious trial lawyers, irrational jurors, and state court judges in the pocket of those rapacious trial lawyers.

Gore's case landed square in the middle of a heated legislative debate in Congress over products-liability law, including a measure that would have capped punitive damages at $250,000. As part of the lobbying efforts to pass that legislation, business groups had focused on Alabama as the nation's leading "tort hell" and the BMW case became exhibit A as to why Congress needed to do something to rein in punitive damages.

In 1996 the justices found that the punitive award in the Gore case was an unconstitutional violation of BMW's due-process rights, largely because it was so much larger than the actual economic harm alleged to have befallen Dr. Gore. The court sent the case back to the Alabama Supreme Court to reconsider. The state court, by then almost entirely remade from Democrat to Republican, took the U.S. Supreme Court ruling to heart: it reduced the $2-million award to $50,000, a fraction of the amount Gore's lawyer spent litigating the case. As a result, for all his trouble and the abuse heaped on him, Gore ended up with exactly nothing from his lawsuit against BMW except that car buyers across the country would now know whether or not their new BMWs had a fresh paint job—and his lawyers actually lost money.

After the U.S. Supreme Court decision, Alabama juries continued to award punitive damages, some extremely large in cases of egregious conduct. But the BMW decision gave the new conservative state supreme court a powerful tool for ensuring those awards are pyrrhic victories for plaintiffs. In 2002 the Alabama Department of Insurance reviewed all the jury verdicts on appeal that year involving punitive damages. There were eight cases, with judgments totaling $6 million. The court reversed all but one. In 2004 the court reviewed eleven cases involving punitive damages. It completely threw out five; reversed and remanded another four; and affirmed two others, one without comment, and the other, it reduced from $1.5 million to $300,000.

Still, tort reform groups never just declare victory and go home once they've won a major lawsuit restriction. *BMW v. Gore* was for them merely a step in the right direction for a more radical goal: taking juries out of the picture entirely.

★ ★ ★

In 1989 a sea captain with a drinking problem named Joseph Hazelwood steered the Exxon *Valdez* oil tanker into Bligh Reef in Alaska's Prince William Sound. The crash punctured the ship's single hull, spilled more than eleven million gallons of oil into the environmentally sensitive coastline, and decimated the area's famous wildlife. In 1994 an Alaska jury handed down the largest punitive-damage judgment in American history at the time: $5.3 billion to be paid to fishermen and others who'd suffered ill effects from the spill. Naturally, Exxon appealed the award, but as part of its legal strategy, Exxon embarked on a new and novel approach to its defense.

The company began funding a battery of academic research that would challenge the competency of juries to award punitive damages. It hired some of the nation's most prominent economists and legal scholars—including University of Chicago law professor Cass Sunstein; Daniel Kahneman, a Princeton University professor who won a Nobel Prize in economics in 2002; and Kip Viscusi, a professor at Harvard Law School—who argued that punitive damages, if they shouldn't be abolished, should at least be placed in the hands of more "rational" judges and not left to the whims of average Americans in the jury box.

Corporate underwriting of scientific research that is used to influence litigation and politics is an old story. The tobacco industry made it an art. But Exxon's project was new in that it focused on social-science research, and because it was designed to undermine the institution of the jury itself. Exxon has never acknowledged how much money it plowed into the effort (and it maintains that it did not have any control over the conclusions of the studies). But, given the scope of the work, it was likely quite expensive. The studies involved eight thousand jury-eligible citizens and six hundred mock juries on whom the researchers conducted various experiments, purportedly replicating scenes from a courtroom. Some of the results were published in a 2002 book, *Punitive Damages: How Juries Decide,* to much fanfare in legal circles.

The authors of *Punitive Damages* concluded that juries, despite their good intentions, were utterly incapable of making coherent decisions when it came to awarding punitive damages. They're capricious, unpredictable, antibusiness. They refuse to listen to instructions, are biased by hindsight, and on top of that, they're poor risk managers, according to the researchers. Simply put, as Cass Sunstein writes, "people do not know how to 'translate' their moral judgments into dollar amounts." Individuals are bad enough at coming up with appropriate awards on their own, he writes, but when they get together on a jury, they're even worse. The research claims to show that deliberations actually increase the final award substantially, which is, naturally, always a bad thing, according to the research. Judges performed all the tasks far better than the mock jurors, according to *Punitive Damages,* which included a group of judges in its study.

In conclusion, the authors recommend that juries be taken out of the process and that "serious consideration should be given to moving away from the jury and toward a system of civil fines, perhaps through a damages schedule of the sort that has been used in many areas of the law, including workers' compensation and environmental violations." Sunstein writes at the end of the book that "perhaps the ideal system of punitive damages would not involve juries or even judges, but specialists in the subject matter at hand who would be able to create clear guidelines for punitive awards."

Most of the policy prescriptions in the book as well as the articles that preceded it are measures that would benefit Exxon's financial picture. Indeed, they are essentially the same restrictions on lawsuits that tort reformers have been pushing in one way or another for many years. (The call for "experts" to replace juries is a frequent one in medical malpractice debates.) The authors of the studies have insisted they were given complete autonomy in pursuing their work.

One academic who took Exxon money, however, was fired after he produced an article that conflicted with the company's political agenda. William Freudenburg, a sociology professor then at the University of Wisconsin (now at the University of California, Santa Barbara), published a paper in early 2005 detailing his experiences with Exxon. As an ethnographic researcher, Freudenburg is a compulsive note taker, and he kept "field notes" on all his conversations and interactions with Exxon during the course of his engagement with the company. In his article, Freudenburg excerpts many of his notes at length, and they show in detail exactly what Exxon was looking for when it contracted with him for academic research.

For instance, Freudenburg recounts his conversations with a man later identified by the *Los Angeles Times* as Terry Gardner, a company official.

According to Freudenburg, Gardner told him that Exxon wanted to commission research that would help in its appeal of the *Valdez* verdict by influencing judges. "With the judges, there's at least a reasonably good chance that they'll be able to see things as they ought to be," Gardner reportedly told Freudenburg.

Gardner indicated that the company was thinking long-term; Exxon believed that the *Valdez* case would ultimately go all the way up to the U.S. Supreme Court. Gardner was open with Freudenburg about Exxon's strategy in shaping judges' opinions. He mentioned the ever-important media campaign, which included placing articles in major newspapers.

Despite misgivings, Freudenburg signed on with Exxon and eventually drafted a paper he planned to submit to the journal *Risk Analysis*. In it he suggested that while punitive-damage awards don't do much for public safety, more corporate transparency was critical to reducing the chance of environmental disasters. After he sent the paper to Exxon, the company terminated his contract. Apparently, Freudenburg's analysis wasn't exactly what it was looking for; Exxon wasn't about to embrace "openness" in its corporate operations—lawyers might find more reasons to sue!

Other academics did, however, publish a number of articles with financial support from Exxon, all of which discussed the evils of punitive damages and the juries that award them. As their research began to trickle out of the academy, other scholars who specialize in empirical research on the legal system were quick to spot significant flaws. The critics' major complaint was that the starting point for the research—that punitive awards are frequent, high, unpredictable, and vastly out of proportion with the actual damages suffered by the plaintiff—conflicted substantially with nearly every other authoritative study on real-world punitive-damage awards. One of the book authors, Reid Hastie, writes, "To our knowledge, there is not a single instance in which our results disagree with findings from other experiments conducted by independent groups of behavioral researchers or with any findings from the statistical analysis of actual trial verdicts."

Not so, countered Duke law professor Neil Vidmar in a 2004 *Emory Law Journal* article. Vidmar, an expert himself in experimental jury studies and empirical research on the jury system, investigated real punitive-damage awards given by juries in Florida between 1989 and 1998. He found what just about every other researcher who has taken a hard look at actual punitive damages has discovered: they're rare, becoming more so, and they're usually pretty small relative to the compensatory awards. And businesses only incur them when they do something really, really bad. Vidmar is no raving anticorporate Nader-ite. He actually worked once for Exxon himself as a consultant on the *Valdez* litigation years ago. While he has done some work for plaintiff lawyers challenging state tort reform laws as unconstitutional, Vidmar's Florida research was funded entirely by Duke University.

In Florida, the numbers simply spoke for themselves. Vidmar, working with American Bar Foundation research fellow Mary Rose, turned up only about twenty-three punitive-damage awards a year, one quarter of which were in drunk-driving and other car crash cases. Vidmar and Rose also discovered that the rate at which punitive damages were awarded had fallen even as Florida's population skyrocketed, and the median punitive award was only about two thirds of the compensatory award. In effect, Elmer Norman was highly unusual.

One of the premises of the Exxon-funded research is that juries are irrationally awarding excessive punitive damages in cases where a business defendant doesn't really deserve them, because it had met a government safety standard, for instance. But when Vidmar and Rose took a look at the facts in individual cases in Florida, they found that most of the awards did look to be very much well deserved. In one case, for instance, a South American airline had removed disgruntled passengers from a flight during a stopover, detained them, strip-searched them, and then left them stranded in a foreign country. In another case, a manufacturing plant had been illegally dumping toxic chemicals into a trash Dumpster near a residential neighborhood. The government had fined the company as a result, and the company claimed to have stopped the dumping. But one day a nine-year-old boy and his friend climbed into the Dumpster to play. They were overcome by toxic fumes and died.

Some of the awards were rather unusual, but these said more about Florida than its juries. Vidmar and Rose had to create a special category for a cluster of lawsuits designated the "improper treatment of dead persons." These cases included one filed by the parents of a Haitian boy who claimed a hospital harvested their son's organs without their consent. In another case, a funeral home lost a woman's amputated legs that were supposed to be kept on ice until she died, so that her entire body could be buried in proper Orthodox Jewish fashion. These cases resulted in the most lopsided ratio between compensatory and punitive damages—about six to one—but that's largely because the economic losses involved were minimal.

Vidmar and Rose did find some extremely large punitive-damage awards, ranging from $6 million to $325 million. But of the twenty largest awards, seven weren't ever likely to be paid, mostly because the defendants were bankrupt, insolvent, or, in one case, facing criminal charges. Three other awards were either reduced or overturned on appeal.

While real juries in Florida proved to be rather predictable in awarding punitive-damage awards, the Exxon mock jurors were all over the map in making decisions about when to award punitive damages and for how much. One reason is that the experiments really didn't replicate what goes on in trials and jury deliberations.

Richard Lempert, a law and sociology professor at the University of Michigan, wrote a critique of one of the early Exxon articles in 1999 in the *DePaul Law Review.* He observes that the trial viewed by mock jurors in a study conducted by Kip Viscusi and Reid Hastie was a video that lasted only fifteen minutes, with a script of less than three thousand words. Given that some complex trials can take weeks—years, in one Monsanto case— with hours of expert testimony on both sides, Lempert writes, "the study's mock jurors receive so much less information than jurors receive in actual trials that there is no scientific basis for assuming that the magnitude of the effects found in the study resembles those found in actual trials." He also notes that in a real trial, the jurors would have heard from the defense counsel, who would have argued against any punitive awards. The researchers often simply left out the other side.

Based on the fake juries' performances, the researchers recommend that judges should take over the function of awarding punitive damages. Viscusi writes that his research shows evidence that "judges are much more willing than jurors . . . to refrain from imposing punitive damages"—which, presumably, is the desired outcome. Again, though, the research conflicts substantially with more than sixty years' worth of real-world data showing that not only do juries and judges both suffer from some of the same sorts of biases, but that when presented with the same set of facts in a trial, they tend to reach the same conclusions.

The most famous study came in the 1950s, when Hans Zeisel and Harry Kalven Jr. undertook a massive study of the American jury system, funded by the Ford Foundation. They surveyed judges in about four thousand real jury trials around the country to see whether and where judges and juries diverged in their opinions. While their research focused on criminal cases, they found that, surprisingly, judges agreed with the jury's verdict 78 percent of the time. Other research since then has come to similar conclusions on the civil side. In 2002 Cornell law professor Theodore Eisenberg and his colleagues published a study comparing the trial outcomes of judges and juries. The researchers found that there was very little difference between the rate at which each group awarded punitive damages or even in the ratio of punitive to compensatory damages. As Eisenberg has written, the rate of agreement between judges and juries is better than the rate between scientists doing peer review, employment interviewers ranking applicants, and psychiatrists and physicians diagnosing patients.

One possible reason for the huge disconnect between the Exxon-funded findings and all the other research on judge-jury agreement is that the judges selected for the study weren't exactly a representative sample. Viscusi and his colleagues surveyed judges who were attending conferences sponsored by the University of Kansas Law and Organizational Economics Center (LOEC), held in Copper Mountain, Colorado, and Sanibel, Florida, in 1997. The LOEC was founded in 1995 with $1 million in seed money from the Fred C. and Mary R. Koch Foundation, one of the charitable arms of the oil and gas powerhouse Koch Industries. Other donors have been the right-wing John M. Olin Foundation and a host of other corporate interests.

The corporations and the foundations foot the bill for judges to vacation in swank resorts and eat crab cakes poolside in exchange for their indoctrination in free-market economic theory taught by other luminaries from Koch-funded libertarian think tanks and university programs. As a result, the group may have been far more likely to take a dim view of punitive damages to begin with compared with other judges.

The problems with the research really aren't so surprising. Even beyond the funding issues, some of the academics chosen for the work were already well-known critics of punitive damages and juries in general. Viscusi, for instance, has been a regular and well-paid expert witness for tobacco companies and is on record supporting the abolition of punitive damages. His free-market sensibilities are such that he once published a study arguing that tobacco companies save the government money because smokers die earlier, thus resulting in lower health care costs. Even the tobacco industry disavowed the work.

All of this would be an obscure academic debate except that the research has had a quiet yet enormous influence on the nation's civil justice system. Because of the huge number of subjects involved in the experiments and the participation by eminent scholars, judges have treated the Exxon-funded research like gospel. In 2002 U.S. District Court Judge Jack Weinstein in the Eastern District of New York cited *Punitive Damages* as if it were the final word on the subject. Writing that in the "pathbreaking empirical multidisciplinary study," the authors had shown that although jurors were perfectly capable of assessing compensatory damages or even agreeing on the moral and ethical features of defendants, "they have no criteria or standards enabling them to translate their findings into dollar amounts."

The U.S. Supreme Court cited the work in an important 2001 case, *Cooper Industries v. Leatherman Tool Group.* An Illinois judge cited the research in 2002, saying, "Random and freakish punitive awards have no place in federal court, and intellectual discipline should be maintained." Of course, no defendant made better use of the research than Exxon itself. Soon after the first articles were published, the research started to pop up in Exxon's own appeals, including one in the *Valdez* spill case in 1997 before the Ninth Circuit, in which Exxon noted that "these articles present recent social-science research demonstrating that jurors are generally incapable of performing the tasks the law assigns to them in punitive-damage cases." While Exxon cited the work, it failed to mention that it had also financed it.

The research investment paid off. In 2001 the Ninth Circuit sent the *Valdez* case back to Alaska, ordering the original judge to reduce the punitive award, which he lowered to $4 billion. Exxon continued to appeal, though, and for good reason. A Supreme Court ruling in its favor that instituted more restrictions on punitive damages in general would help the company not only in the *Valdez* case but in others, including one pending in Alabama involving an $11-billion punitive award. Perhaps the biggest beneficiary of the work, though, was the insurance industry, which beat Exxon to the punch in presenting a major punitive-damages challenge to the U.S. Supreme Court.

Sixty-three-year-old Curtis Campbell was driving north through Sardine Canyon near Logan, Utah, in 1981 when he made the disastrous decision to pass six vans ahead of him on the two-lane road. The ensuing accident left a nineteen-year-old college student dead and another young man permanently disabled. Campbell himself survived, and the injured parties sued him for damages and wrongful death. The injured parties repeatedly offered to settle with his insurance company, State Farm, for $50,000, the limit of Campbell's auto insurance policy. State Farm, however, forced the case to go to trial even though it knew Campbell was responsible for the accident.

The company led Campbell to believe that it would pay for any damages assessed above the limits of his policy. But when the jury awarded the plaintiffs $185,000, a State Farm agent told Campbell and his wife, "You may want to put For Sale signs on your property to get things moving," indicating that State Farm had no intention of paying.

Stunned, Campbell got a non–State Farm attorney, who sued the insurance giant for acting in bad faith. During the course of the litigation, Campbell's attorneys showed that State Farm's forcing Campbell to trial, far from being an "honest mistake," as the company argued, was part of a nationwide policy to meet corporate fiscal goals by capping payouts on claims. The tactics were most actively employed against "financially vulnerable" people—poor racial or ethnic minorities, women, and the elderly, who State Farm believed wouldn't put up much of a fight. State Farm argued that practices in place in 1981 had been abolished, but Campbell's attorneys alleged that they were very much still in place when the case went to trial more than a decade later.

To prove that State Farm's treatment of Campbell was intentional, his lawyers introduced extensive evidence of the company's fraudulent practices all around the country, which included concealing and destroying documents to avoid disclosure of the claims policy, and systematically harassing and intimidating opposing claimants, witnesses, and attorneys. State Farm routinely used its vast wealth to engage in "mad-dog defense tactics" to wear out opposing attorneys by prolonging litigation, making meritless objections, claiming false privileges, and abusing the law and motion process. (State Farm's litigation eventually outlived Campbell, who died in 2001 at the age of eighty-three.)

Harvey Rosenfield, president of the California-based nonprofit Foundation for Taxpayer and Consumer Rights, says when he originally read the Utah judge's opinion, he thought it would have been grounds for State Farm to lose its license to practice in several states.

Indeed, State Farm's behavior was so egregious that the jury awarded Campbell $145 million in punitive damages, or about one quarter of 1 percent of State Farm's wealth. The trial judge lowered the award to $25 million, but the Utah Supreme Court—hardly a bastion of radical liberalism—later restored the original award on the grounds that, because the company's behavior was largely clandestine, it would be punished, at most, in only one out of every fifty thousand cases even though it would affect large numbers of the state's citizens. The court concluded that the verdict needed to be high enough to serve the public interest.

State Farm challenged the award and appealed the decision all the way to the U.S. Supreme Court. The size of the award alone might have been enough to motivate the company's appeals, but State Farm had other incentives as well. Despite all the media coverage of punitive-damage awards in products-liability cases over prescription drugs or cigarettes, it's insurance companies who are most often on the receiving end of big punitive-damage awards relative to the actual damages in a lawsuit.

In 1997 the Rand Corporation published a study on punitive-damage awards in financial-injury cases and found that lawsuits against insurance companies had the largest ratio between punitive and compensatory awards. Their data show that punitive awards in insurance cases were on average four times larger than the compensatory awards, much higher than the median Vidmar found in Florida for all punitive awards. The study also showed why caps that limit punitive damages to three times the compensatory awards are such a windfall for insurance companies: in Alabama, for instance, such a cap would have eliminated more than 80 percent of all punitive-damages awarded by juries in the state in the 1990s.

Americans may not like trial lawyers, but they really don't like insurance companies, as the aftermath of Hurricane Katrina quickly showed. While they sell peace of mind, insurance companies regularly leave customers flapping in the wind and rarely suffer any consequences for it from the government. Even though companies like State Farm engage in interstate commerce, Congress exempted insurance companies from federal regulation in 1945 in the McCarran-Ferguson Act. The industry is also exempt from antitrust regulation, and it even convinced Congress to prevent the Federal Trade Commission from investigating its practices. As a result, the job of regulating the multibillion-dollar insurance industry falls solely to badly outmatched and underfunded state regulatory agencies, which often have cozy ties with the industry itself. In Utah, state insurance regulators testified against Campbell, even though at the time they were supposed to be investigating State Farm for fraudulent claims handling.

Lawsuits like Campbell's—and the threat of large punitive-damage awards—are often the only recourse consumers have to prevent insurance companies from abusing them with abandon, and juries seem to recognize that. The U.S. Supreme Court, though, did not. Rather than defer to the good judgment of the Utah justices, the high court rewarded State Farm for its litigiousness and ruled that the $145-million punitive award in Campbell violated State Farm's due process rights. Citing the Exxon-funded research, the high court recommended that a more reasonable award would be four to ten times the amount of compensatory damages or something more closely related to the size of the state's maximum civil penalty for such behavior. In Utah, that figure was only $10,000.

For a company with a net worth of $32 billion, a $10,000 award could hardly be considered punitive. In fact, the Utah Supreme Court had noted that evidence during the trial showed that State Farm's employees didn't even bother to report a punitive-damage award to corporate headquarters unless it was over $100 million. "The ability to make the punishment fit the crime is very adversely affected by this decision," says Laurence Tribe, the Harvard law professor who argued the Campbell case. "There will be no reason for an unscrupulous company not to do whatever they want to maximize profits."

In 2004, with marching orders from the brethren in DC, the Utah Supreme Court reduced the original verdict in Campbell to $9 million in punitive damages—about nine times the actual damages, plus interest. The award was split three ways, between Inez Campbell and the two other victims of the car crash. Meanwhile, Exxon, which funded the research that helped State Farm, was in for a bit of a surprise. Because of the State Farm decision, the *Valdez* case was sent back yet again to the Ninth Circuit. Rather than reduce the judgment further, however, the judge decided it wasn't high enough and raised it to $4.5 billion.

CHAPTER FOURTEEN

Can I Get a Witness?: Junk Science and the War on Experts

In 1989, Rossville, Georgia, resident Bridget Siharath gave birth to a little girl. While she was in the hospital recovering from a Caesarean section, hospital staff gave her Parlodel, a drug to dry up her breast milk. A young woman raised in the country, Siharath says no one ever asked her if she wanted to breastfeed; they just gave her the drug, and she took it. "I just figured they knew what they were doing," she says.

After she started taking Parlodel, Siharath says she got extremely aggravated, and her blood pressure soared. The hospital staff discontinued the medication without telling her why, and her blood pressure returned to normal. But when she was discharged, her doctor wrote her a full prescription for Parlodel, which her mother helped her fill on the way home. The next morning, Siharath took one of the pills and returned to the hospital to pick up her daughter, who'd stayed in the hospital for an extra day of monitoring. In the elevator up to the nursery, Siharath's mother, Julia Stevens, says Siharath told her that her head hurt so badly that she felt like the "top of my head's coming off."

While they were talking to the pediatrician, Siharath collapsed on the floor, overcome by grand mal seizures. Her tongue rolled back and her face turned blue. She was rushed to the emergency room. Stevens said the hospital staff told her in the chapel that her daughter might not survive. She had stopped breathing and her heart had stopped. Siharath says she doesn't remember anything until she woke up tied down in an ambulance with a tube down her throat. She was on a respirator, having suffered three seizures and a subarachnoid hemorrhagic stroke. "The pain in my

239

head was so bad I begged them to take the IVs out. I just wanted to die," she says.

Siharath spent six days in intensive care and nearly two weeks in the hospital. She was paralyzed on the left side of her body and spent the next year learning how to walk again. She barely recognized the father of her child, who she'd been with for three years and was planning to marry. "They had to show me pictures of my baby because I couldn't remember her," she says. Siharath had always wanted to have a big family, but after the stroke, doctors told her having more children would be extremely dangerous. The brain trauma left her with mental issues that required long-term psychiatric treatment. She's afraid to fly, suffers from serious depression and even today, has difficulty working steadily because of health problems.

Doctors couldn't figure out what had caused the stroke and seizures. Siharath didn't smoke. She didn't have any pregnancy complications that sometimes result in such problems, such as high blood pressure. Most of all, though, Siharath was only 17, and young women rarely ever suffer such postpartum complications.

Siharath spent the next five years trying to piece her life back together, while the origins of her medical problems remained a mystery. But one day in 1994, Siharath saw a TV news show about a woman who had suffered a strikingly similar incident to hers, only the woman ended up paralyzed as a result. The woman blamed Parlodel.

Curious, Siharath went to the hospital and read through her medical records. There, she found a note that said that the staff observed that her blood pressure had gone up on Parlodel from the very first administration. Siharath contacted a lawyer, and she later learned that the FDA had asked Sandoz, the drug maker, to pull Parlodel from the market two weeks before she had her stroke. The government agency had received reports dating back to 1980, when the drug was first approved, that showed 32 women had died as a result of taking Parlodel, and more than 500 others had suffered from serious complications including strokes and heart attacks after giving birth and taking the drug.

When the FDA sounded the alarm in 1989 that drugs that suppressed lactation were dangerous, every other drug company that manufactured them pulled them from the market, except Sandoz (now Novartis), which made Parlodel. Sandoz marketed the drug to hospitals, and between 300,000 to 600,000 women every year continued to use its product. The FDA dragged its feet and allowed Parlodel to remain on the market until 1994, when Sandoz finally agreed to withdraw it as a lactation suppression drug. (It continued to sell the drug for other approved uses such as treating Parkinson's disease.)

In 1995, Siharath sued Sandoz in federal court in Georgia. Given her youth and lack of preexisting conditions, as well as the FDA's case reports of adverse events, Siharath had a compelling case. Researchers had long known that Parlodel was in a class of drugs known to increase the risk of stroke. Animal studies showed that drugs like Parlodel caused arteries to constrict, as did some limited studies conducted on humans. But the litigation dragged on for six years, until March 2001, when a federal judge ruled in Sandoz's favor and threw out Siharath's lawsuit before it ever even got to a jury. He concluded that the battery of scientific experts she'd called on to testify didn't prove that the drug had caused her stroke and seizures, mainly because of a lack of epidemiological studies and human clinical trials, studies the manufacturer had never conducted before putting Parlodel on the market.

The judge based his ruling on a 1993 U.S. Supreme Court decision called *Daubert v. Merrell Dow Pharmaceuticals* that in theory was supposed to keep "junk science" out of the courtroom. The decision instructed judges to serve as stricter gatekeepers, screening expert testimony before letting it go before a jury. It turned out to be one of the most important supreme court decisions of the second half of the twentieth century, and it has had a devastating effect on the ability of average citizens like Siharath to bring lawsuits against big corporations over defective products and environmental pollution.

The *Daubert* decision didn't come in a political vacuum. In the years leading up to the case, tort reform groups had sponsored a wave of publicity designed to convince the public, legislators, and mostly judges that the courts were awash with disreputable plaintiffs' experts—hired guns who were undermining the integrity of the system and swaying juries with bogus testimony. (Defense experts, naturally, were never part of the dialogue.) The clarion call for a crackdown on plaintiff experts came in 1991, when Manhattan Institute scholar Peter Huber published his book *Galileo's Revenge.*

Huber was a darling of the tort reform movement, having published a highly influential book, *Liability,* a few years earlier. An MIT-trained engi-

neer with a Harvard law degree, Huber had clerked for Ruth Bader Gins-
burg on the DC U.S. Court of Appeals for the DC Circuit Court and for
Sandra Day O'Connor on the U.S. Supreme Court. O'Connor would later
cite Huber's work in two major decisions on punitive damages. He also
served as a technical adviser to the Reagan Justice Department on breaking
up AT&T.

Not only was he brilliant, but Huber knew how to turn a phrase, and
with *Galileo's Revenge,* Huber coined the term "junk science," which would
become the mantra of corporate groups looking to discredit plaintiff experts
in litigation. The book created something of a firestorm with allegations that
the courts were overrun with charlatans masquerading as scientists who
would testify to anything for money, all of which was helping undeserving
plaintiffs win millions of dollars and bankrupt benevolent corporations,
which could no longer make childhood vaccines and other useful social
goods. Huber called for "wise judges" to seize control of the situation and
assert themselves as gatekeepers to the courtroom, where they should prevent at all costs such rogues from ever getting in front of a jury.

For all its pithy sound bites, colorful anecdotes about plaintiffs winning money in "cancer by pothole" cases and popular acclaim, *Galileo's Revenge* suffered from some serious flaws. Mainly, Huber offered no
compelling evidence that the anecdotes he presented were in any way
representative of a larger "crisis." No data supported his assertion that the
courts were under siege with junk science, or that juries were unduly
swayed by fringe scientists making outlandish claims. At the time the
book came out, the types of cases Huber complained the most about—
products-liability lawsuits—had been steadily disappearing, having declined 35 percent in the previous six years in federal courts. And for all
their "hired guns," plaintiffs in those remaining cases were getting slaugh-
tered. Their success rates in federal products-liability trials fell from about
41 percent in 1979 to 31 percent in 1989. Plaintiffs fared even worse in
pretrial proceedings handled by judges, losing nearly 75 percent of the
time in 1989, a sign that judges were already doing quite a bit of gatekeep-
ing. In 1993 the Carnegie Commission on Science, Technology, and Government would conclude that the notion that junk science was flooding
the courtroom was highly overblown and that "many of the concerns are
greatly exaggerated."

Nonetheless, Huber became the Moses of the junk-science movement,
and with all the publicity and drumbeating from the tort reform groups, the
U.S. Supreme Court eventually answered his call.

★ ★ ★

In 1974 Jason Daubert was born missing three fingers on his right hand and the lower bone on his right arm. A few years later, evidence started to surface that such limb malformations might be caused by a drug prescribed to pregnant women for morning sickness called Bendectin, made by Merrell Dow Pharmaceuticals. The San Diego boy's mother had taken Bendectin when she was pregnant with him, and when she learned about the possible link, she and her husband filed suit against Merrell Dow in federal court in 1984. Four years later, a Southern California trial court granted Merrell Dow's motion for summary judgment, a move that meant the case was so weak it didn't even warrant getting sent to a jury. The judge found that the Dauberts' proposed scientific evidence didn't support their claims that Bendectin had caused Jason's birth defects. The Dauberts appealed, setting off a long journey that eventually led them all the way to the U.S. Supreme Court.

The *Daubert* decision was upheld on appeal. The appellate court ruled that the scientific evidence didn't meet the "general acceptance" standard for the introduction of expert testimony under the Frye test, in reference to the 1923 decision in the DC Court of Appeals that had governed expert testimony for many years. The Dauberts appealed again, and the case went to the U.S. Supreme Court over a technical question of whether Frye or the 1975 federal rules of evidence governed expert testimony. The federal rules said that courts should undertake a "preliminary assessment of whether the reasoning or methodology underlying the testimony is scientifically valid and of whether that reasoning or methodology properly can be applied to the facts at issue." They made no mention of "general acceptance," and the Dauberts argued that the rules trumped Frye. In 1993 the high court ruled against Merrell and sent the case back to the Ninth Circuit to reconsider the case using the federal rules rather than Frye. But because the federal rules didn't really spell out how judges should evaluate expert testimony, the high court attempted to provide some guidance.

To that end, Justice Harry Blackmun wrote that testimony must be based on the scientific method, and it must be reliable and relevant to the case at hand. To meet these requirements, the court suggested that testimony should be based on peer-reviewed studies with methods that can be tested through accepted scientific methods and a host of other factors, including certain abstract conditions for "falsifiability, or refutability, or testability."

The court emphasized that judges were supposed to focus only on the experts' methods and principles, not their conclusions. Fact finding and issues of causation were the province of the jury. Blackmun recognized that the rules the court was creating had the potential to keep not just junk science but good science out of the courtroom. Writing for the majority, Blackmun observed, "That even limited screening by the trial judge, on occasion, will prevent the jury from hearing of authentic scientific breakthroughs is simply a consequence of the fact that the Rules are not designed to seek cosmic understanding but, rather, to resolve legal disputes."

Daubert went back to Ninth Circuit Judge Alex Kozinski, who then upheld the trial court's summary judgment using the new Supreme Court definitions, but also, by invoking none other than Peter Huber. Kozinski derived his definition of good science from *Galileo's Revenge,* in which Huber, incidentally, had made Bendectin litigation a centerpiece of his argument (this despite the fact that most juries were finding for the drug company in those cases).

The decision was a huge triumph for business groups who'd been backing the Manhattan Institute, particularly the tobacco industry. With *Daubert,* the Supreme Court had essentially passed a major piece of tort reform that would have cost businesses millions of dollars and years of lobbying to achieve through Congress and state legislatures. The ruling set off a flurry of new satellite litigation brought by defense lawyers encouraged to challenge expert testimony at every step under the new rules as a way of forcing plaintiffs to exhaust their resources early in a case, leaving them in weaker bargaining positions or simply shut out of the courtroom.

Just in case some federal judges did take the more liberal reading of *Daubert,* business groups set about educating them, and eventually state judges too, on the "proper" use of the new ruling, which in their minds, was clearly to restrict more plaintiff testimony. For instance, the Civil Justice Reform Group, the leading business lobby working for restrictions on products-liability lawsuits in the 1990s, donated $300,000 to Harvard Law School to create "the Daubert Project," headed by law professor Charles Nesson, who filed a brief on behalf of Dow in *Daubert.* Other donors included Procter & Gamble, which anted up another $100,000 to pay for the group's "educational" seminars for state and federal court judges that it held around the country in the mid-1990s.

The efforts seem to have paid off. In 2001 researchers from the Rand

Institute for Civil Justice found that judges were not only excluding expert scientific evidence more often but that they were then using the exclusions to throw out plaintiffs' cases all together. For instance, judges in the Third Circuit had excluded experts 53 percent of the time in the two years before *Daubert.* By 1996 the court was excluding that testimony in 70 percent of the cases where it was an issue. The result on plaintiffs' cases was striking. In the four years before *Daubert,* judges had granted summary judgment in 21 percent of the challenges to expert testimony. In the four years after Daubert, that number more than doubled, to 48 percent, and nearly all of the rulings—90 percent—went against plaintiffs.

Daubert has not only doomed many plaintiffs' cases that might once have gone forward at least to a jury, but the new rules, which require extensive pretrial hearings and expert testimony themselves, have made products-liability and toxic tort cases so expensive that many lawyers won't take them anymore, regardless of merit. Esther Berezofsky, a toxic-torts lawyer in New Jersey, says the biggest impact is on individual cases, with just a single plaintiff. "Lawyers can't take cases like that. They can't afford it, and [big companies] know that. It's exactly what the overall design is. We've seen the evolution of *Daubert* in keeping people out of the courthouse." Indeed, after *Daubert,* and a follow-up decision by the Supreme Court extending its provisions to all types of expert testimony, not just scientific, the number of products-liability lawsuits filed in federal court fell 56 percent between 1997 and 2000. The number of federal nonasbestos-products liability trials has also fallen, from 267 trials in 1992 to only 87 in 2003.

"*Daubert* has been successful," says David Michaels, a professor of environmental and occupational health at the George Washington University School of Public Health and Health Services, who has testified as an expert in litigation for plaintiffs. "Unless a case is an easy one or it's really large, the case gets dropped. Many people who should be getting in aren't."

Daubert has served Corporate America well. As they've done with global warming research, Exxon and other big companies have found that simply muddying the scientific water for a judge is enough to get potentially significant lawsuits dismissed in the early stages, based solely on challenges to plaintiff experts. For instance, in 2000 a federal judge in Louisiana threw out a case filed by Clinton Chambers, an independent contractor at an Exxon refinery in Baton Rouge who was diagnosed with a rare form of leukemia in 1996. He eventually sued Exxon, alleging that his illness was the result of benzene exposure at the refinery. Benzene is classified by the EPA as a known carcinogen, and its ability to cause all sorts of blood cancers is well documented.

Chambers's lawyer hired three experts to testify about the relationship between the benzene exposure and Chambers's cancer. One of the experts, Dr. Peter Infante, was an epidemiologist who once headed up the Office of Standards Review at the U.S. Department of Labor's Occupational Safety and Health Administration (OSHA), which was charged with setting standards and regulations for the use of toxics in the workplace. Now an adjunct professor of environmental and occupational health at George Washington University, Infante had also written the definitive 1977 study confirming that benzene caused leukemia and planned to testify about a 1995 follow-up study he published that showed benzene exposure caused a four-fold increase in the risk of contracting the rare type of leukemia that Clinton Chambers had.

Jurors never got a chance to hear what he had to say, however, as lawyers for Exxon filed a *Daubert* challenge arguing that the plaintiff's experts had failed to prove the link between benzene and Chambers's cancer with better epidemiological evidence. Infante noted that the cancer is so rare that it's hard to find enough people who died from it for a good epidemiological study, but he'd done just that in his 1995 study.

Nonetheless, in 2000 U.S. District Court Judge John V. Parker agreed with Exxon, stating that the plaintiff hadn't offered any epidemiological studies that proved a statistically significant risk of contracting the type of leukemia Chambers had from benzene exposure. Without the experts, Chambers's case was sunk, and it quietly went away. Meanwhile, after the case ended, more studies confirmed Infante's research that benzene does in fact cause the rarer form of leukemia that Chambers contracted.

Infante says that scientists have known for a long time that benzene caused leukemia, long before they had epidemiological evidence for it. Researchers used things like case reports, clinical observations, and animal studies to draw pretty good conclusions. He says that the first occupational disease ever really documented by doctors was scrotal cancer caused by coal tar pitch. There were never any epidemiological studies, he says, but nonetheless, scientists used observed cases to prove that the tar caused this particular type of cancer.

These time-tested techniques scientists use to deduce cause and effect are being thrown out right and left by judges who are requiring expert testimony to meet standards that even clinicians don't use in their day-to-day practice. Infante says that in the Chambers case, "the court is just simply wrong," noting that his research had appeared in a peer-reviewed journal. "This is a good example of how the judge wasn't competent."

Unfortunately, in such cases, plaintiffs don't have much recourse. In a 1997 decision in *General Electric Co. v. Joiner,* the U.S. Supreme Court followed up on its *Daubert* ruling to decide on the standards for appealing the exclusion of expert testimony. It said that basically, losers could appeal only if the judge had abused his or her discretion, an extremely high standard to meet legally. As a result, appellate courts almost never overturn a trial court decision excluding expert testimony. The Fourth Circuit, for instance, went almost five years, in thirty-two consecutive decisions, without ever overturning a trial court decision that excluded expert evidence, according to a tally kept by attorney and *Daubert*-on-the-web blogger Peter Nordberg. When it did finally break the record at the tail end of 2005, it ruled in a criminal case, not a civil one.

Before *Daubert,* most of the fighting over expert witnesses happened in a courtroom, before a jury, which got to listen to the testimony and cross-examination, along with a host of other information before making a decision. *Daubert* essentially took that process away from the jury and vested judges with vast new powers to affect the outcome of litigation, in part because people like Huber argued that judges were supposed to be better than juries in handling complex scientific matters. The practical results of the ruling are less convincing, however.

A classic example is a case in New Jersey filed by a woman named Kathy Magistrini against her former employer, One Hour Martinizing Dry Cleaning. Magistrini had worked for the dry cleaner for two years in the late 1970s, and through her work she was exposed to the chemical perchloroethylene (PCE), manufactured by Dow Chemical. Two years after leaving the job, Magistrini was diagnosed with leukemia, an unusual cancer in an adult her age. She had to undergo a bone-marrow transplant and total body irradiation treatment that left her suffering from mouth damage, hair loss, infections, and other horrible side effects. The treatment also left her unable to have children at nineteen.

It wasn't until the mid-1990s that Magistrini discovered there might be a link between her old job and her cancer, after her husband saw a TV broadcast on the issue. Shortly afterward, Magistrini filed suit against the dry cleaner and Dow. The defendants challenged Magistrini's experts, who were called to testify about the links between the chemicals and her illness. The judge held a *Daubert* hearing that lasted for four days—longer than some trials. In the proceedings, the defendants added experts to testify about the plaintiff's experts. The plaintiff's lawyer then complained that *those* experts should be subjected to a *Daubert* hearing to see if they were qualified to testify at the *Daubert* hearing. The judge would later reject this motion, noting that the plaintiff had asked "the Court to act as gatekeeper to itself." There were so many experts on both sides—at least six total—that the judge hired a doctor as a "technical adviser" during the hearing.

Despite the layers of experts, the main issue in the hearings was the proposed testimony of Dr. David Ozonoff, arguably the nation's leading expert on PCE. (He was the plaintiff expert featured in the movie and book *A Civil Action,* and had studied PCE for twenty years, long before he ever got involved with litigation.) Ozonoff took a medical history from Magistrini and reviewed her medical records before concluding in a two-hundred-page report that it was likely that the PCE caused her cancer.

After all the testimony, the judge ejected Ozonoff based on a convoluted notion that he hadn't numerically weighted each study he reviewed and evaluated them accordingly. No matter that no one in his field evaluated data that way. The judge thought he should have and, as a result, threw out his testimony. "I think the Magistrini case was a real miscarriage of justice," says Ozonoff, who believes that the law requires judges simply to find that an expert is qualified to testify and not to evaluate him or her based on their conclusions. "To me, [the judge] just put herself in the place of the jury."

The *Daubert* hearings cost Berezofksy, the plaintiff's lawyer, thousands and thousands of dollars, yet never even reached a jury. *Daubert* "is not about efficiency," says Brooklyn Law professor Margaret Berger, who is an expert on expert testimony. She notes that judicial decisions on scientific evidence have been all over the map, and scientists believe that some of them are far out of line with the way science is done in practice.

A bigger concern, though, is who is really making the decisions about the evidence. In the Magistrini case, there was a court-appointed technical adviser who assisted the court in its decision regarding whether the case got to the jury. Yet the adviser wasn't even subjected to the same screening process—i.e., allowing the parties to argue for or against the person's designation as an "expert"—as the experts in question in the *Daubert* hearings. And as Infante and Berger both note, *Daubert* hearings generate an enormous amount of paperwork for a judge, far more than there would be in a regular trial. Federal judges have huge caseloads, which means that for the most part, a good chunk of the scientific evidence coming before the court isn't being handled by "wise judges" but by their twenty-five-year-old clerks, fresh out of law school.

It's not hard to see why corporate defendants like *Daubert* so much. There's no doubt that it's saved them a lot of money and public embarrassment by avoiding jury trials that might expose their more unsavory business practices and sanction them with big punitive-damage awards. Occasionally, though, lawsuits thrown out by a federal judge on a *Daubert* motion over expert testimony will have a counterpart that survives in state court and proceeds to trial. The differences in outcome between the judicial fiat in a *Daubert* hearing and a jury trial, where average citizens are allowed to view a wide range of evidence—and not just scientific evidence—show why *Daubert* has been such a boon to big companies.

Take the case of Parlodel. The drug generated a host of litigation, but as in Siharath's case, judges in federal court have frequently barred plaintiff experts who've sought to testify that the drug caused a plaintiff's injuries. The reasons have varied: some judges rejected the results of animal studies that showed pretty conclusively that Parlodel could cause the conditions leading to strokes and heart attacks. The judges said they wanted more experiments on humans, even though such studies would likely be unethical given the drug's known dangers. Others wanted more epidemiological studies, which didn't exist because the drug company never conducted any. None of the rulings ever found that the experts involved were charlatans or had doctored their credentials or faked data to prove the drug caused strokes—the kinds of things you might expect from a junk-science practitioner.

When the cases have been allowed before a jury, jurors occasionally have taken a much different view of the evidence. In March 2004 a jury in a Kentucky state court heard the case of a thirty-two-year-old woman who'd died after taking Parlodel shortly after giving birth to her second child. Not only did the jury hear from several of the same experts who'd been excluded from the federal cases, but they also heard more about Sandoz's conduct in marketing the drug, something that was largely absent from any of the federal *Daubert* hearings.

In 1987 the FDA had forced Sandoz to change the warning label on Parlodel to reflect an increasing number of case reports of strokes and heart attacks in young women linked to the drug. Yet the Kentucky plaintiff presented evidence suggesting that the manufacturer continued to mask the dangers in its marketing to doctors, instructing sales reps to avoid any discussion of the alleged risks unless questioned by the doctors. Even as it told the FDA that it didn't advocate use of the drug as a standard therapy for most pregnant women because of the possible risks, it nonetheless continued to push hospitals to adopt Parlodel as part of their "standing order" regimens for all postpartum women who didn't plan to breastfeed, even though many of those women should never have taken it because of pregnancy-related complications like high blood pressure.

The Kentucky jury was scandalized and found that Parlodel was the likely cause of the woman's death. Jurors awarded her family $19 million, including $11 million in punitive damages, in part based on testimony from the very experts who'd been excluded in several other federal court cases. The state supreme court upheld the decision to include the expert testimony, saying that the experts in the case were more than qualified to meet the requirements of expert testimony.

The Kentucky case was the exception, though, not the rule. Thanks to *Daubert,* most of the women like Siharath who believe they were injured by Parlodel have never been able to hold anyone accountable for their injuries. Siharath, now 34, remarried (her last name is now Asher), went back to high school after her ordeal, and has worked for a sympathetic employer for the past decade. But she still suffers from the lingering effects of the stroke, and even 17 years later, she's still angry that the courts never forced the drug company to take responsibility for what happened to her and the other women who took Parlodel. "I'm just an underclass working woman and I don't matter to the courts," she says. "They know this pill caused my problems. It's destroyed my life forever and I'll never get those years back. Someone should be punished for it."

Conclusion:
Why It Matters

In the desert outside of Palm Springs, California, in late January 2005, the waterfalls were burbling and the expansive lawns verdant at the storied La Quinta Resort. Beautiful women in bikinis decorated little pools tucked discreetly into courtyards between the resort's quaint white stucco casitas. Palm trees and the mountain backdrop gave the resort an air of 1930s Hollywood. The stars at the resort that week in 2005, though, were among the most vilified of American professionals: members of the Association of Trial Lawyers of America—personal injury lawyers—who came to Palm Springs to lick their wounds shortly after the inauguration of President George W. Bush to a second term.

A fleet of private jets was lined up at the Palm Springs Airport and the trophy wives were on prominent display, but for the most part, the event was populated with middle-aged white guys from such power centers as Wheeling, West Virginia, who'd come to play winter golf under the tax-deductible guise of "continuing legal education." And despite the glorious setting, $1,000-a-night rooms, and on-site Botox clinic, any masters of the universe on hand were vastly overshadowed by the Grim Reaper.

The convention's bread-and-butter sessions focused on such cheerful topics as litigating nail-gun injuries. ("Did you hear about the guy who was sitting in the barber's chair when a nail gun next door misfired and blew a nail through his brain?") Brain-damaged babies, misdiagnosed rectal bleeding, and doctors' use of Super Glue in the brain brought out the nation's ambulance chasers to pick up tips for wooing juries and winning cases. Of course, "winning cases" is a relative term here. As one lawyer noted in a presentation on misdiagnosed cancer litigation, "There is never a winner in these cases because your client is not likely to survive."

In the exhibit hall, passersby were treated to graphic displays of all the new and accidental ways a human can die painfully. "We try not to get too much blood on them, or people get gored out," said a surprisingly cheerful Matt Watts, the youthful national sales manager from the Presentation Group, a litigation-support outfit whose anatomical illustrations help lawyers explain their cases to juries. He held up a poster board illustrating a cervical spine fusion procedure that shows bright red muscle tissue sheared away from the neck of a woman who bears a slight resemblance to actress Janet Leigh. "Routine surgeries go awry," he shrugged, adding that those mistakes occur more often when the doctor was "out partying last night and operating drunk. Happens a lot more than people think."

Down the hall, a computer auto-looped a cartoon of two little boys happily swimming around a houseboat on Lake Powell. It looked like something you'd see on Nickelodeon until the boys suddenly made faces and dropped to the bottom of the lake, dead from carbon monoxide poisoning, which is apparently epidemic among houseboaters.

The Hall of Horrors continued with booth after booth of accident-reconstruction animations: small cars crushed by tractor trailers; bus rollovers and jet-ski collisions facing off with massive barge wrecks; airplanes exploding, trains colliding with pickup trucks, and the impact on the human body intimately re-created in Technicolor anatomical models. Here, too, were palsied babies, lacerated spleens, an animated film of a doctor breaking his patient's neck while inserting a breathing tube. Asbestos victims wheezed into breathing devices on "day in the life" videos while photos of bruised and battered elderly people illustrated nursing home neglect.

To those who have lobbied hardest to put limits on injured Americans' access to the courthouse, the ATLA convention is exhibit A in their argument that the legal system is out of control. In each houseboat cartoon or colorized X-ray, they see a cottage industry of frivolous litigation or a lawyer-driven extortion scheme designed to redistribute corporate wealth to the less fortunate. Indeed, only in America are death, destruction, and the pursuit of justice so intertwined with freewheeling capitalism, which was also prominently displayed in the Salon de Flores. How else to explain the placement of a colon-polyp video next to a booth for "structured settlements," an entire industry devoted to helping successful plaintiffs manage their winnings?

The ATLA hall reveals all that is horrible, opportunistic, and grotesque about the tort system, and yet it demonstrates so starkly why it's so necessary to protect the health and well-being of average citizens. Most countries don't do it this way. The Europeans have elaborate social safety nets to provide cradle-to-grave benefits that help buffer life's unexpected tragedies and the downsides of capitalism. They have government-provided health insurance, pension systems, substantial unemployment and disability insurance programs that make so much personal injury litigation unnecessary. Suspicious of big government and hostile to taxes, Americans rejected a collective solution long ago in favor of a free-market approach based on the notion that "you break it, you buy it."

Americans have chosen to place the cost of injuries directly on those who caused them, primarily through the civil justice system. If the railroad kills your cow, the theory goes, the railroad should pay you for it. If the railroad could have avoided killing your cow but killed it anyway, the railroad should pay even more. And the threat of having to pay for all those dead cows is supposed to provide an incentive to find ways to avoid killing them in the first place.

The story of how that biblical concept of retributive justice got from the railroad and some cows to houseboats and structured settlements is a bloody one. Modern tort law is the product of the Industrial Revolution. The injuries on display in Palm Springs are different—more babies, fewer cows—but the issues are the same as those at play 100 years ago: who should pay when corporations hurt people in pursuit of profit?

Lawrence Friedman writes in his *A History of American Law* that at the turn of the twentieth century, industrial accidents were killing a staggering thirty-five thousand people a year and injuring two million others. Workers bore the cost of all these injuries, almost exclusively. There was no workers' compensation, no Supplemental Security Disability Insurance (SSDI) Income benefits for the disabled, and certainly no big jury verdicts for injured workers. Nineteenth-century tort law came down firmly on the side of business. Legal rules prevented injured people from collecting damages in a lawsuit if they were even 1 percent responsible for an injury. That meant, for instance, that people who were hit by trains couldn't sue the railroad because they'd dared step onto the train track. The "assumption of risk" doctrine protected dangerous industries from workers' lawsuits on the theory that people who work in, say, coal mines, know from the get-go that the work is dangerous, thus barring any claims against their employers.

The old tort rules didn't allow for wrongful death suits, and even when they did, awards were capped at such scandalously low levels that railroad lawyers would jokingly advise engineers that if they hit someone on the tracks, they should back over him again to ensure that the victim was good and dead. Such rules ensured that after the Triangle Shirtwaist Factory fire in 1911, when young immigrant women leaped to their deaths or burned horribly while trapped in an unsafe garment factory in New York City, the few families that were able to press wrongful death claims for their wives and daughters received seventy-five dollars apiece.

As Friedman writes of these early tort rules: "Enterprise was favored over workers, slightly less so over passengers and members of the public. Juries were suspected—on thin evidence—of lavishness in awarding damages; they had to be kept under firm control. The thrust of the rules, taken as a whole, approached the position that corporate enterprise should be flatly immune from actions for personal injury."

When the leaders of the tort reform movement wax poetic about the good old days before the so called "litigation explosion," before Ralph Nader, this is the era they have in mind. Many of the favored tort reforms would return the nation to the days when the courts primarily protected business from workers and consumers, not the other way around. More and more of these reforms are passing every day, both at the state and federal level.

Since 2001, the Bush administration and a Republican Congress have created many new legal protections for favored industries. In the legislation creating the Department of Homeland Security, for instance, legislators included a measure to immunize from lawsuits any company that sold antiterrorism products. The list of such companies, which had to be certified by DHS, is classified, but is known to include most of the nation's defense contractors, which now can't be sued in state court or held liable under any circumstances for punitive damages should their products fail to, say, detect a bomb on an airplane, or result in anyone's death or injury. In 2005 gun manufacturers won legal immunity from lawsuits filed by victims of shootings. And, of course, there have been ongoing efforts to pass the "cheeseburger bill," which would prevent lawsuits against fast-food restaurants alleging that their products cause obesity.

Even when the movement has succeeded beyond its leaders' wildest dreams, as it did in Texas in 2003, tort reform groups never seem to declare victory and go home. They just come up with new demands that would put even more restrictions on citizens' ability to bring and win lawsuits. Elected officials are happy to get on the bandwagon. And why not? There's little downside to bashing trial lawyers and the legal system.

The tort system is an easy target. Overreaching by judges and mistakes by juries are inevitable. And the availability of big pots of money—especially in areas with a lot of poverty—invariably brings out some bad actors, as with the discovery in 2005 that thousands of lawsuits alleging injuries from silicosis by Mississippi residents may have been fraudulently generated.

These stories stick with people because they don't have any firsthand experience to contradict it. Most Americans never use the legal system unless they're getting divorced. Despite their reputation as the world's most litigious population, Americans rarely sue when they're injured. A landmark study by the Rand Corporation in 1991 found that while one in six Americans suffer an injury in an accident that causes measurable economic loss—and one-third of those accidents result in severe injuries that impose significant costs on the victims and society—most of them never bring lawsuits. The Rand study found that only one out of every ten Americans injured in accidents pursue compensation for it, and of those, only two actually file a lawsuit. Only 5 percent of people who think they've lost more than $1,000 to illegal conduct ever file a suit. And of the hundreds of thousands of people injured every year by medical errors, only one victim ever files a claim for every ten instances of malpractice.

Americans are deeply ambivalent about lawsuits. David Engel, now a law professor at the University at Buffalo Law School, conducted a seminal study in the late 1970s examining Americans' attitudes toward personal injury litigation. He spent two years interviewing residents of a small rural community and studying civil cases filed in their local courts. His findings revealed that there was deep-rooted social stigma associated with filing a lawsuit that helped ensure that most people never did it. Residents of the county he studied viewed litigants as troublemakers, not to mention greedy people who violated community norms by trying to "cash in" on injuries they suffered. "Money was viewed as something one acquired through long hours of hard work, not by exhibiting one's misfortunes to a judge or jury or other third party, even when injuries were clearly caused by the wrongful behavior of another," Engel wrote.

The attitudes that Engel documented more than twenty years ago are just as strong today, and they conflict with tort reformers' portrait of the litigious American who needs to be kept out of the courthouse—and the Robin Hood jury. But they are completely consistent with the country's Calvinist beliefs that accidents are acts of God, often punishment for sinning, and thus something people should simply buck up and endure with a stiff upper lip, not a subpoena. The ATLA convention hall would make anyone queasy, but its gaudy juxtaposition of money and injury especially conflicts with these long-held American values. That's one reason the tort system is so vulnerable to the ongoing attacks from business. Americans believe in personal responsibility, and lawsuits seem like just another form of victimology.

These Calvinist views tend to hold sway in jury deliberations, where Americans start debating from a position of deep skepticism about plaintiffs, rather than businesses. Take the case of John Quinby, a forty-year-old quadriplegic man who lived in Bucks County, Pennsylvania. In 1996 Quinby went to see his doctor to have a mole removed from his face. The doctor and his nurse left Quinby propped on his side on an exam table, alone, after completing the procedure. Unattended, Quinby fell off the table and ended up with a broken leg, facial injuries, and, more seriously, a new neck injury above his old one. Where he had once been able to brush his teeth and spend time enjoying the outdoors, even from his wheelchair, the new injury left him dependent on a ventilator. He filed suit against the doctor, but while the case was pending, he died from pulmonary failure as a result of the fall. His wife continued the litigation.

Quinby made the perfect plaintiff: he was young, handsome, and blameless. The case should have been a slam dunk. Instead, in 2003 a Bucks County jury ruled for the doctor. The verdict was so egregious that a state appeals court made the rare move of sending the case back to a jury with an order to award damages, noting that the facts pointed overwhelmingly to the doctor's negligence.

The Bucks County jury's reluctance to vote in favor of a plaintiff, even in light of overwhelming evidence in his favor, is not unusual. According to state court records, between 2000 and 2005, there were forty-eight medical malpractice jury trials in Bucks County. Of those, doctors won all but five. Of the five Bucks County verdicts that did go in the plaintiff's favor, only one was for more than $1 million.

Bucks County jurors were actually more generous than many of their counterparts in the state. Juries in more than 30 percent of the counties in Pennsylvania in those years never once voted in favor of a plaintiff in a malpractice case. (The record in Lancaster was seventeen to zero for the doctors.) Stories like Quinby's, and the data in the Pennsylvania state courts, rarely make headlines. Yet they are far more representative of what really happens in the tort system than the horror stories told by tort reformers. People filing lawsuits face enormous hurdles to winning compensation, particularly in front of juries, who've been exposed to decades' worth of propaganda about frivolous lawsuits and greedy trial lawyers.

So much of this, however, is occurring beneath the radar screen. The real measure of tort reform is what didn't happen—the cases that weren't filed, the jury trials that simply disappeared, the verdicts not rendered. When lawyers stop taking once-meritorious cases, potential plaintiffs simply fall off the map, their stories left untold. Without discovery proceedings in those lost cases, there are no smoking guns revealing outrageous corporate misconduct or identifying the real butchers in the health care system. It's a phenomenon that's virtually impossible to document.

Yet the tort reform campaigns and the media coverage suggest all is well, in part because lawsuit restrictions are having a perverse effect on jury verdicts. Because the tort system is driven by entrepreneurial trial lawyers, it has responded the way any other market does. When one avenue has closed, lawyers have found other potential openings. For instance, in the face of new caps on noneconomic damages, lawyers have found new ways to reclassify those things as economic damages, by, say, comparing the cost of hiring a driver to what a soccer mom does for a child for free. In Texas, lawyer John O'Quinn beat George Bush's cap on punitive damages by proving that a drug company committed a criminal offense. When products-liability laws made smokers' lawsuits lost causes, lawyers found new plaintiffs in state governments, who didn't have to convince juries that they didn't know smoking could kill them.

At the same time, because tort reform makes litigation more expensive by adding new layers of scrutiny to experts and claims at the same time it limits potential recoveries, lawyers have also gotten much more selective in taking cases. Today, only really serious ones tend to go forward to trial. The change has left many injured people with no legal remedy at all. Even when they have tens of thousands of dollars' worth of losses, it's usually not be enough to cover the cost of litigation, so they're simply out of luck. The more serious cases that do make it into the system have resulted in higher verdicts, which are driving yet even more calls for more restrictions on lawsuits.

Tort reformers always bill these proposals as good for consumers. They rarely are, though. If tort reformers were serious about making the legal system work better and more efficiently, there are lots of things they could focus on. Better funding for the judiciary, for one, would help speed up proceedings, cut the costs of litigation, and ensure faster compensation to the injured people who need to pay their medical bills. But most of the solutions to what may ail the tort system aren't legal changes. They're social ones.

Americans ask a lot of tort law. It's supposed to provide a social safety net, a regulatory structure, and a justice system all in one. It can't do them all well; it's a miracle that the system functions as well as it does. There are two good ways to reduce legal pressure on business and the health care system. One is to prevent injuries and financial fraud in the first place, through better enforcement of health, safety, and consumer protection regulations already on the books. Better regulation of financial institutions, pharmaceutical companies, corporations, and bad doctors could prevent literally thousands of lawsuits. This isn't just liberal lust for big government. If the FDA had done its job and kept just one drug—the dangerous and useless diet drug fen-phen—off the market, it would have prevented a $21-billion legal debacle, not to mention saved hundreds of lives. It's hard to think of a single tort reform that could have made a similar impact on either the public or the drug company.

The other solution is to create universal health insurance to take the big money out of personal injury cases that comes from the cost of long-term institutional care and other medical expenses. If people who had brain-damaged babies knew they could get adequate health care and provide a decent quality of life for their disabled children, they might not need to sue their doctors, or at least if they did, the stakes would be much lower.

Unfortunately for the average citizen, the groups behind tort reform are the same businesses that gutted the regulatory system and don't want to pay the taxes necessary for universal health care. That leaves the tort system as the last real obstacle to an unfettered free market in America, and it's losing the battle.

ACKNOWLEDGMENTS

This book started with a hunch. Back in February 2003, the *New York Times Magazine* ran a short feature on the doctors in West Virginia who'd gone on strike alleging that frivolous lawsuits were driving up their medical malpractice premiums and forcing them to leave the state. After reading their comments, I was convinced that there was more to the strike than the doctors were letting on. "Doctors don't go on strike; they're Republicans," I thought. Also, based on reporting I'd done a few years earlier, I'd learned firsthand that the doctors who complain the most about getting sued are frequently the same doctors who get sued all the time—and usually for good reason.

I wanted to write a story about who was really behind the doctors' strike. Convincing editors to look behind the white coats was a tough sell in that climate, when doctors and politicians all across the country were beating up on trial lawyers and injured patients, and the president had declared a "crisis" in the health care system. Two magazines said yes, and then no, before the article finally found a home at the *Washington Monthly*, my former employer. The article was later nominated for a National Magazine Award, an honor for which I thank *Monthly* editor Paul Glastris, who I like to think knows a good story when he sees one. Paul's willingness to challenge conventional wisdom and to publish my stories on lawsuit myths helped get this book off the ground.

My initial stories on tort reform would have remained just that, stories, if it weren't for the good-natured badgering of my agent, Sam Stoloff, who cold-called me one day looking for clients and then proceeded to bug me for two years to write a book. He thought maybe dietary supplements—ephedra was killing athletes at the time—but only flinched a little when I said I wanted to write about tort reform. Once I told him what I had in mind, he was sold and has been a steadfast enthusiast for this project ever since. I deeply appreciate his editorial comments and his encouragement. Likewise, my editor, Martin Beiser, has been a cheerful voice on the other end of the phone, offering smart advice on how to animate a potentially mind-numbing subject.

As a nonlawyer, I've benefited greatly from the assistance of a number of brilliant legal minds: John Vail, Bob Peck, Neil Vidmar, Marc Galanter, Mike McCann, Bert Kritzer, and all the other folks at the Law and Society Association who toil away in obscurity, crunching raw data, surveying jurors, and trying to find out what's really going on in the civil justice system. Thanks go, too, to the dozens of trial lawyers who shared their cases with me, as well as Carlton Carl at ATLA, who has graciously fielded my calls for nearly two years, even when he was busy buying a small town in Texas. Special thanks to Victor Schwartz, the godfather of the tort reform movement, who not only gave me a copy of his torts textbook as a primer, but who graciously lectured me—often in the voice of Bill Clinton—on the nuances of civil justice even when he knew I was writing a book critical of his life's work.

In a debate like the one over the civil justice system, it's hard to find much middle ground that isn't tainted somehow by money, from one side or the other. So I am forever grateful to the Alicia Patterson Foundation and the Fund for Investigative Journalism, which provided research money for this project. Neither group has a dog in this fight, and their commitment to improving the quality of print journalism has given me a high degree of independence that I hope is reflected in the book.

Finally, but most importantly, Erik Wemple, my husband, has, without complaint, put up with hours of tedious dialogue about the collateral-source rule and other sleep-inducing legal subjects. He footed the bill for my research when the grant money ran out. He has read every word of this book at least twice and contributed significant commentary and editing on both the reporting and the writing, all of which are much improved as a result of his input. (Any mistakes are still mine alone.) On the home front, for the better part of a year, he has also done nearly all the cooking, cleaning, grocery shopping, and a significant amount of child care, all while working a demanding job of his own, which he has frequently neglected so that I could work more. Every woman should be so lucky. There is no good way to fully acknowledge the extent to which Erik has supported not just this book but my money-losing journalism career, or to adequately thank him for it. Thank you, thank you, thank you.

ENDNOTES

Introduction

Page

2   *Cornelius's work:* Obituary, *Indianapolis Star,* March 3, 1995.

3   *In 1994 he wrote a mea culpa:* Frank Cornelius, "Crushed by My Own Re-form," *New York Times,* October 7, 1994.

7   *Since 1986, forty-eight states have passed some type of restriction on lawsuits:* American Tort Reform Association, "Tort Reform Record 2005."

Chapter One / Too Good to Check:
Media Myths about the Civil Justice System

Page

11   *U.S. News & World Report editor-in-chief Mort Zuckerman:* Mortimer B. Zuck-erman, "Welcome to Sue City, U.S.A.," *U.S. News & World Report,* June 16, 2003.

11   *The magazine later published only a brief clarification:* The correction was pub-lished July 21, 2003. See also Howard Kurtz, "A Little Snag in Those Frivolous Suits," *Washington Post,* June 23, 2003.

12   *Among the examples was:* Editorial, "Who's to Blame for Rising Costs?" *Weirton Daily Times,* February 17, 2003.

13   *The piece described:* Barton v. American Automobile Insurance Company 132 Cal. App. 2d 317, 282 P.2d 559.

14   *The Insurance Information Institute:* Richard S. Jacobson and Jeffrey R. White, *David v. Goliath: ATLA and the Fight for Everyday Justice* (Baltimore, MD: United Book Press, 2004), 56.

14   *The agency later conceded: Consumer Reports,* August 1986.

14   *The company's executive vice president:* Jacobsen and White, 43.

14   *In 1979 Elizabeth Loftus:* Elizabeth Loftus, "Insurance Advertising and Jury Awards," *American Bar Association Journal,* January 1979.

15   *According to the business owner:* "So Sue Me!" *60 Minutes,* March 23, 1986.

15   *In fact, the real lawsuit:* Steven Brill, "The Not-So-Simple Crisis," *American Lawyer,* May 1, 1986.

15   *It took eleven years:* Ralph Nader and Wesley Smith, *No Contest: Corporate Lawyers and the Perversion of Justice in America* (New York: Random House, 1996), 274.

16   *The psychic in question:* William Haltom and Michael McCann, *Distorting the Law: Politics, Media, and the Litigation Crisis* (University of Chicago Press, 2004), 1–5.

16   *"The most fantastic verdict:* Peter Huber, *Galileo's Revenge: Junk Science in the Courtroom* (Basic Books, 1991), 4.

17   *In one of its early fund-raising letters:* Ken Silverstein, *Smoke & Mirrors* (Public Citizen, 1996).

17   *Of course, ATRA's funding:* "Tort Reform Interests and Agendas," *Legal Times,* April 17, 1995.

17   *ATRA doesn't mention that:* Associated Press, "Judge Throws Out Viewer's Suit against 'Fear Factor,'" March 9, 2005.

18   *Stella Liebeck was an unusual:* The description of *Liebeck v. McDonald's* was taken from several sources, including, *Distorting the Law,* by William Haltom and Michael McCann, *No Contest,* Nader and Smith, and several news accounts in the *Wall Street Journal, Newsweek* and the *Washington Post.*

20   *Typical of the media treatment:* "Java Hijack," editorial, *San Diego Union-Tribune,* August 20 1994.

21   *For instance, in 1995:* "Tort Reform Budget," Covington & Burling, October 3, 1995, Philip Morris document #2041201160, http://www.pmdocs.com/PDF/2041201160_1168_0.PDF (accessed August 10, 2006).

21   *At the time of the products-liability battle:* Peter Stone, "Grass Roots Goliath," *National Journal,* July 13, 1996.

21   *Philip Morris USA was also chipping in:* Philip Morris, letter to Victoria Hughes, vice president for development, Citizens for a Sound Economy, March 7, 1994. Philip Morris Archives, document #2047993206. (Documents produced from the state tobacco litigation are now online and can be accessed at www.tobaccoarchives.com.)

21   *After a brief introduction:* "Lawsuit Abuse Patch Thru Script," Philip Morris archives document #2048768981, February 13, 1995.

22   *Mobil Oil ran:* William Haltom and Michael McCann, *Distorting the Law: Politics, Media and the Litigation Crisis* (University of Chicago Press, 2005), 224.

22   *Tort reformers organized:* Aric Press, Ginny Carroll, and Steve Waldman, "Are Lawyers Burning America?" *Newsweek,* March 20, 1995.

22   *Victor Schwartz the éminence grise:* T. R. Goldman, "Tort Reform: What Happened, What's Next," *Legal Times,* July 8, 1996.

23   *In December 2003,* Newsweek *featured:* Stuart Taylor Stuart and Evan Thomas, "Civil Wars," *Newsweek,* December 15, 2003.

24   *Personal injury and other tort filings:* National Center for State Courts, "Incoming Tort Cases in 29 General Jurisdiction Courts, 1994–2003," http://www.ncsconline.org/D_Research/csp/FRI/Torts29States1994–2003.pdf.

24 *According to the Congressional Budget Office (CBO):* "The Economics of U.S. Tort Liability," Congressional Budget Office, October 2003, 5.

24 *The most recent data:* Bureau of Justice Statistics, "Federal Tort Trials and Verdicts, 2002–2003," August 2005.

24 *In the nation's seventy-five largest counties:* Bureau of Justice Statistics, "Tort Trials and Verdicts in Large Counties, 2001," November 2004.

24 *Just between September 2003 and September 2004:* Terry Maxon, "No Cure All," *Dallas Morning News,* September 26, 2004.

24 *In 2001 they voted:* Bureau of Justice Statistics, "Tort Trials."

24 *That figure, though:* Towers Perrin Tillinghast, "U.S. Tort Costs: 2004 Update."

26 *In a 1992 memo:* Manhattan Institute, Judicial Studies Program, "Mission Statement and Overview," November 1992.

26 *It has targeted:* Manhattan Institute Judicial Studies Program Mission Statement and Overview, November 1992.

27 *University of Wisconsin law professor Marc Galanter:* "The News from Nowhere: The Debased Debate on Civil Justice," 71 *Denver University Law Review* 77 (1993).

27 *As The Economist observed: Economist,* "Order in the Tort," July 18, 1992.

27 *In response to criticism:* Peter Huber, "Huber Responds," Letter to the Editor, *Texas Lawyer,* February 8, 1993.

27 *In 2002, for instance:* Christi Parsons, "Downstate County Is a 'Plaintiff's Paradise,'" *Chicago Tribune,* June 17, 2002.

28 *Two months after the verdict:* John Stossel, "The Blame Game," *ABC News,* August 17, 1995.

28 *A few months after the broadcast:* Lieberman, Trudy, *Slanting the Story: The Forces That Shape the News* (The New Press, 2000).

28 *A classic example:* John Stossel, "Give Me a Break, Trial Lawyers," *ABC News 20/20,* July 23, 2004.

29 *In February 2004:* "Tort Reform Debated at Symposium," *The Daily Oklahoman,* February 27, 2004.

29 *In April 2002:* Steve Taylor, "Marketing Blitz Planned for Doctor Walkout," *Brownsville Herald,* March 22, 2002.

29 *And, of course, millions:* David Mastio, "Prime-time Propagandist," Salon.com, February 25, 2000.

30 *Perhaps that's why:* Lieberman, 23.

32 *In January 2004:* Todd Glasenapp, "Fear of Lawsuit Forces Cancellation of Page's Polar Bear Plunge," *Arizona Daily Sun,* January 20, 2004.

Chapter Two / When the Smoke Clears:
Big Tobacco's Secret Tort Project

Page

33 *It wasn't uncommon for:* Patricia Bellew Gray, "Legal Warfare," *Wall Street Journal,* April 29, 1987.

34 *Often the plaintiffs couldn't:* Sara Guardino and Richard Daynard, paper,

"Punishing Tobacco Industry Misconduct," The Berkeley Electronic Press, 2005.

34 *In documents turned up during:* Jordan, J. Michael, memo to Shook & Hardy attorneys, April 28, 1988, www.kazanlaw.com/verdicts/images/exb_d_sob.gif (accessed April 25, 2006).

35 *He believed, as the TPLP's mission stated:* Richard Kluger, *Ashes to Ashes* (New York: Vintage Books, 1997), 559.

35 *Arnold & Porter, in turn:* Ken Silverstein, "Smoke and Mirrors" (Public Citizen, 1996), 4.

35 *Scanlon, who died in 2001:* Mark Landler, "A Practitioner of Bare-Fisted Public Relations Takes Punches," *New York Times,* February 12, 1996.

36 *Known as the "napkin deal,":* Dan Morain, "Assessment of Brown's Speakership Is a Mixed Bag," *Los Angeles Times,* June 8, 1995.

36 *Tobacco lawyers weren't at the table:* Leo Wolinsky, "Tobacco Industry Gifts after Vote Reported," *Los Angeles Times,* January 9, 1988.

37 *Before it was over:* Kluger, 674.

38 *"The primary purpose of:* Carl Deal and Joanne Doroshow, "The CALA Files" (The Center for Justice & Democracy and Public Citizen, 2000), 14.

39 *Kluger managed to find:* Kluger, *Ashes,* 687.

40 *The sugar growers cooperative:* James Pinkerton, "The Spoils of Tragedy," *Houston Chronicle,* August 2, 1992.

41 *CALA hired Jon Opelt:* Carl Deal and Joanne Doroshow, "The CALA Files," 8.

42 *When the Starr report was released:* Deal and Doroshow, "CALA Files," 10.

42 *The expansion plans were:* Ibid., 33.

43 *The language in the ads:* Cohen, Neal, Memorandum to David Greenberg, Jack Nelson, Bernie Robinson, January 2, 1992, Philip Morris archive document #2023921990.

43 *The ad claimed (without proof) that:* Deal and Doroshow, "CALA Files," 24.

43 *The magazine noted that:* Deal and Doroshow, "CALA Files," 16.

43 *In 1992, Cohen sent a status report:* Cohen memo, January 2, 1992.

44 *By 1995 the tobacco industry's:* "Possible Revised Budget for Expanded 1995 Tort Reform Program," Covington & Burling, January 24, 1995. Philip Morris document #2048769111.

44 *Keith Teel, one of the industry lawyers:* Teel, Keith, "Memorandum to the Tort Reform Policy Committee Re: Possible Budget for Expanded Tort Reform Program," Covington & Burling, January 24, 1995, Lorillard Files, document #91881092.

44 *"Let me tell you about a problem:* John Stauber and Sheldon Rampton, "Radiation Therapy: Cynical Wisdom from APCO & Associates," first published in *PR Watch* in 1996. Available online at http://www.prwatch.org/prwissues/1996Q3/cohen.html (accessed April 26, 2006).

46 *Rumors were also flying:* Teel memo, January 1995.

46 *Vincent Bollon, general secretary-treasurer:* Deal and Doroshow, "CALA Files," 24.

Chapter Three / Mess with Texas: George W. Bush
and the Texas Tort Moguls

Page

48 *Carol Ernst met her husband:* Alex Berenson, "In First of Many Vioxx Cases, a Texas Widow Prepares to Take the Stand," *New York Times,* July 13, 2005.

48 *Company documents revealed:* Alex Berenson, "For Merck, the Vioxx Paper Trail Won't Go Away," *New York Times,* August 21, 2005.

49 *On August 23:* Steven Shavell and A. Mitchell Polinsky, "Vioxx Verdict's Dark Side," *Boston Globe,* August 23, 2005.

49 *At the time of his death:* Verdict sheet, *Ernst v. Merck & Co.*

50 *Another one of Bush's 1995 reforms:* "Obstacle to Justice: Texas Supreme Court Annual Review 2004–2005," CourtWatch, http:www.texaswatch.org/documents/CWYIR2004-2005.pdf (accessed April 25, 2006).

51 *Texas Public Policy Foundation hired the GOP pollster:* Deal & Doroshow, "CALA Files," 8.

52 *More than a dozen home owners:* Bob Burtman, "Slab o' Trouble," *Houston Press,* June 27, 1996.

53 *Richard Weekley, a cofounder:* "Texans for Lawsuit Reform: How the Texas Tort Tycoons Spent Millions in the 2000 Elections," Texans for Public Justice, November 2001, http://www.tpj.org/docs/2001/11/reports/tlr/index.html (accessed April 25, 2006).

53 *A neighboring chemical corporation:* George Flynn, "Firm Sues to Block Enron Plant Restart," *Houston Chronicle,* January 7, 1995.

53 *Jim "Mattress Mac" McIngvale:* Frank Klimko, "Lion's Owner Is Sought by HPD Officers," *Houston Chronicle,* October 17, 1987.

53 *Bob Perry is CEO:* Christy Hoppe, "High Roller Keeps Low Profile in Texas Politics," *Dallas Morning News,* November 3, 2003.

54 *(Rove would continue to work:* Rove deposition, Texas tobacco litigation.

56 *In addition, the year of Bush's:* Keith Teel and Joseph Doss, Letter to Roger Mozingo and Daniel Donahue, R.J. Reynolds Tobacco Co., August 16, 1993, "Re: Budget Projections," Philip Morris document #2025773219, http://www.pmdocs.com/PDF/2025773219_3223_0.PDF (accessed August 11, 2006).

57 *Tort filings in Texas:* "Examining the Work of State Courts 2003," National Center for State Courts, www.ncsonline.org/D_Research/csp/2003_Files/2003_SubCivil-TORTCON.pdf (accessed April 25, 2006).

59 *A 2002 study:* "Nursing Home Conditions in Texas," Minority Staff, Committee on Government Reform, U.S. House of Representatives, October 28, 2002, http://www.democrats.reform.house.gov/Documents/20040830112134-57472.pdf.

59 *A Harvard University study:* David Stevenson and David Studdert, "The Rise of Nursing Home Litigation," *Health Affairs,* March/April 2003.

Chapter Four / We Wuz Robe'd: Unseating Liberal Judges

Page

62 *Jim Wootton, then the executive director:* Peter Stone, "K Street for June 24, 2000," *National Journal,* June 24, 2000.

62 *The company:* Jimmie Gates, "Court Caps Appeal Bonds," *Jackson Clarion-Ledger,* May 10, 2001.

63 *Not so long ago:* Jerry Mitchell, "McRae's Fiery Tenure Ends with No Regrets," *Jackson Clarion-Ledger,* January 5, 2004.

63 *One night in 1995:* Mitchell, "McRae's Fiery Tenure."

64 *In 2002 McRae joined with:* Mitchell, Jerry. "Courts Can Put a Price on the Enjoyment of Life," *Jackson Clarion-Ledger,* June 9, 2002.

64 *Many of the court's liberal:* Shep Montgomery, "Business Lobbyists Find New Battleground: State Judicial Races," *Mississippi Business Journal,* August 15, 1994.

65 *In May 2002:* John Porretto, "U.S. Chamber Targets Mississippi for 'Flawed Legal System,'" Associated Press, May 8, 2002.

66 *For instance, the Mississippi Supreme Court:* "The New Politics of Judicial Elections 2002," Justice at Stake, Brennan Center report.

67 *In 2002 still-unidentified benefactors:* Chuck Lindell, "Pro-police Political Group a Mystery," *Austin American Statesman,* September 12, 2004.

67 *The LEAA ads recycled:* "The New Politics of Judicial Elections 2002," Justice at Stake Campaign.

67 *In one TV ad:* "The New Politics of Judicial Elections 2002," Justice at Stake Campaign, 12.

67 *Charlie Ross, a Mississippi state senator:* Charlie Ross, "Jackson Action," *Wall Street Journal,* September 15, 2005.

68 *He said to the group:* Phil Zinkewicz, "Industry Groups Rally under the Banner of Tort Reform," *Rough Notes,* March 2004.

68 *The impact of Dickinson's ascension:* The description of the Moore case comes from the Mississippi Supreme Court's decision in *Walter W. Eckman v. Linda Moore* 2002-CA-00669-SCT.

69 *The verdict turned Eckman:* Michael Freedman, "The Tort Mess," *Forbes,* May 13, 2002.

69 *Apparently Eckman performed:* Eckman v. Cooper Tire & Rubber Company, No. 2003-CA-02223-SCT.

70 *Dickinson not only refused:* Welsh v. Mounger, Mississippi Supreme Court 2002-CA-01245-SCT.

70 *The lawyers had written:* City of Jackson v. Otha Stewart, Mississippi Supreme Court 2003-CA-01413.

71 *State politicos dubbed 1996:* Dale Russakoff, "Legal War Conquers State's Politics," *Washington Post,* December 1, 1996.

71 *With Rove's help:* Skip Tucker, "Not So Sweet Home Alabama?," *Inside Litigation,* Winter 2005.

71 *The amount of money:* "The New Politics of Judicial Elections," Justice at Stake report, February 2002.

72 *Donald Blankenship, the CEO:* Paul Nyden, "Coal, Doctors' Groups Donated to Anti-McGraw Effort," *Charleston Gazette,* January 7, 2005.

72 *The justices had written:* Adam Liptak, "Judicial Races in Several States Become Partisan Battlegrounds," *New York Times,* October 24, 2004.

73   *In 2003 the Institute:* Laura Stafford and Samantha Sanchez, "Campaign Contributions and the Alabama Supreme Court," Institute on Money in State Politics report, May 5, 2003.

74   *According to studies:* "Obstacle to Justice," Texas Watch Foundation, www.txwfoundation.org (accessed April 25, 2006).

75   *While on the Texas court:* "Death of Plaintiff Could Haunt Nominee," Associated Press, July 15, 2002.

76   *In the fall of 2004:* West Virginia Chamber of Commerce, Court Watch, Fall 2004 and Spring 2005 sessions, www.wvchamber.com/Court WatchFa04Sp 05.pdf (accessed April 25, 2006).

Chapter Five / Cash Bar: The Campaign to Cut Attorney Fees
Page
79   *That year,* American Lawyer *reported:* Allison Frankel, "Smokin' Joe," *American Lawyer,* May 1998.

79   *At the time the Texas tobacco suit:* Wayne Slater, "AG Says Tobacco Industry Could Be in for Fight," *Dallas Morning Neews,* March 22, 1996.

79   *Initially, the tobacco companies resorted:* Robert Bryce, "Nicotine Fit," *Texas Observer,* November 26, 1999.

80   *"I will never understand:* Linda Campbell and John Moritz, "Lawyers to Get \$3.3 Billion," *Fort Worth Star-Telegram,* December 12, 1998.

80   *The only casualty was Morales:* Pete Slover, "Morales Receives 4 Years," *Dallas Morning News,* November 1, 2003.

81   *In 2003, for instance:* Common Good, press release, May 6, 2003, http://cgood.org/assets/attachments/45.pdf (accessed April 25, 2006).

82   *When the group opened its first:* "War on Fake Claimants: Bureau Forming to Check Spurious Suits for Damages," *Chicago Tribune,* January 26, 1907.

83   *In Philadelphia in 1928:* Ken Dornstein, *Accidentally, On Purpose: The Making of a Personal Injury Underworld in America* (St. Martin's Press 1996), 144.

83   *In New York City:* Dornstein, 128.

84   *Assemblyman Horace Stone said:* "Attack on 'Chaser' Bills," *New York Times,* March 22, 1929.

85   *With echoes of Isidor Kresel:* Walter Olson, *The Litigation Explosion* (New York: Truman Talley Books, 1991), 45–46.

85   *Even Congress lost its enthusiasm:* George Rodrigue, "Hearing Opens on Legal Fee Cap," *Dallas Morning News,* December 11, 1997.

86   *His ascent as a media star:* Lester Brickman, "Contingent Fees without Contingencies," 37 *UCLA Law Review* 29–137 (1989).

86   *That eyepopping figure:* David Margolick, "At the Bar: In Defense of Ambulance Chasing," *New York Times,* October 6, 1989.

87   *In 1994, he was telling:* Peter Passell, "Windfall Fees in Injury Cases under Assault," *New York Times,* February 11, 1994.

87   *In 1994 Brickman coauthored:* Lester Brickman, Michael Horowitz, and Jeffrey O'Connell, "Rethinking Contingency Fees" (New York: The Manhattan Institute, 1994).

88 *None did, and the American Bar Association:* See the American Bar Association Standing Committee on Ethics and Professional Responsibility, Formal Opinion 94-389 and *In RE: Petition for Rulemaking to Revise the Ethical Standards Relating to Contingency Fees,* Supreme Court of Utah, Memorandum in Opposition to Petition, filed by Ralph Dewsnup, Edward Havas, and lawyers from the Center for Constitutional Litigation.

88 *In 1996 he was a primary drafter:* Dan Morain, "Prop. 202 Packs a Powerful Potential," *Los Angeles Times,* March 22, 1996, and Richard Reuben, "Fee Caps an Issue That Won't Go Away," *American Bar Association Journal,* May 1996.

88 *(During the 2000 presidential campaign:* Terry Carter, "Keeping 'Em Honest," *American Bar Association Journal,* August 1997.

89 *Bush's lawsuit failed:* Lester Brickman, "Want to be a Billionaire? Sue a tobacco company," *Wall Street Journal,* December 30, 1998.

89 *Brickman was the plaintiff: Brickman v. Tyco Toys,* U.S. District Court, Southern District of New York, 88 Civ. 3936.

91 *The results were compiled:* Herbert Kritzer, *Risks, Reputations, and Rewards: Contingency Fee Legal Practice in the United States* (Stanford, CA: Stanford University Press, 2004).

92 *Among those is Professor Theodore Eisenberg:* Theodore Eisenberg and Geoffrey Miller, "Attorney Fees in Class Action Settlements," *Journal of Empirical Legal Studies,* March 2004.

92 *In a CV he submitted:* "Expert Report of Lester Brickman," In re: Western Asbestos Company; Western MacArthur Co. and MacArthur Co. U.S. Bankruptcy Court, Northern District of California 02-46284, 02-46285, 02-46286.

93 *Brickman summed it up neatly:* Lester Brickman, testimony before the Senate Judiciary Committee, hearings on contingency fee abuses, November 7, 1995.

Chapter Six / Shock and Law: The War on Lawyers

Page

95 *As the campaign heated up:* Anne Marie Kilday and Mark Toohey, "Pennzoil Lawyers Contributed to Justices," *Houston Chronicle,* February 9, 1988.

96 *He finally found it:* David Broder and Saundra Torry, "ABA President Disputes Quayle on Litigation Proposals," *Washington Post,* August 13, 1991.

96 *Quayle's impromptu debate:* David Broder, "Quayle Charges Some Lawyers are 'Ripping Off the System.'" *Washington Post,* September 7, 1991.

97 *In his nomination speech:* Saundra Torry and Mark Stencel, "Bush, Quayle Put Lawyers in Election-Year Docket," *Washington Post,* August 28, 1992.

97 *In 1994, Grover Norquist:* Grover Norquist, "A Winning Drive," *The American Spectator,* March 1994.

99 *The group, called Contributions Watch:* John Stauber and Sheldon Rampton, "Wolves in Sheep's Clothing," *PR Watch,* 3rd Quarter, 1996.

99 *Simpson in July 1996:* Glenn Simpson, "After Flirting with the GOP, Trial Lawyers Go Democratic," *Wall Street Journal,* July 16, 1996.

100 *The group found that Mississippi:* Contributions Watch, "Plaintiff's Lawyers

Political Contributions in Mississippi," February 1996, Phillip Morris document #2046479124.

101 *Of the five top contributors:* Center for Public Integrity, Party Lines project.

101 *According to data from:* Thomas Cohen, "Medical Malpractice Trials and Verdicts from Large Counties," U.S. Department of Justice, Bureau of Justice Statistics, April 2004.

103 *In 1969 John Lyons:* Richard S. Jacobson and Jeffrey R. White, *David v. Goliath: ATLA and the Fight for Everyday Justice* (Baltimore, MD: United Book Press, 2004), 59.

105 *The court later ordered Minor:* Bennie Whitehead v. Food Max of Mississippi, K-Mart Corp. v. Paul Minor, U.S. Court of Appeals for the Fifth Circuit No. 00-601853.

106 *The jury came back with:* Beverly Kraft, "Kmart Told to Pay $5M in Rape," *The Clarion-Ledger,* September 4, 1999.

106 *In July 2003 Lampton:* U.S. v. Paul Minor et al., U.S. District Court for the Southern District of Mississippi, Criminal No. 3:03cr120WS.

108 *A quick investigation:* Tom Wilemon, "Green Oaks Hosted Lawyers and Judges," *Biloxi Sun Herald,* June 8, 2003.

109 *The Mississippi Republican Party:* Beth Musgrave and Tom Wilemon, "Minor Lawyer: GOP Ads Could Taint Jury," *Biloxi Sun Herald,* November 19, 2003.

110 *Whereas ICE PAC had:*Figures on ICE PAC contributions come from reports filed with the Mississippi Secretary of State's office, www.sos.state.ms.us/elections/CampFinc/Reports/.

Chapter Seven / Millions Served: Jackpot Justice and the Jefferson County Juries

Page

111 *In November 2002:* Morley Safer, "Jackpot Justice," *60 Minutes,* November 24, 2003.

113 *The florist:* Jerry Mitchell, "TV Show on Miss. Justice Stirs Suit," *Jackson Clarion-Ledger,* December 10, 2002.

113 *The legend of a Bronx effect:* Neil Vidmar, "The Bronx 'Bronx Jury,'" 80 *Texas Law Rev.* 1889 (2001–2003).

113 *Cornell professors:* Theodore Eisenberg and Martin Wells, "Trial Outcomes and Demographics: Is There a Bronx Effect?" 80 *Tex. L. Rev.* 1839-75 (2002).

160 *A 2005 study:* Thomas E. Willging & Schannon R. Wheatman, "An Empirical Examination of Attorneys' Choice of Forum in Class Action Litigation," Federal Judicial Center 2005.

114 *In 2004 the Center for Justice and Democracy:* Emily Gottlieb, Geoff Boehm, and Joanne Doroshow, "'Tort Reform' and Racial Prejudice: A Troublesome Connection," Center for Justice and Democracy, March 2004, www.center jd.org/race.pdf (accessed August 15, 2006).

116 *Before the Civil War:* Alan Huffman, *Mississippi in Africa* (New York: Gotham Books, 2004) 124–125.

120 *Pickard, a former plaintiff:* "Bringing Justice to Judicial Hellholes 2002,"

American Tort Reform Association, www.atra.org/reports/hellholes/2002/hell-holes_report_2002.pdf (accessed April 25, 2006).

121 *The county recently made:* Ryan Clark, "Study Tags Area No. 1 in Over-weight People," *Clarion-Ledger,* June 14, 2004.

126 *According to a study:* John Beisner, Jessica Davidson Miller, and Matthew Shors, "One Small Step for a County Court," Civil Justice Report No. 7, April 2003, Center for Legal Policy at the Manhattan Institute.

Chapter Eight / Crackpot Justice: The Myth of the Frivolous Lawsuit

Page

131 *Creative or not:* All of the description of Kevin Muhammad's frivolous fil-ings comes from *The Mississippi Bar v. Kevin D. Muhammad 2005-B-842,* filed with the Supreme Court of Mississippi, April 27, 2005.

132 *In 1992, a team of doctors:* Tom Baker, *The Medical Malpractice Myth* (University of Chicago Press, 2005), 78.

136 *Two economists, Henry Farber and Michelle White:* Ibid., 84.

136 *Once plaintiffs do get:* Vidmar, Neil, *Medical Malpractice and the American Jury* (University of Michigan Press, 1995), 40.

137 *"The practical case for loser pays":* Walter Olson, "Civil Suits," *Reason,* June 1995.

138 *If they lost the lawsuit:* "Uncertain and Certain Litigation Abuses," testimony of Theodore Eisenberg, Oversight Hearing on "Safeguarding Americans from a Legal Culture of Fear: Approaches to Limiting Lawsuit Abuse," U.S. House Committee on the Judiciary, June 22, 2004.

138 *In 2004 a University of Texas:* John Council, "The Perils of Loser Pays; H.B. 4 Rule Unpopular with Defense Lawyers," *Texas Lawyer,* October 11, 2004.

139 *One 1992 study found:* Lawrence Marshall, Herbert Kritzer, and Frances Kahn Zemans, "The Use and Impact of Rule 11," 86 NW.ULRev. 943 (1992).

140 *(Ninety-five percent of prison-inmate:* Schlanger, Margo, "Inmate Litigation," 116 *Harvard Law Review* 1555 (2003).

141 *The maker of Budweiser:* Opposition No. 91153387 to Application Serial No. 78/073976, in the U.S. Patent and Trademark Office.

141 *In 2003 the Federal Trade Commission: In the Matter of Bristol-Myers Squibb Company,* File Nos. 001 0221, 011 0046, and 021 0181.

142 *According to the National Center for State Courts:* "Examining the Work of State Courts 2003," National Center for State Courts.

142 *Northwestern University law professor Lawrence Marshall:* Marshal, Kritzer, and Zemans, "Use and Impact of Rule 11."

Chapter Nine / E Pluribus Screw 'Em: Class Action Reform and the Attack on Consumer Protection

Page

144 *In January 1998: Paul Miller v. Bank of America,* Superior Court of California, County of San Francisco, Case No. CGC-99-301917, Statement of Decision.

146 *In September 2001: Gluck v. Bank of America* (San Francisco Superior Court Case No. 308496).

147 *In 2002 BoA settled:* Sam Skolnik, "Nation's Largest Bank Sued over ATM Fees," *Seattle Post-Intelligencer,* September 22, 2000.

147 *In Congress, Bank of America:* "Unfairness Incorporated: The Corporate Campaign against Consumer Class Actions," Public Citizen, Congress Watch, June 2003.

148 *While it's hard to imagine:* Deborah Hensler et al., *Class Action Dilemmas: Pursuing Public Goals for Private Gains,* Rand Corporation Institute for Civil Justice, 2000.

149 *Even as they were:* Summary of Georgia payday lending law, Center for Responsible Lending, www.responsiblelending.org/pdfs/GA_bill_summary.pdf (accessed April 25, 2006).

150 *Despite well-documented evidence:* Office of the Comptroller of the Treasury, http://www.occ.treas.gov/foia/fair.htm (accessed April 25, 2006).

151 *A disgusted California judge: Schwartz v. Visa International,* Superior Court of Alameda County, Case No. 822404-4.

152 *Not long after the verdict:* Trisha Howard, "Groups Blast Madison County Courts," *St. Louis Post-Dispatch,* June 6, 2003.

152 *A 2000 study noted:* John Beisner and Jessica Davidson Miller, "They're Making a Federal Case Out of It . . . In State Court," Civil Justice Report No. 3, September 2001, Center for Legal Policy at the Manhattan Institute.

152 *The drumbeat continued:* Lester Brickman, "Anatomy of a Madison County (Illinois) Class-Action: A Study of Pathology," Manhattan Institute Civil Justice Report No. 6, August 2002.

153 *A 2002 New York Times:* Adam Liptak, "Court Has Dubious Record as a Class-Action Leader," *New York Times,* August 15, 2002.

153 *In 2004:* Jeffrey Birnbaum, "Advocacy Group Blurs Media Lines," *Washington Post,* December 6, 2004.

154 *In 1991 Chicago attorney:* Joe Stephens, "Coupons Create Cash for Lawyers," *Washington Post,* November 14, 1999.

156 *A 2004 study:* Thomas Willging and Shannon Wheatman, "Attorney Reports on the Impact of *Amchem* and *Ortiz* on Choice of a Federal or State Forum in Class Action Litigation," Federal Judicial Center, April 2004.

156 *A 2004 study published:* Theodore Eisenberg and Geoffrey Miller, "Attorney Fees in Class Action Settlements," 1 *Journal of Empirical Legal Studies,* 27–78 (March 2004).

159 *Warwick filed the class: McIntyre v. Household Bank,* No. 02 C 1537, Northern District of Illinois, 2002.

160 *A 2005 study:* Thomas E. Willging and Shannon R. Wheatman, "An Empirical Examination of Attorneys' Choice of Forum in Class Action Litigation," Federal Judicial Center, 2005.

160 *Ten years ago:* Judicial Conference of the United States, Long Range Plan for the Federal Courts, 1995.

160 *Indeed, the Congressional Budget Office:* Congressional Budget Office, "Cost

Estimate, S.5 Class Action Fairness Act of 2005," www.cbo.gov/ftpdocs/60xx/doc6073/s5.pdf (accessed August 15, 2006).

Chapter Ten / Slip and Call: Merchants (Irrational) Fear of Being Sued

Page

162 *In her congressional testimony:* Testimony of Hilda Bankston before the House Judiciary Committee, February 6, 2002.

163 *The news stories on Bankston:* Beverly Pettigrew Kraft, "Hitting the Jackpot in Mississippi Courtrooms," Jackson *Clarion-Ledger,* June 17, 2001.

164 *She was recruited by:* Sue Reisinger, "Ms. Rabiteau Goes to Washington," *Corporate Counsel,* May 20, 2005.

164 *Senator Dianne Feinstein:* Senator Dianne Feinstein, statement "On the Class Action Fairness Act," July 7, 2004.

166 *In 1999 the small rural:* John Beisner, Jessica Davidson Miller, and Matthew Shors, "One Small Step for a County Court," Civil Justice Report No. 7, April 2002, Center for Legal Policy at the Manhattan Institute.

166 *In 2004, after the White House:* James Rosen, "Bush Summit Backs Agenda," *Sacramento Bee,* December 16, 2004.

167 *James Wootton, the former director:* Comments from FTC Workshop, "Protecting Consumer Interests in Class Actions," September 13 and 14, 2004.

168 *The records had been conveyed:* Tom Wilemon, "Judicial Probe Looking at Big Jury Awards," *Biloxi Sun Herald,* June 12, 2003.

168 *Bankston alleged in the lawsuit: Bankston v. Gulf Guaranty Life Insurance Company,* Circuit Court of Jefferson County, Mississippi, case number 99-0157.

169 *One of the talking points:* NFIB Small Business Policy Guide.

169 *Ohio NFIB director:* Roger Geiger, testimony before the House Judiciary Committee on the Small Business Liability Reform Act of 1999, September 29, 1999.

171 *UCLA School of Law professor Lynn LoPucki:* LoPucki's database can be found at http://lopucki.law.ucla.edu/.

171 *In 2003 University of Texas:* Charles Silver, "We're Scared to Death: Class Certification and Blackmail," 78 *N.Y.U. L. Rev.* 1357 (2003).

172 *More than twenty million people:* Paul Brodeur, *Outrageous Misconduct: The Asbestos Industry on Trial* (Pantheon Books, 1985).

173 *Maxwell's family sued Bryco:* Fox Butterfield, "Gun Maker Found Liable in Shooting Accident," *New York Times,* April 23, 2003.

173 *Richard Jennings, the owner:* Larry Armstrong, "No Surrender from Mr. Saturday Night Special," *Business Week,* August 16, 1999.

173 *In 2005, a former plant:* Fox Butterfield, "Fraud Alleged in Winning Bid for Gun Manufacturer," *New York Times,* October 22, 2004.

173 *In 2005 Michael Schumann:* Ellen Rosen, "Taking on Credit Card Fees, with Allies," *New York Times,* October 6, 2005.

174 *Relying on a quirk:* Karen Robinson-Jacobs and Monte Morin, "Attorney General Asks Probe of 'Extortionist' Legal Tactics,'" *Los Angeles Times,* December

17, 2002, and Monk Murin, "Three Accused Attorneys Resign from Bar," *Los Angeles Times,* July 11, 2003.

Chapter Eleven / The Hypocritical Oath: When Doctors Double as Tort-Reform Lobbyists

Page

178 *In a 1983 lawsuit:* DiProsperis v. Zaleski, Circuit Court of Ohio County, West Virginia, Civil Action No. 83-C-872(B).

178 *According to a* Charleston Gazette: "Some of Those Walking Out Cost Insurers Millions," Associated Press, December 21, 2002.

181 *A lawsuit over the case:* Lawrence Messina, "Are Doctors Punished for 'Bad Results'?" *Sunday Gazette-Mail,* May 6, 2001.

182 *As doctors put the blame:* Lawrence Messina, "The Price of Malpractice," *Charleston Gazette,* February 26, 2001.

183 *The paper determined that:* Lawrence Messina, "The Price of Malpractice: W.Va.'s Medical Malpractice Debate," *Sunday Gazette Mail,* February 25, 2001.

183 *In August 2002, the* Gazette's: Lawrence Messina, "Dead, Active Doctors among 'Empty Chairs,'" *Charleston Gazette,* August 27, 2002.

183 *A Public Citizen study:* "Medical Misdiagnosis in West Virginia," Public Citizen's Congress Watch, January 2003, http://www.citizen.org/documents/WestVirginia/Medical_Misdiagnosis.pdf (accessed April 25, 2006).

183 *In the fall of 2003:* "Medical Malpractice: Implications of Rising Premiums on Access to Health Care," Government Accountability Office, August 2003.

184 *As with so much of:* Scott Finn, "Elkins, W.Va., Doctor Leaves Drug Record Out of Congressional Testimony," *Charleston Gazette,* January 8, 2003.

186 *In June 2003:* Daniel Eisenberg and Maggie Sieger, "The Doctor Won't See You Now," *Time,* June 9, 2003.

187 *According to allegations:* Della J. Westfall v. Robert Cross, Gregory Saracco et al., Court of Common Pleas, Belmont County, Ohio, Case No. 97-CV-120.

188 *California doctors ended up:* S. J. Diamond and Harry Nelson, "Doctors Will Get Refunds on Insurance," *Los Angeles Times,* February 6, 1981.

188 *A year later most:* "Med-mal Lawsuits Drop by More Than Half in Three Years," *Associated Press,* February 5, 2005.

188 *A year after Texas:* Mark Donald, "Access Denied: Does Tort Reform Close Courthouse Doors to Those Who Can Least Afford It?" *Texas Lawyer,* January 10, 2005.

188 *The same memo observed:* Memo from Melissa Coker, Regulatory Specialist, The Medical Protective Company to the Texas insurance commissioner, October 30, 2003.

188 *Eventually, malpractice insurance rates:* Diane Levick, "Malpractice Premiums Begin to Level Off," *Hartford Courant,* September 18, 2005.

189 *The Bureau of Justice Statistics:* "Civil Justice Survey of State Courts, Tort Trials and Verdicts in Large Counties 2001," April 2004, www.ojp.usdoj.gov/bjs/pub/ascii/ttvlc01.txt (accessed April 25, 2006).

189 *In 2005 the Kaiser Family:* Peter Budetti and Teresa Waters, "Medical Malpractice Law in the United States," the Kaiser Family Foundation, May 2005.

190 *In March 2005:* Bernard Black, Charles Silver, David Hyman, and William Sage, "Stability, Not Crisis: Medical Malpractice Claim Outcomes in Texas, 1988–2002," 2 *Journal of Empirical Legal Studies,* 207–259 (May 2005).

190 *The stock prices:* Jay Angoff, "Falling Claims and Rising Premiums in the Medical Malpractice Insurance Industry," Center for Justice & Democracy, July 2005.

190 *In Illinois, the state's largest:* Jim Ritter, "State Doctors, Malpractice Insurer Battle over Rate Hike, Board Raises," *Chicago Sun-Times,* April 21, 2004.

194 *Studying 131 cases:* Lucinda Finley, "The Hidden Victims of Tort Reform: Women, Children, and the Elderly," 53 *Emory Law Journal,* 1263 (2004).

195 *The study of the Medicare population:* "Patient Safety in American Hospitals," HealthGrades Quality Study, July 2004.

196 *The case dragged on:* Kevin O'Hanlon, "Court Upholds Constitutionality of Malpractice Cap," Associated Press, May 16, 2003.

198 *In an affidavit filed: Brittany Phillips v. Dean Heller,* Supreme Court of the State of Nevada, Sasser Affidavit.

200 *In New York:* Neil Vidmar, Felicia Gross and Mary Rose, "Jury Awards for Medical Malpractice and Post-Verdict Adjustments of Those Awards," 48 *De Paul Law Review* 265, 268 (1998).

200 *In a more recent study:* Neil Vidmar, Dara MacKillop, and Paul Lee, "Million Dollar Medical Malpractice Cases in Florida: Post Verdict and Pre-Suit Settlements," 59 *Vanderbilt Law Review* (2006) (forthcoming).

200 *In a 1991 study:* Elanor Kinney, William Gronfein, and Thomas Gannon, "Indiana's Medical Malpractice Act: Results of a Three Year Study," 24 *Indiana Law Review* 1275 (1991).

Chapter Twelve / In Big Government We Trust: How the GOP
Learned to Love Bureaucrats

Page

203 *An NHTSA study released:* Keith Bradsher, *High and Mighty: SUVs: The World's Most Dangerous Vehicles and How They Got That Way* (Public Affairs, 2002), 160.

204 *Even NHTSA estimated that:* "Safety briefing on roof crush," Public Citizen, www.citizen.org/documents/Safety%20briefing%20on%20roof%20crush%20final.pdf (accessed April 25, 2006).

205 *Several key agency officials:* Bradsher, 59.

207 *The court found that: Escola v. Coca Cola Bottling Co. of Fresno,* 24 Cal.2d 453, 150 P.2d 436.

207 *The book began by tracing:* Ralph Nader, *Unsafe at Any Speed* (Grossman Publishers, 1965), 5.

208 *Given how frequently cars crash: Larsen v. General Motors Corporation,* U.S. Court of Appeals Eighth Circuit, 391 F.2d 495.

210 *Among the lobbyists:* Saundra Torry, "You'll Never Guess Who Really Won the Liability Fight," *Washington Post,* September 16, 1996.

210 *Clinton said at the time:* John Harris, "Clinton Vetoes Product Liability Measure," *Washington Post,* May 3, 1996.

210 *Michael Kinsley, then the editorial-page:* Michael Kinsley, "Whose Vioxx Is Gored?" *Los Angeles Times,* August 28, 2005.

211 *Before going to the FDA:* "Pattern of Abuse: How the FDA Does Industry's Bidding," Office of Congressman Maurice Hinchey, www.house.gov/hinchey/issues/fdal.pdf (accessed April 25, 2006).

211 *One of those people:* Michael Kranish, "FDA Counsel's Rise Embodies US Shift," *Boston Globe,* December 22, 2002.

212 *In December 2003: Alma Dusek v. Pfizer,* Inc. U.S. District Court for the Southern District of Texas, C.A. No. H-02-3559, Affidavit of Jessica Dart.

213 *Pacesetter lost a motion:* Margaret Clune, "Stealth Tort Reform: How the Bush Administration's Aggressive Use of the Preemption Doctrine Hurts Consumers," Center for Progressive Regulation, October 2004.

214 *In early 2006:* Heather Won Tesoriero and Anna Wilde Mathews, "Lawyers May Change Their Tactics in Drug Liability Cases," *Wall Street Journal,* January 19, 2006.

217 *Engler declined several requests:* Robert Ankeny, "Engler Likes State's Drug Liability Shield for U.S. Model," *Crain's Detroit Business,* November 29, 2004.

Chapter Thirteen / In the Tanker: Exxon's Stealth Campaign against Punitive Damages

Page

221 *As law professors Marc Galanter and David Luban:* Marc Galanter and David Luban, "Poetic Justice: Punitive Damages and Legal Pluralism," 42 *American University Law Review* 1393 (1993).

221 *As West Virginia Supreme Court Justice: TXO Production Corp. v. Alliance Resources,* Supreme Court of Appeals of West Virginia No. 20281, 187 W.Va. 457, 419 S.E. 2d 870.

221 *In 2001, the federal Bureau:* "Civil Justice Survey of State Courts, Punitive Damage Awards in Large Counties 2001," U.S. Bureau of Justice Statistics, 2005.

222 *By then, ephedra:* Guy Gugliotta, "Woman Wins $13.3 Million against Dietary Company," *Washington Post,* February 8, 2001.

223 *Even with Texas's punitive-damage cap:* Nelson Antosh, "Phillips Settles Fatal Explosion Case," *Houston Chronicle,* January 4, 2002.

224 *The British courts, though:* Thomas Koenig and Michael Rustad, *In Defense of Tort Law* (New York University Press, 2001), 25.

225 *In 1988, he argued:* Richard Mahoney, "It's Time to Curb the Courts," *New York Times,* December 11, 1988.

225 *At the time of Mahoney's:* "Dioxin Verdict Following 3 1/2 Year Trial Is Voided," Associated Press, June 13, 1991.

226 *Thirty-four states would eventually:* "Tort Reform Record," American Tort Reform Association, July 2005.

228 *In 2002, the Alabama Department of Insurance:* Michael DeBow, "The Road

Back from 'Tort Hell': The Alabama Supreme Court, 1994–2004," Federalist Society for Law and Policy White Paper, 2004.

230 *Simply put, as Cass Sunstein:* Cass Sunstein, Reid Hastie, John Payne, David Schkade, and W. Kip Viscusi, *Punitive Damages: How Juries Decide* (University of Chicago Press, 2002) 29.

230 *William Freudenburg, a sociology professor:* William Freudenburg, "Seeding Science, Courting Conclusions: Reexamining the Intersection of Science, Corporate Cash, and the Law," 20 *Sociological Forum*, no. 1 (March 2005).

230 *For instance, Freudenburg recounts:* Alan Zarembo, "Funding Studies to Suit Need," *Los Angeles Times*, December 3, 2003.

231 *Not so, countered Duke law:* Neil Vidmar, "Experimental Simulations and Tort Reform: Avoidance, Error and Overreaching in Sunstein et al.'s Punitive Damages (2002)," paper delivered to the 2004 Randolph W. Thrower Symposium on the Future of Tort Reform, February 19, 2004.

232 *Vidmar, working:* Neil Vidmar and Mary Rose, "Punitive Damages by Juries in Florida: In Terrorem and in Reality," 38 *Harvard Journal on Legislation* 487 (2001).

233 *Richard Lempert, a law and sociology:* Richard Lempert, "Juries, Hindsight, and Punitive Damage Awards: Failures of a Social Science Case for Change," 48 *DePaul Legal Review* 876.

233 *In 2002 Cornell law professor:* Theodore Eisenberg, Neil LaFountain, Brian Ostrom, David Rottman, and Martin Wells, "Juries, Judges and Punitive Damages: An Empirical Study," 87 *Cornell Law Review* 743 (2002).

234 *The LOEC was founded:* John Fialka, "How Koch Industries Tries to Influence Judicial System," *Wall Street Journal*, August 9, 1999.

234 *Because of the huge number:* See Vidmar, 2002.

236 *During the course of the litigation:* State Farm v. Campbell, 2001 UT 89 65 P.3d 1134.

237 *In 1997 the Rand Corporation:* Erik Moller, Nicholas Pace, and Stephen Carroll, "Punitive Damages in Financial Injury Verdicts," Rand Institute for Civil Justice Monograph, 1997.

Chapter Fourteen / Can I Get a Witness?: Junk Science and the War on Experts

Page

241 *The clarion call:* Peter Huber, *Galileo's Revenge* (Basic Books, 1991).

242 *At the time the book came out:* Theodore Eisenberg and James Henderson, "Inside the Quiet Revolution in Products Liability," 39 *UCLA Legal Review* 731–810 (1992).

243 *In 1993 the high court ruled:* Daubert v. Merrell Dow Pharmaceuticals (92–102), 509 U.S. 579 (1993).

244 *Daubert:* Daubert v. Merrell Dow Pharmaceuticals, Inc., 43 F.3d 1311 (9th Cir. 1995).

244 *For instance, the Civil Justice Reform Group:* Russell Mokhiber and Robert Weissman, "The Corporate Seminar for Judges," *Multinational Monitor*, March 18, 1998.

244 *In 2001 researchers from the Rand Institute:* L. Dixon and B. Gill, "Changes in the Standards for Admitting Expert Evidence in Federal Civil Cases since the Daubert Decision," Rand Institute for Civil Justice Monograph, 2001.

245 *Indeed, after Daubert:* "Federal Tort Trials and Verdicts 2002–2003," U.S. Bureau of Justice Statistics, August 2005.

246 *Nonetheless, in 2000: Chambers v. Exxon,* 81 F. Supp. 2d 661 (2000).

248 *Shortly afterward, Magistrini: Magistrini v. One Hour Martinizing Dry Cleaning,* U.S. District Court, District of New Jersey, No. CIV.A.96-4991.

250 *The state supreme court: Sandoz Pharmaceuticals v. Gunderson,* Commonwealth of Kentucky Court of Appeals, 2004-CA-001536-MR.

Conclusion: Why It Matters

Page

253 *The old tort rules:* Jacobsen and White, *David v. Goliath,* 34.

254 *As Friedman writes:* Lawrence Friedman, *A History of American Law* (New York: Simon and Schuster, 1985), 475.

255 *A landmark study:* Deborah Hensler et al., *Compensation for Accidental Injuries in the United States,* Rand Corporation, 1991.

255 *David Engel, now a law professor:* David Engel, "The Oven Bird's Song: Insiders, Outsiders and Personal Injuries in an American Community," *Law & Society Review,* Vol. 18, No. 4 (1984).

256 *Take the case of John Quinby: Patricia Quinby v. Charles Burmeister,* Superior Court of Pennsylvania, No. 2382 EDA 2003, 850 A.2d 667.

256 *According to state court records:* Jury verdict data on medical malpractice cases is now posted on the Pennsylvania Supreme Court website and can be found here: http://www.courts.state.pa.us/index/medicalmalpractice/juryverdicts.pdf.

INDEX

ABOUT THE AUTHOR

STEPHANIE MENCIMER is a contributing editor of *The Washington Monthly*. She was previously an investigative reporter for *The Washington Post* and a staff writer for *Legal Times*. A native of Ogden, Utah, and a graduate of the University of Oregon, Mencimer won the 2000 Harry Chapin Media Award for reporting on hunger and poverty.

.

Printed in the United States
By Bookmasters